THE COMFORT OF WATER
A RIVER PILGRIMAGE

All our stories of who we are begin somewhere else, the philosopher of place, Jeff Malpas, has said. This is true of landscapes, which have travelled a long way and shifted their shapes radically since matter was birthed in the big bang, to become what they seem to be around us; and it's true of each of us. We belong as much to where we came from, and how we got here, as to where we've ended up. What each of us means is what each of us was at source, how our journey has shaped (even damaged and tainted) us, and what's left of us when we finally empty into the sea.

Maya Ward has written here a testimony to a river, and the story of us all. She not only travels and bears witness to a river; she thinks like a river in this book. And in the process she asks us to rethink ourselves not merely in time, but in place: as aspects of where we find ourselves. For instance, in a river.

One senses that the way out – if there is one – of the ecological crisis upon us, is the way in: the journey down into our older selves, where each of us is an angelic organism, a piece of and at peace with, creation; the journey back into places. Understanding and redeeming the waters of the world, we will understand and redeem ourselves.

As Matsuo Basho walked and wrote his *Narrow Road to the Deep Interior*, Maya Ward has written her eloquent road into her own deep self. Her road is a river, the Yarra (Birrarung, in the language of the river's first people, the Wurundjeri), and where the river begins, and her journey ends, is the place–if they'll let us in–we all need to get back to. The Yarra has found in Maya Ward the ideal witness. Her account, like her journey, is romantically conceived, thoughtfully executed and passionately voiced. On the way back up to the headwaters of this songline, Maya learns, and teaches us, to think like a river. She has written not just an account of a river walk, but a sacred geography of a river.

The Comfort of Water–a discourse that braids, in the spirit of Terry Tempest Williams and Kathleen Dean Moore, social ecology, bioregionalism, activism and deep deep sympathy for Indigenous ways of knowing–is perhaps the only sort of explorer's journal we have time to be writing–and reading–these late days.

Mark Tredinnick, author of *The Blue Plateau: A Landscape Memoir* and *Fire Diary*

the
comfort
of water

a river pilgrimage

maya ward

transit lounge

First Published 2011
Transit Lounge Publishing
95 Stephen Street
Yarraville, Australia 3013
www.transitlounge.com.au
info@transitlounge.com.au

Front cover photograph: Nathan Kaso www.nathankasophotography.com
Back cover photograph: Maya Ward
Maps: Ian Faulkner
Cover and book design: Peter Lo

Printed in Australia by McPherson's Printing Group

Transit Lounge is committed to sustainable future for our business, our readers and our planet. Papers used in this book are natural, recyclable products made from wood grown in responsibly managed plantations. This book is made from paper certified by the Forest Stewardship Council.

National Library of Australia
Cataloguing-in-publication data

Ward, Maya.

The comfort of water : a river pilgrimage / Maya Ward.

9780980846218 (pbk.)

"Maps by Ian Faulkner".

Hiking--Victoria--Yarra River.
Walking--Victoria--Yarra River.
Rivers--Victoria--Melbourne.
Self-actualization (Psychology)
Yarra River (Vic.)--Environmental conditions.
Yarra River (Vic.)--Description and travel

Other Authors/Contributors: Faulkner, Ian.

551.483099452

I believe that if one fathoms deeply one's own neighbourhood and the everyday world in which he lives, the greatest of worlds will be revealed.

Masanobu Fukuoka

For the ancient walker inside each one of us
… especially those with the littlest legs:
Holly and April, Sam and Sage,
Azzi, Jerome and Mietta.

CONTENTS

Walk the path
And journey to the source
These are not metaphors

They are instructions

PROLOGUE

The circle bay lay open to the sky, and the light fell into the water. The sea was a silver-green mirror for the dome that wrapped the world. Below was not blue water, it was fallen sky. I could fall in there too.

I began at the bay, because that's where I was. Hot evenings, when the sun was near to gone, I'd run from the house, over the black footpaths, towards the water and towards the sun. Over the road that lay along the shore, then a jump from the bluestone wall down to the sand. Across the sand to the sea, I dived in.

This was my game – to race the sun, to swim far into Port Phillip Bay, along the path the sun laid down. The sun's gold path led straight to me; the sun does that for everyone.

As the sun slipped ever lower, the gilded pathway faded, vanishing into the sea like spilt treasure. It was when the sun had finally fallen, taking with it the juicy heat of the sky, I knew that I'd lost the race. But as I floated in the comfort of water, in the silence of the sky's pure blue, I found I had won something else.

I didn't know what it was that I'd won. It lay inside me,

a mysterious wholeness, an unhatched egg. It demanded attentiveness, yet was inscrutable, a smooth, curved unknown. I just had to wait.

In the meantime, there continued the compelling pull of the path. I followed the light at the end of things, I walked the paths through cities and forests, by rivers, through fog, across water, into mountains, along cliffs, up stairs, to edges.

I followed paths, yet never did I truly arrive.

Then, one day, the pilgrimage.

≈

Early in the morning, opening the door onto the gums and sheoaks lit up by the sun, the wattlebirds were yelping and clucking overhead. Shouldering our packs and stepping out the door, I felt the welcome mat, bristly and giving, below my feet. A feeling came up from my soles; of course, the mat worked both ways. That day, only because I was listening, I heard it. 'Welcome to the world.' The echo of that first welcome rang out over the land, and it rang on for weeks, sometimes a pealing, other times a dark rumble, but there was a music sustained, shimmering the air, parting the way. There was an answer to every footfall in the rhythmic pulse of feet, drumming along the taut surface of the earth. The song of it rang on and on, all the way to the mountain peaks, where we arrived at the very end of our pilgrimage.

At the beginning, none of that was known to me. I set off walking westward with Ilan, my housemate and fellow pilgrim. The path we took that April morning was the same I usually took to the shops and the tram. The concrete slabs of the inner-city footpath were lifted up into little hills by the pressure of ironbark roots searching for water below. The eucalypts above were waving in the wind. I felt like waving back at them.

The train was full of rush-hour commuters off to the city, darkly dressed, quiet and contained. Ilan and I glowed at each other in our complicity, our difference, our bright walking clothes. For we were beginning our adventure, on a weekday, in our city.

We'd only just caught the train – we ran the last bit to the station, and while I stuffed coins into the ticket machine, spilling many of them over the urine-scented platform, Ilan held open the beeping doors, ready for me to jump in. As the train pulled out, the sun shone through the old red brick archway onto the gold coins I'd left strewn at Jewell station.

We rolled through the green rise of Royal Park, and down into the Moonee Ponds Creek valley. The railway tracks ran alongside the concrete channel that was once the creek, through the cavern created by the freeway raised high above on pylons. We changed trains to Williamstown. We were alone in a carriage travelling against the city flow. We walked out through the deserted weatherboard station, the end of the line. We walked straight towards the sun, through the high autumn-dry grasses to the water's edge, to Port Phillip Bay.

To one side of us the chimneys and cranes fenced in the bay's rim. Beyond that, the container ships and oil tankers were making their way to the Yarra's mouth and thence to the docks. All the other sides were open to the sea.

Our fellow pilgrims, Kate and Cinnamon, were waiting

for us. We were finally ready to begin our long journey. We were walking, all the way along the river, to the mountains of the Great Divide, to find the source of the Yarra.

HOW THE YARRA
WAS FORMED

Once the waters of the Yarra were locked in the mountains. This huge lake was called Moorool, or Great Water. It was so large that the Woiwurung had little hunting ground. This was in contrast with the Bunerong and the Wothowurong, whose hunting ground was the lovely flat which is now Neerim, Port Phillip Bay.

The headman of the Woiwurrung tribe was Barwool. He resolved to free the land. He cut a channel up the valley with his stone axe. But Baw Baw, the mountain, stopped him. He decided to go northwards, but was stopped by Donna Buang and his brothers. Then he went westwards, and cut through the hills to Warr-an-dyte. There he met Yan Yan, another Woiwurung, who was busily engaged in cutting a channel for the Plenty River, to drain Morang, the place where he lived. Their rivers joined, and the place where the waters of Moorool and Morang met became Moo-rool-bark, the Place Where the Wide Waters Were. They continued their work, and reached Warringal, Dingo Jump Up, the Heidelberg-Templestowe Flats, and there they rested while the waters formed another Moorool. Barwool and Yan Yan again set to work, but this time they had to go slower, because the ground was much harder, and they were using up too many stone axes. Between the Darebin and the Merri Creeks they cut a narrow, twisting track, looking for softer ground. At last they reached Neerim. The waters of Moorool and Morang rushed out. The country of the Woiwurung was freed from water, and Neerim was inundated.

As Told by Billi-Billeri, of the Woiwurung (Wurundjeri Tribe).

The archeologists say this story is as old as the end of the last ice age, ten thousand years ago or so, when the seas rose and flooded the bay. This tale encodes within it an historical event so catastrophic that the memory of it passed unbroken through countless generations.

Billi-Billeri's story is a fragment of the Dreaming, that web of stories, knowledge, lore and songs that held together the culture of a place. Not long ago Billi-Billeri told the story of the creation of the Yarra to the new colonisers. Now scientists are saying that the seas may rise again soon, if we do not change our ways. There is a web, around us, unravelling.

Billi-Billeri's story is from the land I live in. This land is covered now by the sprawling city of Melbourne, a place whose origin story can be securely fastened to the year 1803. That was the year Charles Grimes first rowed up the Yarra during his survey of the place known to the locals as Neerim. As acting chief surveyor of New South Wales he had seen all the rivers on the east coast of Australia. He named this river the Freshwater, describing it as the most beautiful he had yet seen. He then went on to record details of the land, noting its potential and its limitations to grow crops, to fatten lambs, to graze and stock with hard-hoofed sheep and cattle.

In my imagination, I see Grimes standing upright in the prow. The sun reflects off the water. The river ripples with the sway of the boat, the ripples bounce over the white skins of the gums and the paperbarks, they are washed with moving stripes of light. Grimes, with string and weight, thinks he is plumbing the depths of the river.

Grimes found the river there; Barwool had done the work, and the people who lived there knew it, and celebrated it. Grimes thought the river was unmade, and that he, his culture, would make it.

But the river was already made.

That voyage of Grimes' was just over two hundred years ago. An origin story is a powerful thing. A story we may live by whether we know it or not.

Grimes was looking for land. So, it seems, was Barwool.

The two protagonists of these stories, Barwool of the Dreaming and Grimes of the British Empire, were each making the Yarra from opposite ends. Both stories happened a long time ago. Both stories, perhaps, are happening now.

I didn't know how to believe in either story. So I had to make the river for myself.

~

The idea of a pilgrimage for the Yarra sailed into my mind one day, threw a rope and tied it securely to my heart. I'd never heard of anyone doing such a thing; there was no official path, yet this outlandish notion seemed at once utterly obvious and completely necessary.

The notion of walking the length of the Yarra grew from my quest to live with clarity and sanity in the place I call home. To that end, I'd been learning about bioregionalism. From *bio* – life, and *region* – place, these are philosophies and practices of living within local ecological limits. Bioregional writers encourage practical action; explore and learn about where you live, and let that knowledge guide your behaviour. Boundaries of bioregions are often drawn around river catchments, yet rivers play another role, a metaphoric one. Rivers are a symbol of the philosophy, as the river's very nature tells of our interconnection and responsibilities to each other. We are all dependant on the health of the water in our rivers, yet that water is so vulnerable. All that is discarded on the streets or spread through the paddocks, the rubbish and the effluent of a society, eventually washes into a river. The river is witness, the river carries everything, right through the heart of the city.

Knowledge of place was once foundational; people lived more locally, and over a lifetime, rarely ventured far from home. Nowadays many of us live much of each day inside the screen worlds of television and the internet, inside the pages of books or newspapers, inside windowless warehouses, shopping centres or office complexes. Travel too is usually inside cars, trains and planes, where the particularities of the ground and the air are lost. Bioregionalism is about reclaiming what we have only just lost – an innate and inescapable sense of place. Writers in the field talk about knowing the 'boundaries of home' in geographical rather than political terms. Almost all of greater Melbourne lay in the Yarra River bioregion.

The almost-new culture and form of Melbourne did not emerge organically from this old land. We have here a colonial heart and ever-expanding rings of American-inspired, car-dominated suburbs. But there are cracks in the grid. The winding Yarra and her tributaries fracture the rigid forms, force accommodations. In these gaps the wild clings on in the city. These places I loved, yet I knew so little about them. With inadequate tools to understand my surroundings, a sense of displacement and an ache to belong gnawed at me. In my process of searching for a way to sink deeper into my home place, I was drawn to tales of pilgrimage. These journeys took place in other lands; often ambitious, often long, usually walked, they were undertaken by those seeking connection with something larger than themselves.

The pilgrim was a seeker. These seekers sought that which is only revealed over time, through devotion to the task, through mental and physical effort. The period of pilgrimage was an immersion, a concentration, of heart, thought and intention; a preparation for a long-awaited meeting. Devotion bears fruit when finally the pilgrim arrives at the destination. Yet, like listening to a story, there's no use in only knowing the ending. The journey, the whole story, is needed for the ending to make sense. And every step on the path is a word in the pilgrim's story.

There are ancient rituals of walking pilgrimage to holy places in many cultures, including the Buddhist, Christian, and Hindu traditions. Yet sacred walking resonated with what I'd heard of Aboriginal connections to land. The seasonal practices of hunting and gathering meant lifetimes journeying over country, along Songlines. These two different traditions; religions originating overseas, and local, ancient practices – neither tradition was mine. But for me to go on a pilgrimage in Australia, with all of this history in mind, felt like bringing them into some sort of conversation. I was interested in what, if I listened carefully, I might overhear.

A walk was something soft and slow, innately attentive to what lay underfoot. I wanted to meet, each in their turn, the diversity of natural ecosystems that unfolded along the Yarra. And I hoped to find people who were living close and careful with their place, growing with the land, learning to be at home here. I felt a pilgrimage might teach me how to better protect and nurture the land that I loved, and to learn from river-dwellers, all along the way.

Yet I also sought the wisdom to be found in quiet places. The river's way would lead us into the mountains. Wild and silent, guardians on the edge of the world, I wanted to learn from them too.

$$\approx$$

There has finally arrived a sense that we must stop affecting the earth in the way that we do, and do it urgently. The calls to change how we source our material needs are growing ever louder. Yet while society is slowly acknowledging the truth of this, there also seems to be a corresponding simplification and smoothing over of the depths contained in these challenges. It is as if change were an external thing, with all the holes in the web of the world fixed with a few new laws and a switch to 'green' buying. As if nothing needed to change on the inside.

I feel the problems are far deeper than our culture seems ready to admit.

I'd grown up in a family of environmental and social activists. I'd known about the issue of climate change from my youngest days. I kept thinking that awareness and action must surely be imminent. But in the intervening decades, despite growing awareness, we've gone backwards. Growing up, I struggled to communicate what I knew of the dire news, yet I saw bewilderment and dismissal in the faces of those around me. I'd often rail against the unfairness of knowing when so many around me seemed at peace with the way things are. I have come, now, to see it as both a gift and a duty, knowing and understanding that there was never a choice but to work for change. Knowing has given me purpose, commitment and clarity. There is great work to be done all over the world. How is it to be done here, now? In truth, the challenges are so huge that for us to adequately come to grips with them, they must enwrap our entire minds.

What does change look like, feel like? How is the change to be lived? How are we changed in the process? Our actions come out of who we are, how we think, what we treasure and what we fear. I feel that all of this must be explored if we are to know how to be and how to behave in this time. And I feel we must start with the land. Where, exactly, do we find ourselves?

The Yarra was the site of first meeting between the whites and the Wurundjeri. It is still contested ground. The almost-new city of Melbourne is where it is because of this river. What, I wondered, did the old river know?

I sensed that walking the Yarra would help me. In a time when the web that holds together the world I love is unravelling, I hoped a pilgrimage along my river would give me courage.

—

Oh, but it was such a long way! I could barely see my friend at the other end of the map room. We'd gone along to see Melbourne University library's topographicals; we'd requested all the maps that the river runs through. Then we laid them out end to end on the library tables. Luckily the library was virtually empty, as we needed almost all the tables. I realised the vastness of the journey in front of me, as we cooeed to each other over the distance of the maps, me at the mouth, she at the source. The land was laid out there in my imagination, contour lines unfolded into hills and valleys, thin curling blue ink became clear meandering streams that cradled the blue of the sky. I planned my quest for the coming summer.

At a party in Northcote one winter's night, a tall, dark-haired woman with soft brown eyes came up to me and said, 'I hear you are going to walk the length of the Yarra'. She had just returned from visiting Aboriginal communities in Arnhem Land in the far north of Australia. Her experience had affected her profoundly. She'd felt an aliveness, an energy in the land and the people, and she sensed that it came, somehow, out of the relationship between the two. She felt that the land she was born in must have had that type of relationship with people, once.

Kate had returned home with many questions of how we are to live in this country. As a teacher who had taken thousands of children canoeing and bushwalking, Kate had a strong relationship to the Yarra, but it was of a particular quality. She wanted to know other ways. We sat on the couch in the corner for the whole of the party, and as we talked a stream of understanding flowed between us. I saw that Kate loved the Yarra in ways I had yet to experience, and I wanted to learn these ways from this woman. She, in return, wanted to learn from me. It was decided; Kate was coming too.

Soon after, I was talking to my friend Cinnamon, while we ate lunch on the grass in the sun at her workplace, CERES Community Environment Park. I told her my plans, and of Kate joining the journey. I cajoled her, 'Are you absolutely sure you don't want to come?' I'd asked her previously for we had gone on an earlier, much shorter pilgrimage together, to the source of the Merri Creek. She'd said no to the Yarra – too epic, she couldn't spare the time.

But this time she went quiet; she bent her neat head and closed her eyes. After a while, she looked at me, intent. Then she smiled.

'I'm ready for another adventure – somehow I'll make this work.'

I leapt on her; 'Yippee, together we'll be pilgrims again!'

'Hold your horses – there's something I have to talk to you about first.' I settled back on the grass.

'I seriously need to question your idea of walking in summer. I think it's just too dangerous to go in bushfire season.'

'I suppose you've got a point, but summer is best for lots of swimming.'

She looked at me soberly. 'Maya, I've been living in the bush for a few years now – I've got much more sense of the risks. Even if I wasn't coming with you, I'd want you to think about this.'

We spoke to Kate, she agreed with Cinn.

'It was on my mind too – autumn would be a much better time. How about the Easter holidays – the weather is superb in April.'

I was a little reluctant to give up swimming weather, but it would be easier walking in the cooler months. I came round to their suggestion.

We set to work, the three of us, to turn a fanciful vision into the cool practicality of what we called the Long Yarra Walk. Cinnamon was clear-thinking, efficient and super-organised, and Kate, being an outdoor education teacher, knew everything about hiking and camping, safety and weather, gear and logistics. I brought along my enthusiasm. I was willing to approach anyone who could help us in our undertaking, and I had many contacts among communities along the river. We figured we could do the journey in three weeks if everything went to plan.

At first I resisted the organisational process. To measure out a dream into daily allotments of rations and spans seemed to do some damage to the limitlessness at the heart of the vision. But very soon I discovered the worth of my companions. For while we attacked the tangibles; devising problem-solving strategies for negotiating every bend of our 250-kilometre expedition, and delegating responsibilities of research and liaison, we held the intangibles, safe in the space between us. We began and ended each meeting with silence, as if listening out for the distant river. And when we spoke into that silence, it was as if we were searching for words that the river, if it had a voice, might dream of saying.

A pilgrimage along the Yarra was an idea like an untapped spring. Once broached, generosity flowed freely. But first, we had to broach it. Somewhat nervously I rang Parks Victoria, the government department in charge of state and national parks. I was put through to the sponsorship coordinator.

'Really?' she said. 'You want to walk the whole way along the river? What a fantastic idea. Helping projects like yours is Parks Victoria's core business – come in and let's talk about it.'

I was somewhat stunned when I put down the phone. If this is how helpful a government department was, what else might our quest unleash? It became a pleasure to share our plans. I discovered this over and over again, upon calling those whose assistance we needed. Sometimes, after my spiel, there was a small silence. I'd start to feel concerned I had asked for too much, or offended a sensibility. Until a quiet voice said something like this, 'I've always wanted to do that! I've been living by this river for years, and I've long wondered where it's come from. It's great that you're going … I wish I could come too.'

I started to consider our quest differently. It seemed this journey was not an unusual desire at all; I saw we would be living the dream of many. My gratitude grew daily for the kindnesses flowing our way. And in accepting this, in seeing myself as a messenger of a culture that sought to better attend to its place, the pilgrimage grew in ways I could not have imagined. People seemed thrilled with the idea of us staying on their particular patch – maybe because in this way they would become part of the journey. Or perhaps it was the unleashing of the archetype of pilgrimage; the giving freely to strangers in the service of something greater.

Our intention was to follow the Yarra wherever it went, and to stay beside it every night. Most of the river, however, ran through private hands. We had thought the strip of land adjacent to the water was public property. We were wrong; one of the legacies of early colonial legislation meant many properties extended all the way to the middle of the river. Since much of the river ran through the Shire of Yarra Ranges, I contacted their environment officer to ask for his help.

'I think the best thing would be if we sent out letters to the property owners on your behalf – that way they'll know we support this project.'

'Thank you so much, that's very kind of you.'

'Well, what you're doing is helpful for us too – we're always looking for ways to communicate the importance of care for the river's water quality, as well as habitat and biodiversity on farmland. I think your walk is a great way to link people into the bigger picture, to get them appreciating that their property is part of this complex river system. Which reminds me, have you contacted Melbourne Water yet to ask for access to the water catchment?'

'No, not yet. But everyone has been so supportive we think they'll be fine with our idea to walk alongside the dam.'

'I wouldn't be so sure about that. They rarely let anyone in.'

'We'll get on to it straight away. Thanks for letting us know.'

The upper reaches of the Yarra River have long been off-limits.

The branching headwaters bubble up in swampy hollows among mountain forests, protected by the closed water catchment of the Upper Yarra Dam. These wet sclerophyll forests have been protected for over 100 years to ensure clean drinking supplies for the city. We sent a letter to Melbourne Water, asking for permission to walk up to the source, through the closed catchment. Meanwhile, of more than 300 riverside properties contacted by the Shire of Yarra Ranges, only three owners declined access, citing fears for our safety. Luckily, there are two sides to a river, so those few properties would be easy to avoid.

Once we had decided on viable daily walking distances of between ten and twenty-five kilometres, we then planned where we could stay along the way. Parks Victoria allowed us the special privilege of camping on properties they manage. Between us, we knew a number of supportive people and organisations with properties beside the river, but there were also places where we had no contacts, so it was necessary to simply ring up strangers and ask for permission to camp on their land. The spring of generosity ran sweet towards us, and offers kept arriving; laden boats on a clear river.

One day after a meeting with Kate and Cinnamon I walked in through the back gate of my house. Ilan, my housemate, was in the garden watering the lettuces. I joined him in the speckled sunshine under the yellow gum, and, balancing on a log, shared with him the latest Walk plans. As he turned off the tap, he turned to me and said,

'How would you feel if I asked to come too?'

'Really?' I squeaked. I nearly fell off my log in delight

and confusion.

I said I'd have to ask the others, but it sounded like a great idea. Ilan, a dancer, performer and urban planner, loved the river and the bush and was fascinated with the questions of how we can better care for our place. The girls met him, they were happy. And so we were four.

We began organising our gear and food. Cinnamon impressed us with spreadsheets of our requirement lists, immaculately laid out and elegantly fonted. As a last-minute packer, these lists were very useful for me – even when their formality made me smile. We discussed the logistics of carrying all that we needed for three weeks, and decided very quickly it would be impossible. We'd need a support crew. This solution fitted quite naturally into the notion of pilgrimage. The traditional pilgrim accepted the charity and generosity of the community upon the path. Our friends and families would take turns in ferrying our trailer from one site to the next, and provide dinner for us each night; they became the community of support. This would also enable more people to share the pilgrimage with us, for there were many who wanted to join in.

Our departure date of Friday, the fourth of April, was drawing near when we finally heard back from Melbourne Water. They said no. They would not allow access to the water catchment. We could not walk the upper reaches of the river.

This was an answer we didn't expect – we'd thought they, like everyone else we had approached, would be happy to help. We called an emergency meeting, and arranged for Kate and Cinnamon to meet with the person in charge at Melbourne

Water. We were sure a personal approach would give us the desired result.

The girls returned with bad news – Melbourne Water would not budge. There were strict regulations to keep people out of the catchment, to ensure the purity of the water supply. We were devastated by this news. We felt sure if only they understood what we were attempting to do, they would help us, as everyone else had. But time had run out. There was no chance to make any more pleas or petitions. We would need to work out an answer on the journey itself, hoping to stay true to the vision of walking all the way to the source.

And yet our vision had grown. As we plotted together, another, richer layer of shared intention was born. Quite often the first thing people would ask was, 'Why aren't you starting at the source and walking to the sea – wouldn't it be easier to head downhill?'

There were many reasons to start where the river meets the sea. We knew where the sea was, but we didn't know the location of the source, so we needed to follow the Yarra to find it. We'd be walking from where we lived and what we knew into places we didn't know. Away from the familiar, into the unknown. We'd walk from the city into the mountains, away from the noise of people and deep into land where it was easier to hear the sounds of other voices.

And it was more than all of these reasons.

We were starting from the bay, where Grimes had first entered the Yarra to claim the interior as imperial property. Yet we sought a different claim.

We hoped to hear stories from people all along the Yarra, and to share our experience with them in return. So we arranged to meet with up local custodians; municipal mayors, river friends' groups, primary schools, to make connections with communities all along the length of the waterway. Through coming to know the river, we would come to know the river's claim on us.

During one planning meeting, we each spoke about what we hoped to do on the pilgrimage. Cinnamon was taking her new camera, keen to document. Kate, a textile artist, would sketch and write to later work her observations in needle and thread. I was studying Social Ecology (the study of the interrelationships between the personal, social, spiritual and environmental domains), so I'd write essays from my diary entries. And Ilan was taking a video camera to record his dance of each place. He planned on getting up at dawn every day, wherever on the river we had been offered for that night, and dancing the dance of what he found there, and what he felt. All of us hoped to meet the river, each in our own way.

As part of our preparation, we searched the historical records for other Yarra journeys like ours. Robert Hoddle, Melbourne's surveyor, had trekked up the Yarra not long after the colony was established. To prove it, there was a creek with his name on it, somewhere in the Yarra Valley. Forty-two years after Grimes first rowed up the estuary, Hoddle had taken a survey team and set off to the mountains to find the headwaters. When they had walked as far as their rations would take them, he noted the place where they stood. He wrote 'deep gully deep gully' on the map he was making. It was somewhere above the Yarra Falls, hidden away in the thick wet forest now enclosed in the water catchment. It was the third of April, 1845. One hundred and fifty-eight years and one day before our expedition was due to begin.

William Barak of the Wurundjeri had lived high up on the Yarra at Coranderrk, the Aboriginal mission station. He was the *Ngurrung-gaeta* of the tribe – a man of power and influence within his community. He regularly walked down the river that his ancestor, Barwool, had cut into the earth. Barak walked all the way to the new seat of power in his land; the booming city of Melbourne. The city was expanding over his custodial country, filling in the grid that surveyor Hoddle had laid over his land. He walked to the city to petition for the rights of the Wurundjeri. He demanded to know who was the ultimate authority responsible for the treatment of his people. When he found out, he sent a letter to Queen Victoria, seeking justice.

Barak walked much of the length of the Yarra until he was old, and he died exactly 100 years before our journey. After his, we found only one mention of a recorded trek along the Yarra, also about 100 years ago.

Barak had been a child when the colonists first arrived. He had lived to see his people and his culture scattered and destroyed. Knowing the story of Barak changed our journey. It seemed that if any mode of travel could do some small justice to his memory, then a pilgrimage was the way to do it. To travel with the sacred in mind meant walking mindfully, with sincerity, clarity and commitment. These qualities we would need if we hoped to walk in his footsteps. I rang my friend Ian Hunter, a Wurundjeri elder and Barak's great-great-grand-nephew, to invite him to our launch. He said he'd try to get there. In case he didn't he wanted me to know that the Yarra is a Songline.

And I sought out Joy Murphy Wandin, Wurundjeri elder, the great-grand-niece of Barak, who'd been with me when, a few years back, I had first shared my dream to walk the whole river. I'd asked for her permission, back then, to walk this pilgrimage through Wurundjeri country. She'd said to me to also consider the river's traditional name, the Birrarung. I'd said I would. And she gave the Walk her blessing.

The Estuarine Yarra

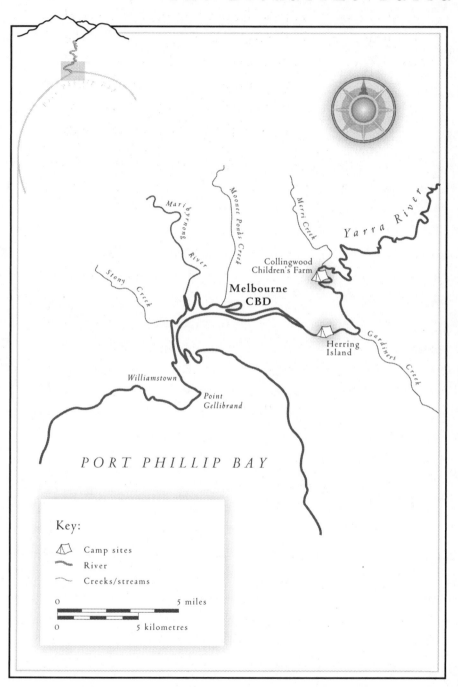

Maribyrnong River

Moonee Ponds Creek

Merri Creek

Yarra River

Stony Creek

Collingwood Children's Farm

Melbourne CBD

Gardiners Creek

Herring Island

Williamstown

Point Gellibrand

PORT PHILLIP BAY

Key:

Camp sites

River

Creeks/streams

0   5 miles

0   5 kilometres

SPIRITS OF THE ANCESTORS

The end of a river is a slippery thing. Point Gellibrand lay alongside a body of water that, at a pinch, could be described as the mouth of the Yarra. The Point was the place where the river opened out into the roundness of Port Phillip Bay, where the river grew into a sea.

Our meeting place was the Timeball Tower. Made of black basalt in 1853, it staked in place the erosional headland, like a spear through the head of a snake. Long ago that tower was a clock that told the time just once a day. It made up for it's lack of other duties by clanging out that one announcement in a manner exceedingly loud.

The timeball dropped at one o'clock every afternoon, the sound of steel on stone rang around the circle bay, and all the ships moored in docks by the water's edge set their clocks by it. An accurate clock was essential to calculate longitude. Those ships carrying sheep and squatters from England, and returning laden with fleeces for the mills, could not plot their sea voyage without this marking of the day.

Ilan and I walked from the train station through the grasses flared gold, the tower silhouetted ahead. At the base of the dark tower Kate and Cinnamon sheltered from the wind. After hugs all round, we separated, each walking out along the beach or headland. Our friends and various dignitaries would soon arrive for the launch of the Long Yarra Walk, but we each wanted some time alone first. I made my way to the shore against the breeze coming hard off the water. Seagulls were hanging above me, suspended in the wind. I walked under them as if they were a mobile dancing in a child's room, as they teetered under the strong and shifting currents of air. I looked back and smiled at their intense and mysterious quest to be balanced against invisible buffeting. Like a room full of meditators.

From the beach the view was wide over the water. On the far side of the bay a few hills rose up in the distance. The Great Dividing Range, the mountains we were headed for, lay further east, not yet visible. I walked into the water and balanced on the broken basalt stones among the wind and the choppy little wavelets. I wished I could have just a quick swim. But really, it was far too cold. Sunlight bounced off water in a thousand directions. I squatted low on the stone and dangled my hands in the sea.

'We're on our way,' I whispered to the waves. I cupped my hands and drew up a little bowlful, and splashed my face. Saltwater dripped. I stayed there, curled on the rock, for as long as I could.

When my time ran out, I stood up on my stone and gave a little bow to the bay. I saw a limpet shell loose in the cold shallows. Built like a miniature hill, it was bone coloured, smooth and worn, with fine brown lines radiating out from a centre peak. The home of this creature that clings to its place I put in my pocket, to keep for the journey, a talisman.

Many Aboriginal tribes throughout Australia define their country along watershed boundaries, and our whole walk by the Birrarung lay inside the bounds of Wurundjeri country. But the land we gathered on that morning was a territorial edge between Bunerong and Wurundjeri country, both tribes of the Kulin – the pre-European confederation of Port Phillip (Neerim) tribes.

Tammy Cappochi, a Wurundjeri woman and Parks Victoria ranger, had been invited to launch the journey, and to speak on behalf of her people. She balanced her little child on her hip as she spoke of the importance in Wurundjeri culture of passing the stories down the generations. Then, at the end of her talk, she asked the spirits of the ancestors to be with us as we walked.

Before we set off, we invited those gathered to write a note in our logbook; messages for us to take to those we would meet upstream. And while they did that, our friends and visitors spoke in turn. One by one, they said how grateful they were that we were giving their beloved Yarra a pilgrimage, while we beamed back and tried not to cry.

As we shouldered our daypacks and started walking, uppermost in my mind was the gift that Tammy had given us. 'May the spirits of the ancestors walk with you.' Somewhere, on the far side of my seeing, the ancestors were beside us, walking with us, seeing through our eyes.

I remembered what Ian Hunter, the Wurundjeri elder

whom I had worked with, had said to me a few days before; the way along the river is a Songline. A Songline is a path of the Dreaming, a narrative of the ancestors, which mapped the land in song. I imagined how stories would be alive in places all along the way, days and days of walking and chanting, walking and chanting, woven together into neural pathways, the brain grooved to the shape of the land. Paths of mind, heart and country, traversed over a lifetime. Stories passed down the generations, regenerated each time the song was sung. The ancestors, the people, the land, becoming one thing, enchanted through chant, grown together through song, and each singing made them anew. The singing of hills (now flattened), bends (straightened), billabongs (drained).

To imagine such a web of meaning once alive in this place, to have read of its dismemberment and its forgetting, yet to be stepping out on a fine morning with the wind and the words of kind people, was to be emptied and filled, blown clear through, free and indebted and with the chance to be true. May I breathe through my feet, lay my skin open, and be there to meet it all. All that is left, and all that is new.

We began.

At the beginning, there by the end of the river, there was no path along the water's edge – shipbuilding and shipping companies and their docks lined the shore. So we walked along the footpath, the Yarra hidden from us. A few extra pilgrims were with us for a stretch, including Greg, my former partner, who was lined up as canoe support, and Jess, Ilan's cousin, who had been MC for the launch. Jess was once a park ranger and taught marine ecology to children. He planned to accompany us for the first days, and we were pleased to have such knowledgeable and handsome (yes, tall and dark) company.

To the surprise of our guest walkers, our first stop came after only ten minutes; take-away coffee for Kate, and snacks from our packs for the rest of us.

'This is the earliest scroggin stop in the history of bushwalking,' said Greg in mock disgust. But we had eaten breakfast hours ago, and with the nervousness of the launch out of the way, we suddenly discovered how hungry we were. And there was a long way to go before lunchtime in the city.

We walked on through the old town of Williamstown with its grand Victorian buildings. Initially considered to be the site for the city of Melbourne, it was without access to fresh water, so that plan was abandoned. I was glad – I like the quiet backwater feel of Williamstown – the sense that you could almost be in the country.

Beyond the town, back by the foreshore, alongside the shipping channel, we walked a concrete path. Casuarinas were probably thick along here when Europeans first arrived; the traditional name for Williamstown being *Koort Boork*, Place of the Sheoaks. Now a couch grass lawn met a retaining wall edging the water.

We looked out over what was formerly a shallow delta. Once a wilder river's rippling mouth lashed to and fro just there, seasonally flooding the low-lying land. But shipping required deep water and stable banks, so the river was tamed and dredged, and the silts were used to shore up the riverbanks of Port Melbourne.

In front of us we could see the cranes (named, I suppose,

after those long-necked birds, and looking like a mechanical distortion of those lovely endangered creatures) for loading and unloading container ships. Obese, steroidal, almost comically oversized, these ships delivered consumer goods from all over the world. For their return trip they were filled with bits of the country cut up or squeezed and sold; coal, ores, trees, wheat, wool, wine.

Kate, with her irrepressible friendliness, talked to all the fishermen we passed, and so was in danger of being left behind. While we waited for her to catch up, we walked over the grass to the water, where on the strip of sand we spied a blue jellyfish, washed up dead after the summer breeding season. Two black swans were standing on the shore. Beyond them I saw Albert Park beach, my childhood beach, nestled in the curve of Hobson's Bay, a crescent cove within Port Phillip, whose edges extended past my seeing.

We veered off our path to take a look at the salt marsh that held to thin bars of sand in the estuary edge. (At our launch, folk from the local council shared how they and the community were working to return and restore some of the estuarine ecosystems along the river.) The sun reflected off the bright sand and the water, and lit upon the white feathers of a solitary spoonbill sweeping her spoon-like beak back and forth, searching for food.

The path continued under the shadow of the tall chimney of the Newport Power Station. It led to the Stony Creek Backwash, an intertidal zone, covered and revealed twice a day with the tides. The grubby little Stony Creek joined the Yarra there. The backwash was once quarried for stone, but now supported a stand of White Mangroves, the southernmost mangroves in the world. The semi-submerged trees were a dark line along the water's edge, ringing the bowl of the backwash, along with a fringe of bright and slimy plastic; rubbish washed in and out by tides. In front of the Mobil Oil Terminal, near where the giant oil tankers docked – this was where the mangroves nestled. To their peril. For the whole ecosystem was destroyed by an oil spill in the 1980s. What we saw that day was recent regrowth. The area had been brought back to life with the help of another local Friends group, yet it was always in danger of further toxic effects, there at the end of the river, where pollution from all the combined waterways passed on its way to the sea.

A white-faced heron walked alone in the middle of the shallow waterbody. The mangroves were shaded by heavy bands of concrete, the cavernous underbelly of the Westgate Bridge. Air and earth rumbled, as trucks passed, high above our heads.

After farewelling our extra pilgrims (except for Jess), we walked a little way back from where we'd just come. That path had ended at a complex of international shipping facilities. We needed to get to the other side of the river; Parks Victoria had arranged a punt for us, and the dock was a short backtrack. The vessel supplied was the same little punt that ran on the weekend for bicyclists and pedestrians, not big enough for all of us. I went over in the first load, and in the boat was a man named Bill, a photographer documenting all the bridges of the Yarra. He was being assisted by Parks Victoria in order to get some photos of the Westgate's underside. He asked us whether we had permission to access the Upper Yarra water catchment, before letting us know he would be taking photos in there. His news gave us heart – surely we'd be allowed to walk through it, somehow!

While we were waiting for the next boatload of companions, we unpacked a few snacks, and ate by the river in the sun and the wind, watched by seagulls, beside the wreck of old wharves. Upriver, car parks lined the riverbank, and behind us were the factory buildings of Fishermen's Bend. It would take a brave fisherman to cast in such water. The river looked rather unappealing, the more so every step inland, away from the cleansing sea. Apparently the water quality had improved dramatically over the last few decades – only recently some wharves had toilets that emptied straight into the Yarra. Recent sediment samples have been found to contain DDT and other non-biodegradable pollutants, and pathogens like E. coli and salmonella were still in high concentration.

We packed up our snacks and trekked on through the car parks, where the asphalt was poured all the way to the river's edge. Over the other side of the wide Yarra we saw the confluence with another river, the Maribyrnong.

That section of the Maribyrnong used to be the Yarra, too. Prior to the building of the docks in the nineteenth century the Birrarung and her sister-river ran together through the sheoak, banksia and tea-tree scrub. Later the Coode channel was dug, and the Yarra was relocated, becoming shorter, straighter and deeper. The Birrarung once meandered in the vicinity of Footscray Road, where the traffic now flows. Once, the water was stained dark gold with tannins leached from the trees, like wild rivers in other parts of the state.

Further into Fishermen's Bend we approached a grove of young trees planted at the end of a narrow riverside reserve, which backed onto a collection of industrial buildings. In the sheoak closest to the path, a large squat bird with black, white and soft ochre plumage hunched between the fine needles. It was a Nankeen Night Heron, staring out at us from the shadowy foliage. I was thrilled to see this bird surviving in such terrain. After years of watching for birds on forested banks of the Yarra, I'd seen that species only once before, yet the new planting was already habitat.

The Birrarung beyond the trees was closed to us, hidden behind tall metal fences and industrial estates. I said a silent goodbye to the river, then turned to follow my companions up the footpath beside Lorimer Road. More of a highway than a road, trucks loaded with shipping containers sped past. Their speed raised localised gusts that buffeted our bodies forward. There was no use trying to talk, it was too noisy. Railway track remnants were embedded in the footpath below me, signs of an earlier transport system, and I felt nostalgic for times I have not known, when freight was confined to tracks, not let loose on the roads, each carriage hauled by a smoking beast.

We were getting rather weary after a few kilometres of such conditions, but it got worse before it got better. We approached a large construction site on Birrarung's banks. The whine of power tools and plumes of concrete dust filled the air. We picked up our pace, shuttering our ears from the battering noise. I pulled my ineffectual hat low as we were heading north at midday, and the sun was shining straight into my eyes.

Very suddenly the noise, dust and fumes abated. It was

the end of the building works, and a wide footpath lay along the water's edge, lined with slick new high-rise apartment blocks. All was hard and clean and straight and calm, and the buildings led into the sky. I looked up, thinking how difficult I would find it to live so devoid of green and growing things. Yet I suppose dwelling so high would be a chance to learn about the wind and the clouds, the sun and the sky and the storms. To watch birds fly past your face, and far below, watch the wrinkled river smear the vivid lights of the city into a blur. As if living on the edge of a cliff, like a raptor.

We hiked along the river's edge beside Southbank's new Melbourne Exhibition Centre, nicknamed Jeff's Shed for the former premier who had it built. It was a massive structure that leered towards us at a fashionable angle. I mentioned to my fellow walkers how before I was born, when my dad lived with my mum in Albert Park, he used to walk this way to work in the city. He passed by decaying wharf buildings made from curved corrugated iron. One day dad snuck in and planted a grove of eucalypts next to them on the river's edge. All through my growing up, when dad would drive us back to his house in Brunswick, we would pass his trees, and it was the highlight of the journey for my sister and I, to see the trees that no-one but us knew he had planted. As we grew up, so did they.

'They were planted about here, under our feet I reckon. They were cut down when Jeff's Shed was built.'

We crossed Spencer Street and walked on past the casino complex, crossing over the footbridge to the Flinders Street station side. By the bridge the remnants of the creek that once flowed down Elizabeth Street emerged. Oily water bled out from a bluestone-lined tunnel, where it joined the sluggish Yarra. Once that little creek flowed in just above waterfalls. The falls had separated the sweet from the salt water, but were dynamited away to try to stop the flooding that periodically swept the city. Those falls were the reason Melbourne's historical core is situated where it is, so those very first settlers could drink the Yarra's fresh water before it spilled over the falls and into the brine.

We left the riverbank to walk through the underpass below Flinders Street station, crossed the city streets, ducked down Degraves Street and onto Flinders Lane. I led my companions past Ross House, where I worked, and through an arcade and into my favourite Japanese café (ah, the trials of bushwalking!). I'd arranged for my workmates to meet us for lunch. One reason I liked Japanese food so much was their tradition of eating smoked eel. I loved eel; apart from being delicious, it was a food indigenous to this area – eels lived in the Yarra, and were a vital food for the Kulin. Smoked eels were traded around Victoria for thousands of years, and eaten on the banks of this river, perhaps right where we sat.

While the others finished eating, I darted off to buy a hat with a broader brim – my own limp thing was fading already. I found one in a quiet shop off the busy lane, thick with shoppers like me, buying up the contents of those shipping containers we'd watched unload back down the river. I ran into a friend in Flinders Lane, and I felt the bizarre incongruity between my everyday working self and my pilgrim self. In the dark, canyon-like street, where bands of sunlight burnt through to patches on the ground, I explained to her that I was walking to the mountains by following the river, and as I spoke, I felt the city, almost new in river time, grow insubstantial around me.

We said goodbye to my workmates and walked across Swanston Street to Federation Square – to the National Gallery of Victoria located by the river. There was someone we had to visit. We gave our backpacks to the cloakroom attendant, and entered the ground-floor level – the contemporary Indigenous art gallery. In our hiking boots and hats we sat in a row on the sleek new gallery floor to listen to Joy Murphy Wandin. Her image was showing continuously on a screen just by the entry.

'*Womenjika wurundjeri balluk kiamin kundibik*. Welcome to the lands of the Wurundjeri people.'

She'd been filmed somewhere outdoors, and by the look of the environment, towards the headwaters of the Yarra, not far from her home close to Healesville. The images that accompanied her welcome were of tall forests and a clear fast-flowing mountain stream. The appropriateness of the imagery seemed a good omen for our journey, and, in conjunction with Tammy's blessing, a serendipitous start to our quest. With a thank you to the ever-welcoming Joy, we continued on our way.

Leaving the gallery, we climbed down stone steps, out of Fed Square and back to the river. I breathed my relief, finally away from commerce, car parks and construction sites. There were parks on both sides of the river, stately old trees and shady pathways. This was the Yarra that most Melburnians knew; the tourist shot, the place of festivals, water pageants and celebrations.

We sauntered under the curvaceous lemon-scented gums,

then the avenue of Moreton Bay figs right by the water. Pied cormorants were sitting on a litter trap that had been secured to the riverbank, which was filled with floating debris; drink bottles and polystyrene oddments. These birds' preferred perch is in trees where branches overhang the water, where they can spot the movement of dinner in the river below. In the absence of the indigenous red gums, which lean far over the water, the birds use what they can.

Over lunch I'd leafed through a little book Jess had given me that morning; *The Yarra River: A Natural Treasure* by David and Cam Beardsell. It quoted an early commentator who wrote about this part of the river in the 1840s as 'an immense cordon of she oak, gum and wattle tree forests through which the river ran with blackfish, bream, flounder and herring'. Lucky cormorants back then; damn fine fishing.

The river was once much narrower, and wound back and forth between the riparian (riverside) forest. This whole section had been the subject of a large engineering project at the turn of the nineteenth century. Now it was one wide curve. The cut-off bends on the south side of the river became the ornamental lakes in Melbourne's Royal Botanic Gardens. The northern bends were filled in with soil from the new river channel, and became the site for the famous sportsgrounds of Melbourne. They built the Morell Bridge in 1899 on solid land, and then dug the new channel for the river beneath it, lining the sides with bluestone slabs.

We stood on the Morell Bridge, now just for pedestrians, and looked upriver. A flock of white cockatoos screeched overhead. And we sang too, for we had a song for what we saw ahead, although it was warmer than eleven degrees that day.

Paul Kelly wrote the music, and I saw the film clip of the silos on the telly as a kid, and I remember still the shock of seeing something from my world sung about, a mapping of part of the landscape I knew. They tried to take the clock down from the silos a few years ago – Melburnian's wouldn't let them. Maybe because this place has a song.

We approached Herring Island in the sideways glow of late afternoon. Once this was one of the many bends of Birrarung, until flood mitigation measures deemed it interfered with the flow of water to the sea. The bend was cut through and became an island, heaped with the dredged silts. Mr Herring decided that the new island be used as a scout camp – thousands of urban children had gone there for bush adventures in the city. But that was years ago, when children were occupied differently. Now it's a sculpture park.

On the little jetty built for the punt that services the island, we saw someone waiting with a bulging picnic basket. The figure was portly, and grey hair crept out from under his cap: the face was kindly, lit with joy at his surprise for us. It was Noel, a friend from CERES, with gin, tonic, lemon and ice, and tall glasses.

We sipped our drinks with delight, sitting in a row on the jetty and swinging our legs over the Yarra in the sun. Soon Greg arrived with our transport to the island. It was the blue canoe from Collingwood Children's Farm, where Greg worked. It was battered and scraped, with a slow leak after years of service.

We found our trailer on the street, delivered earlier by a member of our support crew. We said goodbye to Noel, and one by one, with Greg playing ferryman, we took over the gear we needed for the night. While we were loading another friend arrived with a big pot of sweet potato curry.

Once on the island, we spread out and explored our water-ringed camp. I found a place to sit looking back over the way we had come, gazing westerly into the riverglow of reflected sun. A heron flew past, a tram rattled across the Yarra over the Church St Bridge. A moon, a thin yellow crescent, was slowly setting over the freeway, just like the famous moons seen in the *The Age* newspaper in the cartoons by Michael Leunig. That day reminded me of one of his poems:

> Go to the end of the path until you get to the gate.
> Go through the gate and head straight out towards the horizon.
> Keep going towards the horizon.
> Sit down and have a rest every now and again.
> But keep on going. Just keep on with it.
> Keep on going as far as you can. That's how you get there.

We ate dinner among the trees, sitting around the island's picnic table, while flying foxes and microbats flapped overhead, eating the airborne insects. Greg had sourced local historical documents, and he read aloud, of how people have long worked to protect the river from pollution, of environmental pioneers in the 1850s, just two decades after colonisation, and of dolphins in the river at Richmond, emus in Collins Street.

I imagined, for a moment, my body borne up with the bats, and I looked down, and saw us. One candle on the table surrounded by a dark wedge of trees. The flowing water, wrapping like arms around the rough-cut edges of the island. Then beyond, all around, the lights, the roads, the carved-out blocks of land filled with house, or factory, or apartment.

Barwool did not cut the shape of Herring Island. That cut came with those who followed Grimes up the river. In such a short space of time, it'd been cleared, quarried, reshaped with fill and salty silts, and lastly revegetated. So many changes. Yet even so, of all the sites we'd seen that day, the island was perhaps the place where the ancestors could have glimpsed a fragment of the whole they once dwelt within.

What is a fragment, an island, when the surrounding land and its stories are buried, replaced by a million myriad tales of a sprawling metropolis? Grimes had indeed brought the British Empire to this river. The British Empire, as late as 1910, covered more than a quarter of the globe. The ideas Grimes brought with him in his boat up this river were laid out over continents. Only islands of the old ways are left.

Yet the islands exist. And like our island, there are no bridges. My journey upriver was fired, in part, by a desire to look into these islands of old ways clinging to the edges of my city. If I want to know the island, perhaps, like a bat, I must fly over water, listening to faint echoes, through darkness. Into darkness I must feel my way, other senses guiding me, to new land, old land.

THE FIRST NIGHT

A strange, nocturnal thing, pliant and wild, is growing in the darkness. The night mind. The patterning, dreaming mind is casting about feathers I must gather, to draw together into wings, to carry me to islands, many islands.

In the limitlessness behind my eyes I glimpse fragments as wholes. There is a pattern made, not of my devising, yet a known thing. As if the day just passed had happened since before I were born. The bright coins spilt as if into a temple bowl, the sun and the gums and the grasses, the tower and the sea, the windborne gulls, the herons – the grey and the nankeen night, the city and the slanting light. They were all there, inevitable and true. They are possibilities, always, and yes, I may see them. But in my ordinary life, why is it that the things of the world do not link themselves together, as if they were words of a song?

It felt as if the world saw us leaving the house, and said, 'here they are, finally, after all these years, they are coming'.

TO BE HERE

I woke to the chime of bells, tumbling over the island. I poked my head out of the tent; the magpies flew off. Thin mist hung in drifts among the eucalypts. A flock of magpie-larks burst through the trees, along with the shafts of first sunshine. The freeway buzzed behind me.

I wandered the island alone before breakfast. One sculpture drew me in. It was of thin layers of pale brown slate stacked perfectly in the shape of an unopened pinecone. Finely balanced, it felt as if it had been there forever. I sat beside it, as if to absorb some of its knowing. A kookaburra came and perched nearby, landing on a flimsy branch. While the branch wobbled under his weight, the kookaburra's head stayed uncannily still, watching me.

The day was calm and shining. The blue sky, reflecting up from the river, made everything extra brilliant. As we breakfasted and packed, we pottered around as if we had oceans of time. After all the logistics of the week's prior, on such a day, it was beautiful to just be.

'Cooee! You lot up yet?' It was a voice, shouted over the water.

'Hours ago, you cheeky bugger.' I hollered back.

It was Jess. I'd canoed him over to the mainland last night after dinner, but he'd returned to walk with us again. Paddling back over to fetch him, I rippled through the perfectly mirrored landscapes that lay below the boat.

Eventually we'd canoed all our gear to the south bank of the river and loaded the trailer. While we packed, lycra-clad Saturday cyclists drank lattes at the bike path café just near us – a converted toilet block. The riverbanks, moving upmarket.

My belly was complaining for lunch by the time we were ready to begin our walking day. Luckily we didn't have far to go – our camp that night was my old home, Collingwood Children's Farm. Upriver we set out, past ancient scented paperbarks sloughing off delicate layers of bark in sheaves, as if they were birthing books. We crossed the river to join the walking trail wedged between the freeway (hidden behind a high concrete wall) and the Yarra.

On the other side of the river the cliffs up to South Yarra and Toorak were high and arrayed with fine old houses and lush falling-to-the-river gardens. In between these were development sites scraped clean of vegetation, and mansions were emerging, big and boxy. Some houses had their own personal docks on the riverbank, with a pleasure-cruiser attached.

We came to the junction of the Yarra and Gardiner's Creek. The confluence was hidden under a giant freeway bridge – it was a cave of echoes, the river threw dancing shadows, and a grid of stone paved the edges of Birrarung. From my research I'd gathered that the junction is approximately the furthest reach of Bunerong tribal land; from onwards of the watery meeting place, both sides of the Yarra are Wurundjeri country. I grew up downstream from that place, crossing the river back and forth from my mum's house to my dad's, and I thought of how my cultural territory of the inner city seemed to reflect the ancient tribal boundaries between Wurundjeri and Bunerong lands. Friends often spoke of being 'north of the river' or 'south of the river' people, and I hear folk say of the river that it is hard to cross, as if there were a border between these lands. As if the Yarra wasn't criss-crossed with bridges! It feels sometimes as if an old cultural way is persisting, despite so much change.

The river curled away, and we walked on, relieved that the freeway had finally let the Yarra alone (although poor Gardiner's Creek now has to bear that ever-present cacophony). Soon we came to a stand of fat and leaning remnant red gums. Around them were new plantings of wetland species, and pond depressions that, in the drought, were completely dry. We chose for our lunch spot the shade by an old gum. Its insides had long ago rotted away, and there beckoned an archway, just big enough to squeeze through. I crawled in. I stood up in the darkness, in the secret heart of the tree.

After lunch, Ilan and I dawdled, peering in at a circus set up in the riverside park at Burnley. Cinnamon, Kate and Jess were arriving at the Corroboree Tree, the historic Wurundjeri gathering place, when we caught up with them. This spot was on the other side of the tracks from the circus. It seems that the riverside flat is still being used for shows and celebrations. The big top comes and goes with the seasons, like the Wurundjeri who gathered there. The tree was no longer alive, barely even a stag, just a tall stump, covered with the spiky protrusions of old red gums. Colour had long faded from the Corroboree Tree. The five of us linked arms around the base – we could just embrace its girth.

Then on into Yarra Bend Park. The Silurian cliffs were high above the river, the trees lean and dusty green with dryness and thin soil. The wriggling white branches of the red gums danced over the cliffs. It looked as if these trees, when bending low over the water, saw themselves reflected in that rippling mirror, and liked the wiggly look, so took it on and grew that way.

The river flowed tan brown with suspended sediment. In one of the documents Greg read from the night before the Yarra was described as a 'clear, pellucid stream'. The clay particles of the soil are so fine that any run-off with silt clouds the water. The tilling and building of the European settlers broke the web of plant roots that once held all the soil tight, and ever since the water has looked like mud.

We followed the little track curling around the cliff, Ilan and I flying ahead, skipping and running and flapping our wings and screeching like cockatoos. The path descended towards the riverbank; the land opened up to a broad track among a thick stand of elms, a few remnant gums among them. The long factory of Carlton United Breweries squatted on the opposite bank, the concrete chimney a beacon steaming above the suburbs. The factory hummed, and a biscuity sweetness was in the air. Perhaps it was the toasting of hops in ovens the size of rooms, or bubbling vats of malt.

I have memories of walking that stretch with my father as a

child, learning from him the names of things; the trees, the rocks, the shapes of the leaves. I'd heard the argument against 'naming' things; that if we focus on learning the names of things we then become attached to the name, and might then think we 'know' it. We might fail to see its deeper reality. Yet in our culture, which pays little time or attention to the particulars of place, I felt it to be a worthwhile place to start. Naming can be a first stage of seeing, like an introduction, a courtesy. On the way to really seeing it, in the place where no words are needed.

I was with Jess, and we played a game; all the birds we could think of with a colour and a body part included in their names. We sang out their names as we skipped along.

'Orange-bellied parrot!'

'White-faced heron!'

'Red-browed firetail!'

'Um, um, yellow-tailed black cockatoo.'

'White-naped honeyeater.'

'White-throated treecreeper.'

'Ummm, redback spider!'

'Cheat!'

Just as we approached the Gipps Street Footbridge I thought back to my last evening of living at Collingwood Children's Farm. That night I walked the beloved landscapes, and on the footbridge I came upon an old man in a wheelchair who was looking over the river. We were curious about each other, so we got talking, and I found out that he lived across the bridge at the Salvation Army Hostel.

'I come to watch the birds,' he told me. Then he let on

that he knew an old cypress in the park where three tawny frogmouths lived. He said he couldn't tell me where, he would have to show me. I agreed, and in agreeing, I found that I had to push his heavy wheelchair around the corner and up the hill and then along a bit, and then along a bit more.

'Crafty chap.' I thought to myself.

But it was worth the work, to see the big, bark-coloured birds, asleep, perched in their daytime stick position, appearing almost identical to the stumps of dead branches. And it was worth it, to see the enthusiasm of this man, and the clever way he got to see his friends the tawny frogmouths.

A few years later, walking on Gipps Street towards the footbridge there was a garage sale in the house by the river. I stopped to check it out, and one of the men chatting there said,

'Gidday, remember me?'

It was the Tawny Frogmouth Man. He looked healthy, so much younger, and there was no wheelchair.

'Oh yeah, I got better. I've found myself a nice flat over east a bit, but I come back to visit me mates. You really liked those tawnies, didn't you? You know they're not there now, the bloody council chopped down that tree.'

We crossed over the footbridge from Kew into Abbotsford, then down the three flights of concrete steps. Just as we arrived at the bottom of the steps a child rode up on his bicycle. It was Will, son of our friends Thais and John, who were just riding up behind him. Thais and John each had another small boy on the backs of their bikes. While Will turned around and shot off along the path ahead, John and Thais got off their bikes and walked with us.

Thais and I knew each other from working together on an event she and others had begun at CERES Community Environment Park. The event, The Return of the Sacred Kingfisher Festival, is held in honour of a tiny azure and white bird. It celebrates the time of year when sacred kingfishers return to Victoria after spending the winter in the north of Australia. But it was much more than that. CERES, a chaotic, creative and colourful sustainability village, was located on top of a former tip alongside the Merri Creek. The Merri wound through the industrial northern suburbs, becoming a dumping ground for chemical sludge and washed through with whatever detritus the drains delivered. The red gums were felled, the water ribbons, which ran along the creek's surface like green streamers, were poisoned. But over the last few decades, massive community work had transformed the CERES site along with wider rehabilitation of the creek. Large-scale replanting reinvigorated the local ecosystems. The migratory sacred kingfishers, which hadn't been seen on the Merri for decades, were found to be returning each spring, nesting and breeding once again. So the festival was also a celebration of the repair work of the humans, and the reward; wildlife returning. Thus Thais wrote in our logbook:

> Hello to the sacred kingfishers upstream and say farewell to them from us as they leave on their migration journey into the unknown, as you continue on your journey into the unknown! Happy walking, swimming, resting on soft moss, feeling soggy, and hopefully not too prickled by blackberries…

During the years when I worked at CERES on the Kingfisher Festival, Ian Hunter, Wurundjeri Elder, was our cultural advisor. He introduced traditional stories and together we wove them into the theatrical event, the dusk ritual, down by the creek, where the birds and the repair community were the heart of the party. Sometimes, Ian would come with new stories, what he called contemporary Wurundjeri stories. Sometimes, we would add to traditional tales, with Ian's assistance and permission.

There is an old story, of Bunjil the wedge-tailed eagle creating the world, but forgetting to add colour. That came later, with his wife, Branbeal, the rainbow. When we performed the story, Branbeal came in with her helpers, the rainbow lorikeets, whose feathers, when they fall, replenish the colour of the world.

I don't know, now, whether the bird bit is new or ancient. I worry about that sometimes. I celebrate it, at others. Like when I pick up a feather from a rainbow lorikeet. Or when I leave it there, breaking apart, coloured filaments combing into the earth.

That particular year at Kingfisher, I was one of a group performing the character of Waa, the crow, who played an important role in traditional Wurundjeri culture. On the day of the show, I opened my front door, and two crows were waiting in the sheoak. As I walked the three kilometres through the Brunswick streets from home to the performance site on the creek, the two crows followed me, flying from tree to tree, most of the way.

Maybe that sounds sweet, but have you ever looked closely at a crow? One of the birds that day was young; untidy, dark eyed. Yet I knew he would soon smooth his sleek feathers, his muddy eyes would pale and harden, and he would look at me like ice. I felt, that day, the seriousness of the land I live in.

≈

Together we approached the farm. By an avenue of poplars, four horses with riders were flanking the path, awaiting our arrival. Frank, the horse-riding instructor from the farm, had ridden out with a welcoming party of three young riders. I was flush with pride and excitement as we walked with our equine escort to my former home. I had lived at the farm for four years, in the old bluestone house built in the 1850s. I had loved farm life – I missed it still, years after moving away, but I am lucky that my farm is a public farm, and I can revisit whenever I need, along with the hordes of city children.

We followed the main Yarra trail that bisects the farm. Anglo-Nubian goats, Guernsey cows, Leicester sheep and a couple of donkeys watched our mob pass by (there were eighteen of us by then, counting the horses). We passed the apple orchard and the pigs, and then turned in to the side gate. Greg Barber, the mayor of the City of Yarra (and the only Greens mayor in the country), was waiting for us under the peppercorn trees by the barn. We were hot and tired and sweaty and thirsty, but there were photos to be taken, sitting on straw bales with the horses lined up behind, and conversations to be had with the mayor and the council's environment officer. Greg Barber gave us a handful of his cards, suggesting we may like to give them to others we would meet on our journey, to foster discussion between caretakers along the length of the waterway. We were happy to take them. He wrote in our book:

To the people upstream…everybody lives in a catchment, and we all live in this one – we need to get together!

Trees, fish, water, birds, ecology, economy, humanity, all are one.

Then down to the big old oak tree, below the farmhouses, where we were to camp for the night.

Before it got dark, Jess and I planned to have a paddle – our support crew had dropped the blue canoe back to the farm that morning. We hauled the boat down the track past the house, the orchard and the overgrown gardens. We launched at the place where farmer Greg had once made a path down to the water, just below the oak. Under the wattles the river was dark and very still, and as we paddled off downstream, the escarpment was perfectly reflected in the water.

We started back when the sun had set, the cold air sinking off the land and onto the water. As we approached, I remembered all the times I had returned to the oak at dusk, and the delicious excitement of coming home, all the years I lived there. Often the flying foxes would be thick overhead, as they commenced their nightly migration along the waterways in search of food. And once, a few years back, I heard the sound of drums and marimbas floating across the water; it was our large and colourful party, tiny under the encompassing limbs of the great oak.

It was my birthday, and we were gathered under our party tree. Two friends were playing Eastern European folk music on accordion and fiddle, and we were singing, when Greg noticed someone lurking behind the oak. It was Bill, an elderly Macedonian man with a round leathery face and a roving eye, who grew tomatoes and chillies, zucchini and chicory in his garden plot at the farm. He'd been having a quiet drink alone in his tiny shed on his plot when he heard the music and came to investigate. Greg brought him into the circle.

'Do you know any Macedonian songs?' I whispered to Sophie.

'I know the perfect one,' she replied seductively.

She began playing a melancholy tune on the piano accordion strapped across her breast, and Bill turned to her in wonder. He stood there among us, in front of the fire, and sang this song he knew well, a beautiful song of mourning for homeland, while tears ran down his face.

A few years after finishing high school I flew off to Europe. I was keen to experience something of the land that created the culture that had so recently colonised Australia.

I wandered through Turkey in the spring, at Easter time, when the fields were a fairytale of flowers, and young rabbits bounced through lush grass. High in the hills of Tuscany, I scythed the meadows of summer with an anarchic crew of back-to-the landers; all loincloths and nut-brown skin. In the herb fields and forests around the house we collected herbs for tonics and nettles for soup. Then I headed north. I wrested

Karrote, Pastinak (parsnip) *und Rote Bete* (have a guess) from German mud, as the harvest moon sank behind coppery beech forests. And I picked the only greenery to escape the white of winter, the fir and the holly, to decorate the long nights of Christmas. I swelled in happiness through the cycle of the year, and felt a rich sense of rightness, of homecoming. Culturally familiar, almost clichés, I wondered how it was that these experiences felt more real than anything I'd yet known.

It was at a large festival in Ireland that I came to some understanding of what I felt. Thousands of people had gathered together to celebrate Lughnasa, the birth of the goddess, in August when the crops ripened. This ancient Celtic celebration had been held for millennia, there in the centre of Ireland. Food was shared out among the thousands, at a vast humming circle in the valley. Gypsy children rode their massive horses around the ring, and from their wagons fiddles, flutes and thin, bad-tempered men tumbled out. In that wet green land the windblown clouds brought rain a dozen times a day, and rainbows arced over the hills. At the end of ten days the full moon rose, and raucous, careering dancers spiralled all the night long. I realised that these were people ancient in this land. Yet they were modern people. So, perhaps like a dim memory relived, a game played, in earnest but not without irony, these people were aligning themselves with their indigenous identity. Through the bulk of my ancestry, I too once belonged here. This was home.

But it wasn't. As the European winter descended, and my senses were dulled by cold I'd never known, I grew desperate for the smells and seasons of my birthplace. The eucalyptus oil my German boyfriend dropped into a steaming bowl and laid in front of me to clear my sinuses brought on a gale of tears. I was homesick.

When after a year I came back to Australia, I saw anew the gum forests, the way the light dripped through the loose and shining canopy. Yet beyond that, there seemed an emptiness. It appeared that we did things backwards here. We had Easter, which originated in a spring festival, in autumn, we celebrated a sweltering Christmas with feral fir trees and fake snow on shop windows. In Europe, so much of the culture that I had grown up with made sense for the first time. The stories I read as a child, the rituals of the year, odd and unconnected in Australia, became true over there. The plants of Europe; blackberry, dandelion, fennel, were not rampant weeds as in Australia but useful wild foods for the farmers I worked with. In Melbourne I did not have stories for the native trees, or for the seasons. I didn't know how to eat without damaging the fragile ecosystems of the place where I lived. I longed for a sense of community that was more than people, one that included all things.

My boyfriend came from overseas, to see if we could live together, here in my country. Or, if not here, whether I would return with him to Germany. I took him down the dusty narrow track to Galatea Point in Yarra Bend Park, among the red gums, to sit by the river of my home. I said that I could not leave here, that I had work to do, learning how to live here well and wholly. And he was a gardener in his country, he knew all the stories of the trees, and could read the land. He belonged somewhere. That was much of why I loved him. He went back to Europe without me.

I stayed in Melbourne, and explored what it meant to be

here. I wondered if, and how, the traditions of my European ancestors could better fit in this land.

Prior to the introduction of Christianity, agricultural societies had recognised and celebrated the cyclical transitions of the year – the solstices and the equinoxes. Christmas replaced the traditional winter solstice celebrations, and took on many of the symbols of a far more ancient tradition. An example; in Denmark, I was told that the story of Santa Claus evolved from northern European shamanic traditions; of eating hallucinogenic fly agaric mushroom (those fairytale ones that grow under pine trees, red with white spots, the colours of a certain overweight gentleman's suit) and going on journeys to contact the spirit world, guided by the rhythm of bells. Fleeting visions of flying reindeer seem an obvious consequence of such practices. Other traditions such as Christmas trees (the only green thing in a European winter, and so a symbol of life), gathering together to share rich food (such as puddings full of dried fruit from the autumn harvest) and the importance of fire – candles and coloured lights – are a response to the place and the season, a response to the longest, darkest night of the year, the winter solstice.

In Australia, my friends and I began to celebrate the equinoxes and solstices. On the 21st or 22nd of June we would gather under the bare oak tree in the darkness, and we would kindle a flame at dusk. It became a practice of aligning ourselves with the world's changes, bringing awareness to the pendulum swing of the year. We would make a wish, and affirm the gifts of the night; depth, introspection, a gathering of energies to spend in summer. It felt good to be there, with friends, with veggies baking in the camp oven on the coals. It felt more like what Christmas was meant to be.

At the same time I began to get serious about my education; learning how to live in this place. I planted trees, grew food, ate bush tucker, studied maps and books, and asked endless questions. I found friends who shared such passions, who taught me, who let me teach them so that I could see what I had learned. We sought to connect with local Aboriginal people, and we were guided by their knowledge and wisdom. We gathered together and began to celebrate a shared sense of place.

One day Ian Hunter asked me if I would help him harvest bushfoods from the Latrobe University wetlands. I agreed, keen to learn more about native foods. We drove there on a hot day to cut cumbungi, a water plant that grows in wetlands and billabongs and quiet bends of rivers. We were out to harvest the tender bases of the cumbungi stalks at the place where they emerge from the mud at the bottom of the dam; roasted in the coals, these stalks would taste deliciously like a mild, nutty leek. We were up to our waists in water, wearing wetsuits, and wielding heavy machetes. We bent low to cut the stalks from the murky water, taking care not to slice our feet off in the process.

While we chopped then threw the stalks into a heap at the side of the dam, Ian told me stories of growing up as a person of Indigenous heritage in Melbourne in the 1950s. He told me about the remnants of language his family managed to preserve, of times exploring the bush and the river with his older relations. I listened and worked. Each time I bent down to the black water to cut another stem my face was reflected back at me, and it seemed to be asking – why have you not heard these stories before?

After we had finished harvesting, he took me exploring around the wetlands, and everywhere we went, he showed me food. We dug up club rush corms from around the edge of the dam, small round tubers with a taste like water chestnuts. We ate crunchy wattle seed out of their dry purple-brown pods. Ian peeled away the corner of some hessian sacking that worked to smother the weeds, but it also made a home for our next treat – we squatted down and ate the sweet ends of sugar ants. In the university car park Ian and I snacked on lerp, the delicate sugary shells the sap-sucking insects spin onto the eucalypt leaves.

We piled the cumbungi stems into the back of his four-wheel drive and drove into the city along Plenty Road. As I wound down the window to catch the cool change, I was thinking of the time in the forests of Italy, and my enthusiasm for picking wild greens and strawberries along the forest paths; foods from my cultural tradition, even though I am fourth-generation Australian. I felt that enthusiasm again, I felt something burningly real, yet this time it wasn't a cliché. For everything I learned was new.

It was as if Ian had peeled away a corner of the 200-year-old blanket that Europe had thrown over this land and over me. I had seen, for a moment, what lay beneath.

At that time, when I was living at the Collingwood Children's Farm, news came that developers were going to turn the Abbotsford Convent into a housing estate. They planned to build over many of the paddocks by the river that the farm currently grazed; four-storey townhouses, right on the boundary. We were horrified!

We immediately joined the campaign to try to stop the development. Greg joined the Abbotsford Convent Coalition Committee and became a vital part of the team. He had the idea of holding a bonfire for the winter solstice – a public one, where all the community could come down and make a wish for the convent. With Greg coordinating, volunteers came from all directions to help; making lanterns with the children, building the bonfire in the top goat paddock near the convent, making posters, cooking food. I spent all solstice day in the farm kitchen making spicy lentils. As dusk neared, I struggled up with the big pots, dropping them off at the farm food stall. Then I ran, flute in pocket, robes flying, to get into position, to be the piper leading the children's lantern procession.

It took many years of hard work by hundreds of people, but the convent was saved. And now the bonfire burns every winter solstice, a celebration of the community's victory. But the bonfire has its own life, an ancient European ritual reignited in modern times, and each person will have their own meaning for it. For the seventh bonfire, I asked Ian Hunter if he would be part of the celebrations, if he would do a welcome to country for us, and tell the creation story of the Yarra before the bonfire was lit.

'And Ian, how would you feel about making the fire with firesticks, and then we could light the bonny from that? I mean, it might be too difficult, being winter, and it might be raining ...'

'Nah, of course I can do that. No problem. And tell you what, I've got a song that goes with that story in language –

should we teach everyone that?' offered Ian.

'Yes! Fantastic!' I replied.

Yani duwi baan.

Baan yana baan yana.

Yani duwi baan.

Baan yana baan yana.

'What it means is, it's asking the water to go away, 'coz you know how it was stuck up there in the mountains? Before Barwool came along with his stone axe and cut the river down to the bay? Well, the story is the mob up there didn't have anywhere to hunt. They just had all this water everywhere. So I reckon they were pretty bored with just fish to eat, so these are the English words:

> Sick and tired of eating fish
> Eating eel, eating fish
> Come on wombat come on 'roo
> We want to eat you too.

'It's great for kids, they love this song – they like to know what it means, but they'll sing it in language. There's a clapstick rhythm that goes with it, on the one and the three and the four, CLAP … clap, clap, CLAP … clap, clap, CLAP.'

'Yay Ian, that's perfect, because we imagined the lantern parade being the Yarra, so the parade then becomes the freed water pouring down from the mountains on it's way to the bay. We can teach the song to all the people around the bonfire, and get them to clap the rhythm.'

'Goody good,' said Ian.

＝

The second night of our pilgrimage we hosted a gathering for friends with a campfire and meal under the oak tree. My sister arrived, carrying, as ever, mountains of delicious food.

'All your Enid Blyton dreams come true hey?' I scowled at her, embarrassed and happy, grateful to be known.

THE SECOND NIGHT

I am walking with my sister near the coast of Turkey. We are in a wide river valley, an untamed estuary stretching over many miles of rushes and reeds, flush with spring life. We find a beautiful clear pool, a river backwater. It is warm, there is no-one to see us. We take off our clothes and slide into the water. It is sun warmed and silky and a clean pale green, and surrounded by tall bright reeds. I open my eyes underwater.

They stay open. My blood soughs, tingling and tinkling through my ears, my brain, my chest, and there it washes my heart. I am clear, all the way through. And then I grow, beyond my edges. For my eyes are open wide in a pool of tears. The salinity of the water matches my eyes exactly. I fit, exactly, where the sea and the river meet and mingle. The boundary between above and below vanishes, water is my home as is the land. I leap and dive with amphibian joy. I fall face forward with my eyes wide open, over and over into the green water. Tears spill from my eyes, tears, the perfect gift. Tears belong, as I do.

The Yarra is estuarine all the way to Collingwood Children's

Farm. Just beyond the farm, at Dight's Falls, that's where the sea can climb no higher. In my home estuary I would not open my eyes. I would not even swim, although I have dunked myself up to the neck a few times in desperate heat, and been grateful. But the estuary is too polluted to swim safely, and is thick with sediment. If this estuary matches the salinity of my tears, I will never know.

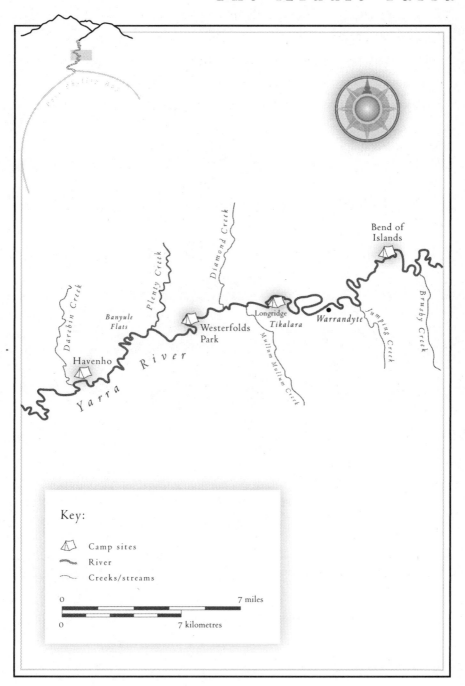

Key:

⌂ Camp sites

~ River

- - Creeks/streams

0   7 miles

0   7 kilometres

WHAT THE RIVER SAYS

During the night, in the hours when sleep eluded me, I dragged my mat and me out of my tent. So in the morning I woke, cosy in my sleeping bag, among the long grass, under the generous spread of the oak. In the sunrise glow I looked up into the intricate branches, at the sharp turns of the limbs; elbows bent, wrists testing their limits. The thin fingers, the thousands of tiny branchlets, all swept towards the earth. In spring each finger sprouted a bunch of bright leaves which, by late summer, had darkened under months of sun.

Jess, stretching outside his tent, saw me awake. 'How about another paddle?' he whispered.

We lugged the canoe out from under the farmhouse and back down the river path. We slid it down the steep bank, over the weeds to the water. The river was shrouded with a mist that caught in the breeze, to be combed thin by the wattles before vanishing into the trees. Black ducks played in the rapids upstream. I scrambled down the rough-cut steps after Jess to the bank, slippery with mud left by the retreating tide. I held the boat while Jess got into the navigation position in the rear. Happily, that meant the front seat was for me, where

I could just sit and watch and not have to think about the delicate business of steering. Jess pushed us off into the flow – onto Birrarung, River of Mists.

I was tired. I'd been awake half the night, mulling over the day before. So after breakfast, as I wandered around the farmhouses and the gardens above the great oak, around the place once my home, I was more than a little sentimental.

I remembered our unusual pets; how I would stand on the kitchen table and pat the sleeping possums through the holes in our ceiling, where they lived, curled and furry, during the day. By night they tap-danced on the tin roof, and I liked them less. Then there were the blue-tongue lizard babies eating out the strawberry patch, while their mum came and curled up on the crimson velvet cushion by the fireplace.

I crept into what was once our garden shed, now ramshackle. There on the wall were words Greg had written in chalk on The Garden Talk Board, our noticeboard once used for recording planting times and watering rosters;

'It's over. Goodbye dear messy shed, covered over with the glory of the morning. Memories of baths, baa's, seedlings, hippy hothouses, and good gardening times.'

The morning glory was creeping down the slope to cover what had been our enormous vegetable garden, where we'd grown almost all our food, where my grandmother used to come and help before she became too vague and got lost on the way from the train station.

I circled back to the oak. I'd been there in storms and in stillness, at times of frost and dull flyblown heat. I'd eaten many after-party breakfasts there, on the ashes of the party fire; goose egg pancakes with homemade yoghurt made from farm milk; Guernsey milk so creamy that an inch of delicious soured cream would settle at the top of the big jar. Or farm eggs and scorched bread and wattle seed tea, made by a friend from indigenous silver wattle seeds he collected from the riverbanks.

In my mist of memories, I stirred up the fire from the night before, and cooked eggs for a quick second breakfast. The blue smoke rose through the branches. While we packed, Jess sat straight backed under the oak, writing in our log book.

What an amazing adventure the past three days have been! I've journeyed with you in anticipatory thoughts about this trip since the very first time I met you Maya. Now to be on the river doing it is amazing and yet so natural too. It's been such a pleasure to contribute – being your MC, paddling the canoe back and forth, backing up trailers, putting up tents – I love all this stuff! The feeling of connectedness for the river has grown for me over the past few days, and I'm sure for you it will grow even stronger. Also the growing between you walkers that I've witnessed has been beautiful, and I'm sure there will be much more there too. Blessings on your sacred journey. May your pilgrimage to the source reward you with all the inner treasures you seek.

Lots of love, cousin Jess

It was late (not quite as late as the day before, but closer to the afternoon than we'd hoped) when finally we were ready to leave. We said goodbye to the farm, and set off along the river. I walked backwards for a while; taking leave of the oak.

The river tide had retreated even further since we'd been canoeing – under the Johnston Street Bridge we could have walked across the stones with the water around our shins. The underside of the bridge was, as usual, a running battle between the graffiti artists and the council – the council had the upper hand that day; the wall along the track was a smooth grey. Multicoloured runnels, the sole trace of the art that had been blasted off, meandered over the concrete path and dripped over the edge. The stories and the scrawl, the messages and the chemicals, ran down to the river.

We turned sharp left at the end of the bridge, to take the steep and secret path up to Johnston Street. We wanted to walk on the other side of the Yarra, and that was a good way to get there. Johnston Street's traffic was a reminder of the world we weren't seeing by following the river – it was a relief to get to the end of the bridge, and return to the world of Yarra Bend Park, shady and inviting.

We stepped off the footpath onto the grassy swathe and turned upriver. Not fifty metres along there was a bluestone deck with a fragile metal railing, decorative in an old-fashioned way. It was the remnant of the previous Johnston Street Bridge, too narrow for modern traffic, demolished long ago. There was a cutting originally made for the old road; it went through mudstone, tan-brown, very similar to the colour of Yarra. After a solid rain, the river took on even more of this colour, and in that place, it was easy to see why.

The track upriver was old and unpaved, and the rock face rose sharply on our right, with the river flowing far below us. The sedimentary rock that formed the land mass to the east of the Yarra dates from the Silurian period, which means that it is at least 400 million years old. For much of that time, this area was underwater. The rocks around us were formed by layers of sediment deposited in the sea by ancient rivers. The Yarra itself is a very old river, more than 100 million years in parts, which means it was here in Gondwanan times. And for much of that time it has been wearing away at these cliffs, cutting ever deeper into the valley, and carrying with it these silts. Somewhere, at the bottom of the bay, layers are building again to one day become rock. And among the silts will be other things that may become strange fossils; beer bottles, coat hangers, carburettors, outboard motors.

The sedimentary rock had been warped and twisted over millions of years, causing the rock to curve into synclines (smile-shaped layers) and anticlines (rainbow shaped). Some of the softer, older layers had worn away, leaving rock arches. Ilan clambered up the cliff and draped himself provocatively along a particularly fetching anticline, and gazed lizard-like into my camera. As we walked on we passed a place where the rock layers had twisted through ninety degrees and stood like dark fluted columns. The softer layers were pale, some so fragile I could prise out little pieces with my fingers.

We climbed around the bend and up the slope to the parched north bank of the river, to steep mudstone cliffs carpeted with lichens russet brown and faded green. The cliffs overlook Dight's Falls, where water tumbles over jumbled stone, and rubbish is wedged between the rocks. There we had a view of our destination, the first since Williamstown.

'This is incredible what we are doing!' Ilan exclaimed, and I felt a shiver of recognition; of how he too loved this quirky mission. Together we sat on the cliffs and looked to the far distant mountains, a humble smudge on the horizon.

The crash of the water below almost masked the sound of another freeway – the Eastern. For that road to be built, they had to change the course of the Yarra, and they built over historic sites precious to the Wurundjeri – the location of the first native school, and the place where hundreds of tribespeople gathered in the early days of settlement to discuss what they could do about the white invaders on their land.

When I was about six years old, I remember being at the freeway protest where the mayor of Collingwood was arrested and dragged off in his mayoral robes. I remember the fury and the sadness of my father and the other protestors as they lost the battle to save the park from eight lanes of traffic.

~

Freeways are built to carry the cars that a city like Melbourne, designed for horse and tram, simply cannot accomodate. The only areas not subdivided and built upon in the early development of the city, apart from parks, were the creeks and rivers. So above, alongside and amidst the waterways they fit their new roads. The riverside zones were also the only places where remnants of the original vegetation could hold on.

My dad became interested in indigenous vegetation before its current rise in favour. He found some rare plants one day while exploring the Moonee Ponds Creek, and so he set about protecting and enhancing the area. Council provided some more indigenous species, and with friends he began to revegetate ever larger areas of the creek banks. He spent time there almost every day for ten years, eventually revegetating ten acres of what was formerly wasteland. Then one day came the news. The Tullamarine freeway was widening. They bulldozed his little piece of bush. He stood beside the freeway holding a sign while the torrent of cars roared past. It said, 'You killed my garden'. He left Australia not long after that, and has lived overseas ever since.

≈

We continued down the cliffs, back to the water's edge. Not far above Dight's Falls is the confluence of the Yarra and the Merri. Cinn and I stopped, remembering our earlier pilgrimage. There on the other side of the river we had set off three and a half years before, on an adventure that was the seed of our current quest.

≈

Our destination had been the headwaters of the Merri Creek, in the Great Dividing Range north of Melbourne. It was a seven-day journey, mainly through the grassy plains, and for me its abiding joy was the openness of the land, the way we could almost always see the mountains, our destination, up ahead, and how every day they would inch closer. When we made it to the source, and looked down over the other side of the Great Divide, into the vast Murray River watershed, all of us just wanted to keep walking. We did not want to leave the pilgrim life, this magnificent walkabout. But Greg was waiting for us in the old station wagon; we had to go home. We drove back down into the valley, through Wallan

East and Donnybrook and Woodstock, the road not far from the creek and the way we had walked. We pointed out to Greg the sights, the highlights, the places we had stayed, we tried to tell him the stories linked to the places that whizzed by the car windows. It was too fast.

'Slow down Greg!' I pleaded.

'Cut it out Maysie, we're only going sixty.'

I slunk low in my seat when we came to the suburbs and the creek was lost to sight. After we had dropped Freya and Cinnamon at their houses, Greg in his kindness drove to the confluence of the Merri, where it meets the Yarra, and he left me there. I sat on the little footbridge for a long time, talking to the creek, telling a little of what I had seen. Then I walked the mile back to the farmhouse along the Yarra.

Part of the reason for that creek pilgrimage was to raise awareness of the new freeway planned for the Merri valley. We had linked up with the anti-freeway campaigners and were getting good media attention and spreading the message of preserving the creek without a traffic sewer running alongside it. In my heart I did not believe we could prevent it – the road lobby is ferociously powerful, and there was lots of money to be made for a few people who live nowhere near it. And so I did the pilgrimage back then with one thing in mind; to remember the creek the way it was, quiet under the sunshine, unravelling down from the mountains through the open woodlands, black-shouldered kite hovering silently above the plains.

When we returned from our Merri pilgrimage we made a presentation at the hearings into the freeway. While we waited nervously for our turn, I watched in sadness as people of heart and care tried to convert their love into scientific jargon, attempting to speak the language of their opponent, presenting dry, factual points they hoped the panel would consider. One by one they were dismissed. When it was time for our presentation we nervously set up our slide projector and told our story; three pilgrims who went walking into wonder, and who came back changed, gifted by the grace of the land. We expressed our fervent hope that this experience could be known by people into the future, and told of the hundreds of children who accompanied us at various times on our journey. To our surprise it silenced the panel. I could see they were moved. But we couldn't save the creek.

A few years after our Merri journey I went on an expedition to Galada Tambore, the Merri Creek gorge, with some Merri Creek Management Committee friends. I hadn't been back since our Long Merri Walk.

Galada Tambore is one of the most significant examples of the original basalt grasslands, the most endangered of all Australian ecosystems. That day we saw one yam daisy, flowering along with the other wildflowers. One tiny plant is all that we could find of what was once the staple food of the Wurundjeri, that once flowered in a golden flood over the plains. We crouched down, hunkered against the unseasonably cold wind, to see the delicate yellow daisy in a field strewn with burnt-out cars, the deafening sounds of the new freeway being built through the Merri Creek valley only a few dozen metres away.

～

We said goodbye to Jess at the top of the ridge. I was a little sad to see him go. As my naturalist companion, we observed the world together; the natural becoming cultural – our culture of recognising and admiring the live things around us. It was midday when we said our farewells, the light sharp and pure streaming down. A shadow passed over us and we all looked up; black-shouldered kite, circling the sun.

Jess turned back down the path, and we were left where the bush track met the Yarra Boulevard. At that point the gorge went almost straight down to the river. It would have been impossible to stay beside the water there without climbing gear, which is why the path came up to the road. There was a honey-coloured mudstone structure in front of us, and affixed to it was a plaque with these words:

> This cairn was erected conjointly by the Kew, Collingwood and Heidelberg City Councils, as a memorial to Charles Grimes, Surveyor General of New South Wales, and party, the first white men to discover the river Yarra, reaching the Yarra Falls on 6th of February 1803. Also, to mark the crossing of the river near here by the first overlanders, John Gardner, Joseph Hawdon and John Hepburn, in December 1836.

The cairn didn't have a date, but by the style of construction I guessed it to be from the 1940s or 1950s. I couldn't imagine such a cairn being built today in Melbourne, with the greater awareness people now have of Aboriginal stories. It is not that the cairn says anything untrue. Yet it tells only part of the story.

It felt to me as if the strata of history, each of which were deposited over the top of the previous layer in parallel lines, were becoming bent in these times by massive forces, becoming twisted into new shapes. It can be a tortuous process; layers arch and rupture, or turn right over. In time, these strata are revealed. And like seeking out synclines and anticlines, sometimes, we see them. We see smiles and rainbows.

We left the cairn and walked just a few dozen metres along Yarra Boulevard to the gate into Galatea point. I had watched this river bend change over the years as it became the focus for weeding and revegetation programs. The bush was looking gorgeous. Tussock grasses were perky humps along the water's edge, and young wattles sheltered under large white-limbed gums.

I had ventured often to that piece of bush. Here I came with my German boyfriend to say goodbye. I once found a nest of baby willie wagtails in a kangaroo apple bush, and the mother flew at my face, scolding furiously. Here I came to help a weekly working group of Kew women plant trees. Here we hooted and clapped under the full moon after we swam the silky water on a stifling summer's night.

We circuited the bend, then climbed back up to the road, to walk the path to Studley Park Boathouse. There it was quite a scene. Nestled in the bush, crowded with exciting active mammals – humans. A Sunday jazz band played; Kate and I joined in the dancing on the lawn in the sunshine, falling over each other in our hiking boots, and laughing.

After, we rested by the boathouse and I read to the others from our Yarra River book:

Yarra Bend Park, a wonderful natural remnant bushland, was reserved *circa* 1877. It was Victoria's first conservation park and is the closest natural bushland to central Melbourne. It is an important reservoir for wildlife in the region … Yarra Bend is a gorge, and a meeting point of sedimentary hills, coastal and volcanic plains.

They grazed sheep in Yarra Bend Park up until 1977. They must have still been there when I first began visiting the park with my dad and his friends, on the weekends when my sister and I stayed with him. I don't remember the sheep, but I do remember the rides in the rowboats that we hired from Studley Park Boathouse, and I do remember the cubby house. My sister and I and some other kids spent one long day building an elaborate bush cubby out of fallen branches. It was round, tipi shaped; we squashed inside its dark, crackly interior. We didn't want to leave at the end of the day – we clamoured at the adults to be allowed to stay and live forever in the park, by the river. Not surprisingly we were unsuccessful, but every time we came back to the park we would seek out our cubby. It took years for it to finally sink into the earth and vanish.

$$\approx$$

Imagine living here all your life. And I mean *here*, in this Yarra River country, not in the other worlds of television and books, or in the internal spaces, the life lived between walls. Imagine the land as it was then. No buildings. No shopping centres, sushi bars, car washes, morgues, pubs, flats, temples, terraces, take-aways, cafés, churches. No eight hours of televised sport every day of summer, no BBC historical dramas, no 'reality' shows or surreal SBS offerings. No internet or Google Earth™. No overseas trips. No overseas even imaginable! And no books on anything. No books.

Then imagine all the energy you ever expended on any of those things, those other places, imagine focussing all that attention to this very terrain. Know yourself as one of the people who lived here for tens of thousands of years, who lived *here* and nowhere else. Your mind is keen and complex, with at least the same capacity for remembering, for imagining, for understanding as any literate modern. And all that you ever knew your whole life long was this place, the country of your tribe, the boundaries of home. There were stories passed here from nation to nation; tribes passed on news from perhaps thousands of miles away, there was trade of goods; smoked eels, stone axes. But there was no outside; no outside because there was no inside. It was all home. Everything, the only thing that you knew, was home.

When I was a kid I wanted to be an architect. For my ninth birthday mum gave me a book of house plans, and it was my favourite present – I would pour over the patterns of rooms, the arrangements of spaces. I searched through that book as if I was looking for something. As if somewhere there was a plan, a pattern to be found that would answer a question, a question perhaps not yet asked.

At university, studying architecture, my tutor referred me to a book called *The Timeless Way of Building*. The first few pages of the book described walking along a narrow country road on a sunny day, accompanied by a gypsy-like caravan, pulled by horses. It wrote of the special feeling when the road is laid out ahead, the destination is unknown, but there exists the perfect freedom of the moment. This perfect freedom, the author asserted, is the essence of architecture. Memories of that book came to me as I walked the Yarra. Maybe this walk was my essence of architecture. A delicate feeling for the walls of the air; the boundaries, perhaps, of home.

〜

We passed but did not cross Kane's Bridge with its perky red railings. The path wound on among some healthy bush, obviously well cared for by the local rangers. We took the little track along the water's edge, and as soon as the bush thickened up, we found the place we were looking for. The spot for our first swim of the Long Yarra Walk. (I was happy to swim in this reach of the river, upstream of the particularly filthy Merri.) We couldn't dawdle, so it was just a quick wetting. While I squealed with the cold, Cinnamon relaxed on the riverbank, smiling in the sunshine.

A few years back, a friend told me that when she went to India she swam in the Ganges, as the Ganges is a holy river. That same friend wouldn't swim in the Yarra because she considered it too polluted. Impartial sources would probably agree that the Ganges is more polluted than the Yarra (there are far fewer half-burnt corpses in our river), so perhaps the issue was 'holiness'. I wondered what it could mean to me if I swam in my river mindfully. It seemed that holiness could be a practice, an intention. So I started swimming in the

Yarra. And it felt right, even if the water was a touch slimy sometimes. And while I can try on holiness all I like, in the lower reaches, always I keep my head out, and my mouth firmly closed.

After towelling dry, we followed the path that squeezed past the crumbling cliffs. It wound tantalisingly among stone, snaking around the bends. Soon we came upon a place we'd not considered; a few houses that owned land all the way to the water's edge, there in the centre of the park. We'd neglected to arrange permission to pass through them.

We discussed what to do, deciding to walk in, thinking that people would probably be supportive of our adventure, and we could explain our mission on the off chance we met anyone. All went well until we came to the last house, perched high above the steep bank. Some little children saw us. 'There's people walking down there, there's people', they shrieked. The adults ignored them, so we kept going until someone finally took notice of the kids.

'We're walking to Baw Baw', I called up, hoping to allay any property-minded stroppiness.

'Well you wont get there that way', replied a woman in pink on the balcony far above us. But then she turned back to her Sunday barbeque on the terrace, so we continued on, over our first barbed wire fence. We won't get there that way, she reckoned. I'm afraid that is precisely what we intended to do!

We were soon back in the park; we were due to meet Ilan's mum at Fairfield and we were late, so he marched on ahead, leaving us to stroll.

As we three walked, we spoke of our busy lives at home

(only a few kilometres distant, yet they felt so far away). We talked of how we loved our different jobs in the field of environmental education, but shared the common outcome of overwork and stress, burnout, ongoing fatigue. How crazy it all seemed, compared to following the river in the dappled shade, the forest business going on all around us. The heads of rainbow lorikeets poked out of tree hollows as we passed by, looking, and behaving, like clowns, with their red noses, blue faces, yellow-green wings and screeching, clambering antics. Swallows flew by, eating insects above the water, and taking flying sips of river. Then one currawong called in the distance.

I stopped in delight; I'd heard currawong only a few times in Melbourne. I'd first heard that bird in Sydney, where they cry with such wildness, such plaintive joy, echoing through the narrow streets, I wondered how they did not topple society. But Sydneysiders are used to wildness – all that ocean, all that stone. (Currawongs have, in the years since the Walk, multiplied throughout the city. Now you can sometimes hear them away from the thin strip of wild abutting the river and the creeks, their cries have even, once or twice, shivered through my home in Brunswick. They call most often at dusk, as if, with their golden eyes, they summon the setting of the sun. Some call currawongs weed spreaders, small bird killers. Some people don't care for song.)

Soon we got to the pipe bridge and crossed over to the Fairfield Boathouse – the *other* boathouse on the Yarra. There we met up with Ilan's mother, who had found a prime outdoor table among the lunchtime café crowd. She'd bought us treats – piles of hot fried potatoes and some salad, and we supplemented our picnic with these.

Over lunch she told us stories of living beside the Yarra in Ivanhoe. Before the river was dammed, when she was quite young, the river flooded, and the wild water brought a white horse, which struggled out of the torrent and galloped away up her street. She told us too of her father's sadness when the freeway was constructed, and their house was compulsorily acquired and then demolished. She thought it broke his heart.

The day continued clear and summery. Pale gums stood out against the grey and yellow mudstone. High above us the wisps of cirrus cloud, Kate told us, meant that the weather would soon change – probably the next day. In the meantime, we tramped along the southern bank, searching for the best place for another swim. We found a spot, just across the river from Rudder Grange Park in Alphington, where once a third boathouse stood, until it was demolished in the 1960s. Many years back Greg and I had lived in Alphington, in a street that ended at that park. Canoeing there, we watched a tiger snake swim through the river. I remembered the way a snake swims, and what the water says about that. The water says, 'I will show you ghost snakes, slithering away in the pattern of her body, rippling away on either side, wave forms fading'.

As we were swimming, some friends from the house we were planning to stay at that night arrived from upstream in a canoe. They were off to the boathouse for a coffee, but assured us they would be back for their duty of ferrying us across the river to Ivanhoe later on. Then some rowboats came past.

'You lot can't be from Melbourne?' the rowers called out. Obviously we couldn't be, for Melburnians know that the

Yarra is too dirty to swim in.

'Brunswick, Ivanhoe,' we yelled from the water.

'You're crazy!' they replied, and tipsily rowed past.

When we left Yarra Bend Park it was late afternoon. We'd spent the whole walking day inside it. We passed underneath the Chandler Highway Bridge, which once carried the outer suburban loop train line. The path then ran straight, between the Eastern Freeway and a canal-straight Yarra. The river rerouted again for the freeway. I walked with Ilan and we sang wordless songs together to the rhythm of our feet and the swoosh of the traffic noise. At last the river bent north and we followed it, leaving the freeway and its roar. Ilan was on a mission – to find the Kew billabong, where his mother came as a girl. We pushed our way through the undergrowth and found the billabong. We came to the water's edge, and we thought our own thoughts, for a short while, together there.

Further on we came to a very high chain-link fence. It was the golf course, where Ilan's mother was a member. She was going to accompany us; we would be her guests, and so have permission to be on this land, but she had to change her plans. There we were, with another moral conundrum, like that of earlier when we did our little spot of trespassing. Somehow the tall fence did its bit to reinforce the fact. Cinnamon managed to climb up and over, while Kate, Ilan and I went down to the water's edge, where the fence did not quite meet the river, and we could just squeeze underneath. When we got back to Cinn, she'd come a cropper on the wire, tearing her pants and sustaining a long scratch on her leg. She looked a bit shaky as we continued on.

The sky turned pink as we approached our home for the

night. We were on the wrong side of the river, so we cooeed over the water. Our friends hollered back from the open windows of their grand Edwardian house. Right on the banks, they'd dubbed their rented dwelling Havenho. I had visited and slept over often. As soon as the owners were ready it was to be knocked down and replaced with a huge new residence, the trees bulldozed to make way for a four-car garage.

We watched our friend launch the canoe; he would fetch us one by one. I placed my hands on Ilan's shoulders as he sat looking over the river, where the light of evening lay. He reflected: 'There is not enough time just to sit and think Maya; there is not enough time to just be! We are so busy with people, with schedules, with everything!'

I considered that. We had created many commitments in our eagerness to share the journey. We now held responsibility for the community created around this walk. Even though the help and support of lots of friends smoothed our path, we also made ourselves extra work, having to coordinate and word up many different helpers.

'It'll calm down upstream', I mused, an attempt at consolation.

The dusk had settled on the water by the time it was my turn to cross. I realised I'd seen both ends of the day from a canoe. And we'd passed, that day, a few remnant scar trees, where once the Wurundjeri had fashioned their craft from large slabs of red gum bark. Canoes had plied this river for eons, people floating over this water, between these trees.

I stepped out of the boat onto a mudstone slab jutting up from below, and I sat for a time by the water alone. The world was full of the calls of the white-striped freetail bat –

thousands of tiny pipings.
    And the roar of the freeway.

THE THIRD NIGHT

Years before, at Havenho, with my friends. Down at the water's edge, the rock ledge, I feel the slinky Yarra. And then I'm in, flailing and squealing; I join the others. We can only just stand on the sandy bottom, we circle, we sing together. Then letting go we flow with the current, floating slowly down river on our backs.

The river reds above do not quite meet; they reveal a strip of stars.

My friend calls to me over the dark water, 'We could be in Kakadu!' But no, we are here, in the river, in the suburbs of Melbourne. However we choose to live, we are the continuation of 50,000 years of humans dwelling in this place.

THE PATTERNS, FLICKERING

By the side of the river he trotted as one trots, when very small, by the side of a man who holds one spellbound by exciting stories; and when tired at last, he sat on the bank, while the river still chattered on to him, a babbling procession of the best stories in the world, sent from the heart of the earth to be told at last to the insatiable sea.

Kenneth Grahame, *The Wind in the Willows*

Once, a friend and I were messing about in boats, canoeing on the river at Havenho. The boat glided silently; we fell under her spell. We drifted up to a water rat, and watched him slide in and out of the water – sinuous, sleek and oiled, entirely elegant, both in water and on the bank.

I remembered this as I lay in bed, the sun streaming in. My thin mattress was jammed in the window seat, my favourite spot in the house, where my friend and I once read to each other the tales of Ratty and Moley and their adventures upon a willowy river on the other side of the world.

My feet pointed east. I looked over them to the sun shining

through the lacework of leaves, through garden trees. I saw that my hat had become habitation, overnight spun round with spider web. And webs were sparkling everywhere outside too, shimmering among the trees.

It seems to me that spider webs are denser this time of year, as the nights lengthen on the descent to early winter. A few years back I worked as part of a revegetation crew at Westerfolds Park, starting early, the mornings icy and clear, the replanted bush a shining tangle of dewy web.

That place, Westerfolds, was the destination for our fourth night.

The Havenho kitchen was busy with breakfasters; both pilgrims and housemates. We had lots of appointments on the river path that day, so we couldn't dawdle. But where was Kate? She slipped in just as we were nearing our time to leave. After we had gone to bed she had walked to her home, a little flat just a kilometre away, to sleep there.

'Last chance for my own bed,' she smirked.

A farewell party accompanied us down the steep slope to the river, down steps cut into the bank, to gather on the mudstone shelf just above the water's edge.

The sunlight was bouncing off the Yarra, casting reflections of the river's ripplings onto the undersides of the red gums, limbs leaning over the water. All along the Yarra, light off the water means that shadowsides are lit up, and things not usually noticed are picked out in sharp relief. There were flickering patterns of light dancing over the trees, and dancing over us too, as we stood on the stones, looking upriver.

We set off along the path that wound through the gardens of the Ivanhoe houses, along the riverbank. There was no public walking track, but the local residents allowed each other access. The path disappeared into a weedy bower; *tradascantia*, a dark-green ground-covering weed, had smothered the bush, and dense willows and a bay tree stood above. I picked a few bay leaves for cooking and stuffed them into my pocket – as I did every time I visited that part of the river. The way grew dark and narrow, and there was a tiny creek to jump before we entered Wilson Reserve. There the official river path began again, heading towards Ivanhoe Golf Course. We were protected from errant balls by high mesh fences that curved over to roof the path in places. The dull freeway groan grew as we walked – traffic noise swelling as we passed under Burke Road Bridge, then thankfully fading as we followed the river north. That was where the freeway left the river, to thunder over the Koonung Creek. I remembered exploring the lush Koonung valley as a child, before they built the freeway.

The path was fine gravel, comfortable for walking, with a satisfying crunch underfoot. The day was muggy despite the wind.

Close by, on the far side of the river, beyond our sight, was Bolin Bolin.

≈

A large billabong, Bolin Bolin was where Woiwurrung-speaking people once gathered for the eel migration. For every year around this time, millions of mature silver eels feel the urge to migrate downstream to their breeding grounds of the Coral Sea, off the coast of North Queensland. The eel migration was a sure source of rich and plentiful food, so great gatherings of people took place. During the eel run, marriages were arranged between members of different tribes, disputes were settled, and ceremonies performed. They built stone weirs, with efficient traps slipped in the gaps, over the creeks and river. An *arrabine* was a name for the traditional woven eel trap, made from the strap-like foliage of plants that grew along the river. The trap would guide many eels in, but only let them out one at a time at the other end. A hunter would wait for the eel in the water, and as it slipped out the end, he would grab its slippery length, put its head in his mouth and break its back with his teeth.

Over a thousand people might camp at Bolin Bolin for up to three weeks every April. Tribes from beyond the Great Divide, beyond Kulin lands, sometimes came for the eel gathering, including the Taungurung from the Goulburn River country hundreds of kilometres to the north. According to tradition, the tribes made camp around the billabong in the direction from which they had walked; closest to their country. After whites took over their land, the spread of disease and despair drastically reduced the numbers of the first peoples, and so the gatherings got smaller every year. Then, around 1842, a man called Unwin bought three square miles of land around the Yarra, which stretched from Bolin (now known as Bulleen) to Templestowe.

The Assistant Protector William Thomas, appointed by the British government to monitor the treatment of the Aboriginal people of the Port Phillip region, protested against this purchase. He wrote to his superiors: 'when Bolin and the few lagoons adjacent become private property it will be one of the most serious losses experienced by the blacks'. He was unsuccessful in securing access for them, and the Kulin lost another traditional gathering place.

≈

Over on the other side of the river, in April 2003, we'd arrived at the Banksia Street Bridge. There was no path under the bridge, so we had to cross the six-lane road. It seemed ages since we last had to deal with traffic; I felt nervous of the danger, like a child again. We took each other's hands and we managed to cross the road.

We were running a bit late for our meeting with Ivanhoe Primary, so we hurried, striding along side by side, discussing our teaching plan. The day had turned overcast and humid, so we were sweating as we pounded along the path. Then at the chosen place, the children were there, waiting for us, a throng of sweet little people in blue hats and shorts and yellow T-shirts. We waved as we approached; with our sweaty shirts, backpacks and maps we must have looked the part.

We each took a group and told them the unfolding story of the Long Yarra Walk; where we had come from and where we were going. We asked them how long it takes them to get into the city by car or train; 'half an hour' they said. Then we told them that it took three days of walking to get here from the city, following all the bends of the river. I would like to say they all looked at us, wide-eyed in wonder, but some of them just looked baffled. Others, however, considered the implications of our words, and asked questions of such intelligence that we saw, as we would so many times on our journey, how the river wound deeply through the hearts and minds of so many who lived alongside it.

After our impromptu lesson, we all set off together to walk the bends of Birrarung. This the kids loved! They were like a king tide racing up the river, and I was riding the wave. I raced to get to the front of the pack, to stop them from going completely wild. But no, that's not completely true. I wanted to join in their fun, to run the river with them, to be free for a while of responsibility and logistics and appointments and sensible behaviour. To be one of those naughty ringleaders that the teachers kept trying to rein in by hollering at them from the back. I wanted to run as a child, to run forever along the river.

We came to a dead end down a narrow path; a tight curve of the Yarra where a deposit of white sand had created a beach. To continue our river walk we all had to back out; an interesting exercise with fifty children. Under oak trees we found insect cases emerging from the earth – cicadas birthing into the air from their underground homes where they had lived for up to eleven years. They then live for only a week of singing and mating, before dying. 'Hence they have to make so much noise', grinned Kate. I picked up a case, it was full of stinking rotten cicada juice that ran out over my hand. The smell stayed all day, no matter how much I scrubbed at it.

The children journeyed with us to the end of Warringal Parklands – Dingo Jump Up, where Barwool had once rested from his labours. Before the kids left we took a photo of our fellow adventurers, asking them to point upriver and shout 'to the headwaters!' in solidarity with our trek. They gleefully obliged.

It was something of a relief when the kids departed and we could have a peaceful lunch. Kate and Cinnamon, being teachers, were used to working with children, and they had watched my over-enthusiasm and my consequent exhaustion with amusement. We compared our experiences. Kate told a story of a boy who wanted to know how many days we were going to be walking. He was confused. He didn't quite get it. 'Tell you what, I'll cooee to you when I get to the top. You listen out.' He caught the magic of it then, and beamed at her. 'I will!' he replied.

After lunch we headed off, to find that just around the river bend the valley opened into a wide roundness. We'd come to Banyule Flats, the biggest billabong in the urban region. To the north of us was a grand mansion looking down over the flats; the old Banyule homestead, built in the 1840s. Two men were walking towards us; it was Pat Vaughan and Paul Baker from Banyule City Council. We had arranged to meet the bush crew at the Banyule wetlands revegetation site, and these two were scouting ahead looking for us. (Maybe they doubted that an appointment made weeks ago over the phone to meet on a riverbank with someone you had never met would actually happen. I, too, was surprised and delighted when people were there, waiting for us by the water.)

Pat and Paul lead the way to where the crew was gathered; a mob of burly blokes wearing work clothes the colour of dry reeds, and heavy-duty sunglasses. The Banyule Bush Crew worked hard to re-create a tiny piece of an ecosystem that had been, until recently, methodically and systematically destroyed. Melbourne's waterways were once all fringed with wetlands.

In the floodplains and billabongs that lay alongside the

Yarra and her tributaries, almost fifty different species of birds once thrived. The rivers themselves do not usually provide very well for waterbirds. They need the succession of shallow flooding and slow drying that occurs in the swamps, where the growth and submergence of aquatic plants in warm water sustains a food chain of micro-organisms, frogs and insects, which then feed fish, turtles, rakali (water rats) and waterbirds. Wetlands are one of the most highly productive wildlife habitats in Australia – yet this wetland existed only due to fierce local action to preserve it.

With the growth of the city, the swamps at West Melbourne, Burnley, Hawthorn, Kew, Heidelberg and Templestowe were filled in. Wetlands were drained so that the rich land could be used for grazing sheep and cattle, but there was another reason. In the nineteenth century, swamps and wetlands were thought to emit noxious vapours called miasma, considered to cause disease. We know now that there is no such vapour, rather it is polluted water or mosquitoes that carry diseases. But the word swamp still carries strange and unhealthy connotations.

'What do you need to make these wetlands thrive?' we asked.

'Give us more water! Turn the tap on, up at the dam, so these wetlands can get the flooding they need. In dry years Melbourne Water takes almost 70 per cent of the river for our taps, but that damages the ecosystems all along the Yarra.'

'Write that in the log book!' we said.

The bush crew informed us that sugargliders were recolonising due to the work the crew had done re-establishing their habitat. Sugargliders can soar many metres from tree to tree. They are nocturnal – all I have ever seen of them is their telltale scratchings on the trunks of eucalypts; tiny claw marks that scale the white curve of a gum, as they ascend to eat the nectar-filled blossoms. I can imagine them gliding through the night air, their tiny bodies as taut as a sail in the wind. In my heart's eye I see one leaping from a red gum, over the river, the moonlight reflecting up from the water onto her pale belly, the patterns flickering.

Accompanied by the bush crew, we headed upriver to meet our next group, Viewbank Primary. The school has had a long and productive relationship with the bush crew, and arranged regular planting days together. And so these young custodians shared many stories with us, of birds they had seen, and spring snake sightings.

Perhaps because those kids got down to the river more often, maybe it was the heat of the afternoon; whatever the reason that bunch were a lot more sedate. We ambled with the children through dense stands of replanted wattles and gums alongside the high banks of the river, the sluggish water far below was shallow and brown.

We walked until we came to the junction of the Plenty and Yarra Rivers, where once upon a time Barwool had met up with Yan Yan, who was cutting a pathway for the waters caught up in his country. The Plenty River was not looking very plentiful. I suppose it hadn't for 100 years; in 1903 the Yan Yean Reservoir was built to supply Melbourne with water, and so most of the river was held back in the hills far to the north. It seemed bit cheeky to name the reservoir after Yan Yan, considering by damming the Plenty they were undoing all his hard work.

There we said farewell to the kids; they stood and watched us as we carried on up the Birrarung. The day was at its hottest and very humid, so we were keen for a swim; we saw a good place just a short way along, but the kids were still watching us and waving, so we thought it best to keep walking, to show we were serious adventurers. Later I wished we were less concerned about impressions; for the rest of that stifling afternoon, there was no place we could swim – the steep weedy banks went straight down to the water.

~

When I got bored of the way architecture was taught at my university (too much about the object, not enough about context), I transferred to landscape architecture. In my studies, I first got to know something of the Plenty Valley through what was called a 'design studio'. Our hypothetical project was to design a settlement, a new town on the Plenty River. The large site was north-facing, oriented towards the sun, undulating, and divided by three unnamed ephemeral waterways that ran down to join the Plenty. I modelled a series of small interlinked villages designed on the principle of an aqueduct; streets subtly sloped towards the creeks, lined with small interlocked houses that followed the contours – rings of dwellings encircling hills. I imagined the rainwater run-off streaming along a channel indented in the centre of the bluestone street – tiny waterways – also ephemeral. I envisioned the rain that ran from streets would flow down to irrigate food crops that wound along the contours below the town in terraced gardens; snakes of colour across the earth. I saw the ridges that ran through the town free of buildings but covered with trees instead, wildlife corridors from the village heart all the way to the river. The tops of the hills would be parks; gathering places where people could view the human and natural systems. I dreamed of a settlement that helped people to learn how to live in this land, mindful of each other and of sun and water, of where their food came from, and the wild that interweaves their lives. My teachers thought it fanciful, saying it is impossible to make the modern person adapt to this degree of local attentiveness and responsibility, and adopt communal rather than individual values. Perhaps it was. But it showed me what I desired deep down – to make places that fostered people's connections to natural systems and to each other.

~

The river upstream of the Plenty looked as if it had been recently revegetated with wattles, perhaps fifteen or twenty years old. They looked sickly. Being a pioneer species, fixing nitrogen in the soil that will benefit the plants to succeed them, they don't live long. It seemed strange, however, that they all should be dying at once. I resolved to ask the rangers at Westerfolds Park; they had invited us for morning tea the next day. Among the wattles by the river, we found one massive red gum, branches low to the ground and curled and contorted with time. The trunk was cream and honey coloured, dripping with dark syrupy sap, crunchy bits of broken bark on the earth below. We all grabbed our cameras before climbing among the branches.

On through the Yarra Valley Parklands, the path veered away from the river where it was choked with blackberry bushes. We could not have followed the river through that without machetes, so we stuck to the path, which joined an old rough road. Suddenly it felt as if we had left our parklike path through the suburbs and had arrived in the country. After walking to the top of the ridge we looked down on the way we had come, back over the Yarra and Plenty Valleys. We could see for miles over the gentle folds of the Heidelberg hills and the silvery riverwater sliding away towards the ocean.

'I get it!' cried Kate.

'What?' we chorused.

'The Heidelberg School, the artists, this is what they saw!'

We could see it now, the lovely land, the grey-green trees, the way the valley led the eye into the distance. The view from that spot captured the essence of some special paintings; a certain transparency, a shimmering, the sense of something beyond the temporal form. For me that view held the memory of the way we had come. It was the past, yet it was present, right now. It was time, held, preserved, released.

We turned back to the path, which led back to the river. Ahead rested a large and elegant 1930's building that looked down over the river where the Ruffey Creek flowed in from the southeast. There were signs; 'Odyssey House', a drug rehabilitation centre. It seemed a hopeful place to get well. Just in front of the house was a narrow suspension footbridge with bright yellow railings. It swayed with us as we walked into the middle. Below us pacific ducks and water hens were playing in the rapids, along with one garden escapee, a white duck with a yolk-coloured bill. He was quacking loudly, swimming in circles. Oh the comfort of ducks! So accomplished at setting the heart at ease, at bringing darkness into the play of light. I wondered if the patients at Odyssey House, on their difficult journey, came here to visit the river doctors.

We were nearly at Westerfolds Park, where it was to be just the four pilgrims for the first time. We set up camp on the edge of the car park, so as to be beside our trailer that had been delivered by our crew. We erected a shelter from the side of the trailer to fend off the threatening sky, which loosened a few gentle drops of rain. In some ways it was a relief to not be someone's guest, or to be with friends. Even though they would be taking care of us, it still required social energy, which could be tricky at the end of a long day.

I made dinner underneath the tarp, pottering around the camping stove in bare feet, mincing on the sharp stones, wearing a singlet and a sarong, the day's heat held in my body.

After dinner we sat cosily around our trailer and talked. We talked of wildness, of the edges of the known, and the conversation stalled, heavy with the unsaid, the unsayable.

I thought then about the other side of the river. Walking along, we travel, of course, on only one side. Sometimes it is an arbitrary choice, but far more often we walk on the only side available to us. The other side may be privately owned, or there is no path, or fences that are impossible to scale, or no bridge to access the bank. There is a certain intrigue about the path not taken. I came to think of the other side of the river as the place where all the other possible ways we could walk were embodied, unrealised. The side to walk secretly, illegally, at night, naked, alone, unseen, unknown. A walk much closer to the edge.

I dreamed into my own mind, I turned inside to my body, and I wondered how I'd walk this path if it were only me. Part of me ached to be singing and dancing and crying, bare and keening and falling, deeper into the dark river, and then striding on, and on, forward into the mountains. To be invisible to the eyes of humans, to be seen, instead, by the world.

My thoughts took me away; I needed other company.

I walked up the hill above our camp to find a place to be alone. I sat inside a grove of trees, where I watched the night city. Now outside of the city, I could look back onto it. Those first days, so full of memories, made it difficult to be in the moment – I felt hauled through emotions; my past inscribed into the riverbanks. But as we walked, it was as if I were collecting up the strings of my life as I had lived it so far, and weaving from them a cloth that lengthened with every step. Until then, I'd known many places along the river, a patchwork of places. Now I was joining them together. I hoped, here on, to trail this precious cloth behind me, so that I could meet the world, naked of memory, yet holding it safe.

I left my bower and climbed to the top of the slope in the darkness. At the top of the hill a large historic house looked down over the river. It had become the Mia Mia Gallery, showing Aboriginal art from around Australia. As I approached, the security lights came on, and the trees were lit up. A light wind blew, and played with the trees, the shadows around me flickered.

Tired, I turned to go back down the hill, to find Kate's bivvy bag that I had borrowed for the night. To bivouac means to camp without tents, so a bivvy bag was simply a cover for a sleeping bag. I lay it down among the gums of the park, with the lights of the suburbs twinkling in the distance. I lay down in the warmth and in the forest, I lay down, open to the sky.

THE FOURTH NIGHT

I wake to the wet in the middle of the night – rain, finally come. It brings comfort and release, the release of heat and the comfort of water, for me and for the dry land. I cannot sleep for the bliss of it.

SCENT OF DEEP RIVER

Dawn arrived, heavy and dark. I was keen to look upon a moist world, as it hadn't rained for a while. Not that it was a particularly soaking rain; the deeper earth would still be thirsty.

I struggled into my damp clothes, taking care not to wake Ilan, and tottered out of the useful second door of his little tent. I'd taken refuge there after finally getting too wet in the bivvy bag – I'd tried Cinn first – she had no room. I took my diary and headed downhill through the grasses, following the fall to find the water. I fell in beside a swift creek, churning with the run-off from last night's rain. I followed it to the confluence. The air was heavy with the scent of possum and eucalyptus. High winds hurried the clouds. Rain began again as I sat there, it painted my diary pages, smearing my letters and lines. So I put my book under the mat I'd brought to sit on, and clambered down to the water's edge.

A rough mudstone shelf jutted out where the waterways joined. The stone was smoothed with silt; fine, dust-soft silt, ready to wash into the water. I squatted there, dangling my hands in the wet – it surprised me with its warmth. A tiny azure kingfisher dived over the water, a blaze, a shock of ochre and electric blue through the gloomy morning. The invitation was impossible to resist, so I took off my raincoat, hid my clothes under my coat, and entered the river. *Chickachickachick* said a willie wagtail, his warning call. The rocks were sharp and slippery below me, a cool breeze lifted leaves. The water suddenly seemed cold, it no longer felt like a day for bold action. I lingered there in the drizzle, up to my waist, and went no further.

Back at camp during pack up Ilan seemed grumpy – had I invaded his privacy by taking refuge in his tent? I followed the others disconsolately up the hill, trailing through the wet and clinging grass. I soon forgot my drama when we arrived at the top of the hill, and saw the mountains of the Great Dividing Range ahead. Our still distant destination was that bit closer, and excitement for our quest flared again. I took a photo of my companions, pointing at the distant hills, pointing back to the way we had come. We couldn't delay; we were hurrying to another rendezvous; morning tea with the park rangers, so we took a short-cut through the fields of the park.

When we arrived at the park office, we were shown through to the staff room and found half a dozen park staff there to welcome us. After the handing around of teas and coffees and a chorus of thanks from us, we spread out and chatted to different rangers. I had questions arising from the first four days of walking and I hoped for some answers. I asked about the wattles I had seen dying along the river the day before, and was told that they were an early attempt at revegetating the river, but that the wrong seeds had been used

– the wattle was actually a South African plant. The park was waiting for them all to end their natural life span, and then mixed indigenous planting would go back in. They reminded me that the concept of revegetation was a very new thing when this park was established; techniques were still being developed, and these ecologies were still relatively unknown.

Along the waterways of Melbourne, often the process of revegetation means taking out European plants that have culinary or medicinal uses and replacing them with indigenous plants that at present have little cultural or practical meaning to most people. All of the native plants were of course known or used by Aboriginal people, but such knowledge has barely entered into the colonising culture. Not simply because the new culture didn't want this knowledge – but also because the native food sources are akin to the land – sparse, thinly spread and lean. There are few easy pickings.

Sometimes it seems that revegetation is an activity of a nature-loving, aesthetically minded middle class. People who have lived lives dependant on their own hands for their food, including many of Melbourne's Mediterranean migrants, don't seem to see land that way. When I lived at the Collingwood Children's Farm, I would often chat to the Turkish, Greek and Italian old folk who came down to gather the edible weeds. With big plastic bags they walk along the river, collecting nettles, dandelion, milk thistle, marshmallow – especially in spring, when the fresh new growth of these plants makes traditional tonics, the new leaves full of iron and vitamins.

All along the rivers and creeks, these European plants are poisoned and replaced with natives. I love watching revegetation take hold and thrive, I love to see the birds and animals come back. But our own food is grown elsewhere, it's trucked in from the Murray food bowl. That great river is dying partly because of the irrigation that grows our food. We preserve our dear Yarra, we make sure it looks nice and stays healthy. But, on a river we seldom see …

If we didn't have a fossil fuel–based economy that happily hauled food all around this vast country, what would we do? What if we had to survive on the land around us? What would transpire on these fertile floodplains?

We asked about the history of the park, which had until recently been farmland. The development plan was to subdivide the whole area for suburban subdivision, but huge community opposition secured the area for parkland. Apparently it was a close call. So much of what we loved on the journey had been fought for, and hard won. I sank into my seat, grateful for the unknown many who had worked to preserve openness, and wildness.

As we were leaving the building, we stopped by the aerial photograph in the lobby. It took up the whole wall, and showed the river from Yarra Bend Park all the way up to the end of Warrandyte State Park (still two and a half days' walk away). Most of the land by the river was managed by Parks Victoria. Slowly it was reconnecting isolated blocks into an extensive linear parkway, the green lung of the city. Our walk so far had been wonderfully enabled by this vision.

The ranger pointed out Tikalara Park on the wall, an area still closed to the public, but open for us to pass through; we should arrive there by afternoon. She shared some details of the Tikalara's history. Early on the land was claimed for a homestead. But because the site was rich in food resources, there was also, unusually, an almost-permanent camp of Wurundjeri people. The clashes between the whites and the Wurundjeri were not documented, but the rumours were grim. 'I wonder whether you'll feel anything there,' she said.

After we left the park headquarters we backtracked, to rejoin the river close to where we had camped. The four of us crawled in under the silver wattles and sat silently for a while on the bank, reacquainting ourselves with the river. We decided to walk separately for the morning, stringing ourselves out along the track, for some much-needed solitude. It had been such a busy time, with so many engagements; we were all a bit tired of company.

I didn't know Westerfolds well, so there were fewer stories to remember as I walked alone. My mental quietness drew me in to listen to what was around. Plish and slosh said the river as it ran over the stones; rapids up ahead. I walked under a bridge; Fitzsimmons Lane, a rumbling highway, and on into Candlebark Park. Candlebarks are tall and elegant gums with smooth white trunks that sometimes turn rich pink around the end of summer. They looked so similar I couldn't tell them apart from the more numerous manna gums, trees that also thrive in the relative damp of the river's edge.

The path turned into a timber boardwalk, to protect the steepening slopes from erosion. The wood of the walkway was fading to grey, and echoed satisfyingly underfoot. Peeking through the trees I could see a creek entering the Yarra on the other side – Diamond Creek. I'd walked that creek at a number of places on its journey down from the area of

Kinglake National Park.

Our path took us on past Petty's Orchard. Once common in the area, the orchard was now an historic remnant. Rows of heritage apple trees marched down to the riverbank. Ripe and ready for picking, apples had already fallen into the grass. A faint smell of fermentation reached us, rich and delicious. There was a knee-high iron gate set into the bottom of the tall fence – for the wombats, who would force their way through if allowances weren't made for them. If one is willing to learn from wombats, there are rewards.

Kate and I got down on our knees and butted our way, wombat-style, through the heavy little gate into the orchard. We thought that a few fallen apples wouldn't be missed – and I loved them. Sweet, semi-fermented and rose-scented; they cannot be bought in shops. So with pockets bulging we squeezed back through and returned to the path. I walked along rather uncomfortably after that, as the apples in my coat pockets battered my knees, punishing me for my thievery.

We soon stopped for lunch, where we found that apples worked really well in salad sandwiches. Our lunch spot was a timber-deck lookout, placed to view the junction of the Yarra and the Mullum Mullum Creek. As we packed up our lunch things an elderly and energetic pair who were out dog walking joined us at the lookout; they asked where we were headed so we told them of our quest. I think they were not sure the motley-looking walkers with all the apples were telling the truth.

We came to a narrow wooden footbridge over the murky Mullum Mullum Creek. Then abruptly the path we'd followed for most of the last four and a half days – stopped.

In front of us was a gate, with a Parks Victoria sign, informing us that the area beyond, Tikalara, was off limits to the public. But not to us! We climbed the gate, childishly triumphant. As I jumped down onto the other side, my senses pricked up. Unknown territory. We entered through an archway of trees by the gate, and saw on our right an old homestead, surrounded by paddocks of tall dry grass. The building had no face; its windows were boarded up, and despite its age it looked sterile and charmless. To our left, the riverbank was fenced off and there was a dense collection of green plastic guards indicating recent planting. A few old wattles sheltered the baby plants.

As of one mind, we turned away from the old homestead, jumped the fence and wove through the tree guards to the river. We sat on the bank and were silent for a long time. We were thinking of what the ranger had told us about this place, each in our own way.

I thought of Tammy Cappochi, a Parks Victoria ranger and descendant of the Wurundjeri, who came to our launch at the bay. I wondered what it meant for her, to ask the spirits of the ancestors to be with us on our journey to the source. Since I couldn't know, a more useful question was, what did it mean to me? If I imagined the ancestors travelling beside us, sharing each step that we took, then I must imagine them seeing all that we had seen. The changes wrought on the Birrarung and her environs over the last 158 years – just a few generations – what would a hunter-gatherer make of this? I imagined them witness to this place now, the strange inedible plants and the undrinkable river, gone quiet with no songs, but known once again by the traditional name – Tikalara.

I listened with my hands laid upon the earth, feeling with my fingers into the soil, moist with yesterday's rain. I felt the wetness of my eyes, the heaviness of my heart, there in that place, that time. I kept listening.

When I looked up, there were pacific ducks plying the water. Known as *dulum* by the Wurundjeri, I felt grateful to know their name, and to address them as such.

'To the headwaters?' one of us said quietly. We rose and clambered back over the fence, and continued on the track through Tikalara. The path soon petered out, and we spread out, finding our own paths through the bush by the water.

I was by myself when I found it – a tiny house, or very large cubby, built of sticks and bark. I crawled in and sat, hugging my knees, nursing the silence, on a nest of bark.

I didn't want to go anywhere for a while.

I turned at the sound of wings. A yellow robin was perched on the window ledge.

'Can I move in?' I whispered to the bird. He stayed there, watching me with his huge eyes. I'd heard that robins are one of the first birds to wake in the dim pre-dawn, so they need especially large eyes with which to see. And they are curious birds, who often emerge when a person walks the wet sclerophyll forest paths where they usually make their home. They will perch sideways on the trunk of a tree, tilt their grey head, and study you. We gazed at each other like the new friends we were becoming. We sat there companionably in the cubby.

A cooee came through the trees. Robin flew off.

I went on my way towards the call.

Back with the others, and walking in front, in a cleared area underneath some high-tension powerlines I almost stepped upon an echidna. It was digging through the dirt, hunting for ants. He got wind of me close by, and started to dig himself into the earth, spines flared. By that time the others had caught up. Silently, grinning, they fanned around to have a look. Ilan knelt alongside of him, and wiggled his bum in the air and thrust his nose in the dirt just as the echidna was doing. And when the echidna dared sneak a look to see if we were still there, so did Ilan-the-echidna, and they looked at each other while we stuffed our giggles back down our throats. We left the little fellow alone to resume his anting, and found a wombat track down by the river to follow.

Onwards, the day fading around us. On the other side of the river, soft light shone through the slender white shafts of manna gums. The forest extended for as far as could be seen. For the first time it felt as though the wild was far deeper than a narrow band along the river. It wasn't just visual. I felt a dreaming stillness of trees extending, like something humming beyond sensing, an imperceptible quivering.

Crossing another fence, the little dirt tracks along the bank wove and multiplied. We were back on Parks Victoria land, and close to our campsite, Longridge Park. Excited, we picked up our pace. I knew Longridge from my visits years before, when I had come out with a group of friends to visit the ranger. Lucky man; he lived in a house within the park.

∿

At that time I was playing and performing music, and had got together some musician friends who, like me, wanted to know more about the land. I had been inspired by the work of local naturalists who were promoting a concept called Timelines. These naturalists had been studying the knowledge of Aboriginal people around Australia, who naturally understood seasonality differently from the imposed European model of spring, summer, autumn and winter. For indigenous societies, the seasons were indicated by changes occurring in the environment. And in any ecosystem, a change in one area triggered off changes throughout, the entire system linked through the intertwining of myriad species responding to one another.

Members of the Gould League undertook the detailed task of looking back through years of record keeping by many naturalists, who had marked down such things as the flowering times of the wattles, the arrival and departure dates of migratory birds, the hatching of butterflies from cocoons and the frequencies of storms, here in this bioregion.

As they collected the data, they noticed emerging patterns. Spring actually arrived earlier than was officially recognised; flowers and birds began to burst into their respective songs around the beginning of August. So they called that time Early Spring. There was another flurry of activity at the start of October; this next season they named True Spring. December, the solstice month with the longest days, became High Summer, but divided this from February and March – Late Summer – often the hottest time. The naturalists considered the word autumn inextricably linked to foreign notions of the losing of leaves and the going to sleep of the trees. Autumn here works quite differently; the 'autumn break' (the farmer's term for the rains at summer's end) signals a new round of growth from plants that were often almost dormant during the heat of summer. The naturalists termed the 'autumn break' time Early Winter. Deep Winter was reserved for the short dark days of June and July.

But they made a provision to these new groupings. If the rains come late, then often the season is delayed until they break. In this land, life is on hold without rain.

These ideas, born from detailed, consistent observations of place over time, inspired me to learn about and help promote the 'Six Seasons' of Yarra River country.* I thought that anything that asked us to look with fresh eyes on our place, rather than unquestioningly live by the systems that came with European settlement, was a thing worth knowing. I was living at Collingwood Children's Farm at the time and going on lots of walks in the surrounding inner-city bush, working as a tree planter and carrying my bird book everywhere. I wondered whether music could be made, inspired by the sounds of the bush in each of the seasons. With a group of like-minded musician friends, we set about educating ourselves.

* I found out much later about the Seven Seasons! Coordinated by Museum Victoria alongside local Aboriginal people, this marvellous project documents traditional cultural information about the seasons of the tall wet forests and grassy woodlands around the Upper Yarra and the Dandenongs. This precious information is on display in the city, at the Melbourne Museum, amidst a re-created forest within the museum buildings, where a tiny creek flows, tawny frogmouths perch and bowerbirds nest.

One of our first activities was to come out to Longridge to visit Glen Jameson, resident ranger and one of the key naturalists who had worked on defining the Six Seasons. We sat in his living room with the blinds pulled down to keep the High Summer sun from beating in on us, and he told us stories of living on the long ridge, watching the weather come in; of the needle-tailed swifts, who always arrive at the front of a storm, eating the insects that fill the air when the atmospheric pressure drops. Later that year, in Early Winter when the morning mists are often swirling over the river, we returned to Longridge. We set up our tents down near the water with our recording equipment close by, hoping to catch the calls of the night birds. Most especially we wanted to hear powerful owl, who Glen said lived and hunted at Longridge. And we did, we recorded the owl, scrabbling through the bushes in the darkness, trying to get close without him hearing (as if). When we listened back to the tapes, far louder than the owl was the sound of cars, driving distantly through the valley.

⁓

That evening of the pilgrimage one of our support crew was Nic Morrey. He was an old friend of mine, who as it happened was one of the musicians from the Six Seasons project, with whom I had followed the calls of the powerful owl in the pre-dawn darkness, there in that very spot. He came with his brother Ant, whose trailer it was we'd been using for our overnight gear. As we came along the trails and into camp, the boys were already there, and Nic and I gave each other a huge hug.

'Carn Maysie, come with me to the river!'

We ran down the slope and sat curled up in the spot where once, years ago, we had performed music for a bush wedding. In front of us was a small island crowded with manna gums, their brown bark dripping, heaped high around their boles. And beyond, the swimming hole, a place called Laughing Waters. Nic and I had often swum there in summers past – lying in the water, watching the manna gums blown by north winds, their leaves shimmering like sequined dancers, loose and shining, reflecting light like millions of mirrors.

When Nic and I returned to camp it was completely dark, and the soup his brother had made from his home-grown pumpkins bubbled on the gas burner. I squeezed happily onto the plank bench. Just then a voice called out from beyond the glow of our candles – it was one of the rangers from Westerfolds Park, who had brought along a bottle of his homemade wine for us to share. He joined us at the table and we shared stories. I soon flopped on the table between the dishes, dozey and giggly with fatigue, but Kate and the ranger chatted into the night.

THE FIFTH NIGHT

After dinner the four walkers trudge down to the river by torchlight. I fancy to sit on the bank and face the river; the others want a circle. There are undercurrents between us, dark and swirling and muddy. The hearts of these people feel as out of reach to me as the secret underground watercourses that run somewhere below. I must trust that what is turbid will clear when the time is right, for I do not have energy to delve into the minds of humans.

On this night, my heart is not with people. I am enchanted by the place, by the sense of voices just below my hearing. I just want to float in the cold and the dark and the beauty, immersed in the scent of deep river and my unquenchable happiness, here at Laughing Waters.

A BEGINNING PLACE

A quintessential Early Winter moment on the Yarra, the sky clear, but mist thick in the valley. Wisps, tinged pink with the first hint of sun, curled among the creamy gums. I scrambled out of my nest into the chilly air, pulled on some woollies, and headed down the track to the river. Mist rose as I descended – the tendrils were climbing out of the river and swirling up towards the ridge, where they vanished into the blue.

The sun had climbed the ridge by the time we left. It hadn't found the forest floor yet, so we rugged up against the cold and set out, keeping close to the bewitching river. The water began shining brightly below us once the sun's heat had burnt away the last of the mist. Grey fantails danced above our heads on the path, a quivering flight of dives and steep ascensions. Their fantail feathers and tiny wings were splayed; the sun shone through them. Their call was spread way up and down scales, as aerial and acrobatic as their flight. The sun shone through that, too.

We climbed around the base of the slopes of Longridge and on into the steep dry cliffs of Warrandyte. It was tough

terrain and the sun beat down. We shed clothes in the climb
– layers and layers of them, all tied around our waists. Around
us, the dry and skeletal cliff soils hosted a tree we'd not yet
seen – the red box.

Round or heart-shaped grey-blue leaves – the distinctive
colour of the red box tree marks the line of leanest land. When
I first encountered the ecosystem that had adapted to the
dryness and thin soils of this part of the river, I was repelled
by its harshness, the uniformity of the palette, the lack of
brighter greens. But walking through all the different terrains,
watching them change with the soil, the slope, the sunlight,
had its own fascination, and an immense satisfaction. This
was not a place to be understood in isolation, but rather as
one of the many interlinked terrains the river runs through,
all with ecosystems perfectly adapted to their conditions. Now
I found I particularly appreciated the red box tree, for telling
the true story of its place.

The bank by the water steepened sharply, so we clambered
to the very top of the ridge, seeking a way through. A woman
whose garden we skirted around asked what we were up to;
she kindly offered us a cup of tea, but we had appointments
to keep. We strode along the dirt road that serviced the cliff-
top houses and soon came to Pound Bend. This was a bend in
the river so looped that it nearly met up with itself. A handy
parcel of land, easy to enclose. Early on after white settlement,
the land was deemed a mission station for the local Aboriginal
people. Not for long, though. Soon came the gold seekers,
who turned this land upside down.

In 1851 gold was first discovered in Victoria, at a place called

Anderson's Creek in Warrandyte, not far upstream from Pound Bend. The early technology of the miners was simple; a tray for panning the gold from the sandy riverbeds. But by the 1870s, after thousands of men had scoured all the land around the creeks and gullies (and I mean that literally – the earth was dug, sluiced, crushed, flayed to release the precious metal), gold became scarcer, and techniques more ambitious. Thus the Pound Bend Tunnel was constructed, to manoeuvre the entire river through a 200-metre tunnel dynamited through the mudstone cliff. After diverting the river with sandbags, five kilometres of riverbed were exposed, allowing for a thorough search of the silts that lay beneath. Their speculation proved ill-founded; they found little gold.

Walking from the ridge back down to the water's edge, we scrambled around on the uptilted mudstone shelves to take a look inside the tunnel. It was long, narrow and dark, a coin of bright daylight shining at the far end. A portion of the river flowed through, noisily rejoining the rest after it tumbled down the waterfall – an unusually pleasant by-product of a mining scheme. I'd heard tales of people navigating the tunnel when the river was low, canoeing or floating through on tyre tubes – but also tragic stories of people drowning there when the river flooded. The tunnel looked almost as exciting as a cave, but I was not seriously tempted, although the idea of naughtiness was nice. We rested there awhile on the rock, while Ilan entertained himself and us, dancing the place, dancing the waterfall, dancing himself.

We needed that rest after scrambling steep and pathless slopes. But we had many miles to go before we reached camp.

Kate was looking at the map.

'What time are we meeting the Mayor at Black's Flat?' she asked me.

'Eleven-thirty.'

'You know it's ten-thirty now?' asked Cinn.

'Yep.'

Cinnamon voiced what we all realised, 'We're not going to get to the Flat in time if we walk Pound Bend'.

'Don't worry Mays, we'll come back one day soon and walk it.' And we did, Kate and I, when the wattles began their flowering in Early Spring.

So we climbed to the narrow ridgetop and cut across the land, the tunnel hidden somewhere beneath our feet. Upstream of Pound Bend, not far along the riverside path shaded with elegant gums, we met an elderly walking group coming towards us. I find it hard to pass a smiling elderly face without a chat, let alone a dozen of them, all curious about our packs and questful energy, but I was pulled along by my sense of responsibility for what we had set in motion further upriver. The others stopped to swap stories; I was glad that stories would be shared, but a little jealous too. The irony of racing along on such a beautiful day while the river sauntered beside me so peacefully!

The others soon caught up and we joined the people of Warrandyte as they walked the river. This was the place for *passegiata* – the Italian tradition of walking through the village each day to catch up on news and stories. *Passegiata* in Warrandyte was the meeting of river and community, a chance to check out what the natural world was saying, the gossip of the rapids, the chatter of the crows. We didn't feel out of place there, and it gave me a greater sense of what it would be like if the river were more a part of urban people's lives – from where we walked we could see snatches of the main street where the faces of modest old buildings peered out from under wide verandahs. I could see both good and bad – it is good for the wild creatures to have to river for themselves, to go about their animal business uninterrupted. But the custodianship encouraged by the river running through the heart of town was a powerful way for the humans to meet the local ecology.

At one point, bits of bark and chewed tree were strewn across the pathway, and more fell as we walked along. Looking up, three black cockatoos were disembowelling a dying wattle to get at the fat grubs that were the cause of the tree's decline. Warrandyte folk, picnicking.

Then on to Black's Flat, the continuation of the Parks Victoria river reserve on the other side of Warrandyte township. It was long ago named for the Wurundjeri who gathered there. As we walked the dirt track, we could see about fifteen local river custodians, including the mayor and council staff, waiting for us on the riverbank. It was so incongruous to see a big group of people waiting in the clearing, some in suits and office clothes, that I laughed out loud, laughing too in gratitude that they would join our pilgrimage in this way. The mayor introduced himself, and handed each of us a Shire of Manningham water bottle and lapel pin, which I stuck onto my blue Bonds singlet. All the people introduced themselves, and the role they played in looking after the region. Landcare and revegetation, environmental planning and design, and community education were all represented.

They shared their morning tea of hot cross buns, and told

us that they would walk with us to the next picnic spot, where they would provide lunch. We were thrilled they were going to come with us. Our large party started single file down the narrow track. I placed myself so that I could talk to Cam Beardsell, a local ecologist who had written the book on the Yarra that I carried – the one Jess had given me. I'd found his number in the phone book and given him a call; he'd come down at our invitation. Cam was highly respected for his knowledge of and commitment to these areas, and was willing to satisfy a barrage of questions. He told us that Murray cod lived in the river around these parts, and that theoretically they can grow up to two metres in length. To think that I might be swimming with a fish larger than me, but the sediment in the river meant that I might never see him!

We lunched at Bluetongue Bend. The kookaburra that swooped up as soon as the food was laid out was obviously an old hand at picnics, as she kept diving for people's sandwiches. The most she got was a mouthful of lettuce, a sad result for a carnivore. While we were eating, we asked these folk for advice on where we could stay a few nights further on, in the region of Yering Gorge. We had yet to make contact with anyone, and time was running out to find a place. There was some ringing around on mobile phones, and very soon a suitable site was located. Coincidentally, the campsite found for us was on a farm belonging to the brother of a friend – a friend we were going to be staying with, further along the river.

'Sorry, people, I can't go any further, we've got to talk about it!'

We'd only just said goodbye to the crew when Kate burst.

We had no idea of what was going on, but, with worried looks, we found a place to sit, and circled around her, under the paperbarks. Kate explained that the night before, over dinner, she felt that she was left alone to talk to our guest, the ranger, and that we avoided the responsibility. She felt unsupported, and considered it a lack of care for herself, but more importantly, for those who we meet on the way. Kate, the most naturally gregarious of the group, upheld a pilgrim ethic of openness and generosity, no matter what it cost her personally. We were all tired, and in need of our rest day. I realised that what she said was true; last night we were less naturally hospitable than she. Kate's voicing of her frustration helped us. We each expressed how sometimes it was hard to be as open as pilgrimage seemed to ask of us.

I know I have boundaries, walls within. I'd spent much more time walking through the city where I'd studied and worked, newsstands screaming, advertising infiltrating, beggars pleading, than I ever had in the bush. The city can be an exhausting, numbing assault. To walk as a pilgrim, onward through barriers and over fences, felt as if it were eroding some of my internal walls. I felt as if I could barely keep pace with the person being freed inside me. The best way I could manage was to know nothing, and let the person emerging inside me take the lead. A soft, awake one, just being born.

As we shared our stories, I saw that we were all holding responsibility for the pilgrimage in ways unseen by each other. I grew to understand that others did what I could not, and to be grateful for this. There is no knowing all the ways we are held.

A little further on, by a bend in the river, Ilan spun round, caught our eyes, and raised his hands, stopping us to silence on the track.

'Can you hear it?' he asked, and a smile opened his face wide.

'What do you mean, I can't hear anything.'

'Exactly. No cars.'

For the first time on our journey we couldn't hear even a faint rumble of machines.

The path we were following ended, replaced only with the miniature tracks that the wombats made. The valley sides were growing steeper. I was up front, clinging to trees to steady me on the slope, when Ilan called me back. Cinnamon was upset – she was unnerved by the difficult path, and was afraid that if we kept to the river and the slow scramble it entailed, we would be walking long in darkness. We decided to shortcut onto the ridge. Cinn was worried she was disappointing me, but I said 'not at all' and meant it truly. The part of me that had held tight to ideals and structures was loosening her grip. To adjust to what was needed was far more satisfying and real than being caught in an idea. To flow, to move fluidly around obstacles.

Like a river.

We trekked on, into a broad afternoon. The ridge proved to be a marvellous choice (once we recovered from the climb up the cliff); after being down by the water, we all enjoyed the qualities of openness and vista it provided.

We came upon whole slopes covered in transparent green plastic bags held to the earth, each by three stakes. The scale of the revegetation project was inspiring – to remake the bush along the Yarra, where not long before it was bare cattle farming country. Among the tall grasses the kangaroos stood and watched us, turned and bounced away, turned back to watch us, decided we were definitely humans and then took off.

Soon we entered areas regrown thick with burgan, the local tea-tree. Burgan springs up to quickly colonise bare land, but without regular bushfires, it prohibits the growth of a more varied ecology. With suburbia encroaching on all sides of the Warrandyte State Park, control burns were not a well-accepted option for opening up the country. The Wurundjeri regularly fired the land, to encourage new growth, which in turn attracted game and allowed freer walking.

This land, alas, was not fired for walking. But by following wombat and wallaby ways, worming under thickets, we found the paths of least resistance. Kate and I would stop every now and then to confer over the map, with an eye always to the sun and its setting, aligning ourselves away from the light as we followed the sensed line of river, flowing from the east. I felt as if the energy of rain running down to find the river had entered me; fastfreeflowing, I was drunk on the rhythm of our footfalls drumming in time on the earth, and the scent exuding from the eucalypts all around.

Finally we broke through the burgan scrub into a hillside paddock with great white gums and calm white horses and a pale indigo sky. We sensed we were close to our camp. From there we found a path down to the water's edge, and we could hear Jess's welcoming call; our dear host, our fellow journeyman, waiting for us. The sun had just set behind the ridge. And so it was a twilight swim across to the other side of the Yarra. Body submerged, my eyes skimmed the surface to find a touch of gold resting in the west, showing us the way we had come.

We'd arrived at the Bend of Islands, where Jess and Ilan's grandfather had a block of land – just bush, no house. The boys had visited since childhood, swimming and camping. The block was its own bend, a peninsula of land, a cliff one side that sloped gradually down to the water on the opposite side, and the river wrapped around.

We walked the narrow path up through the blue-shadowed forest to the clearing on the ridge. Jess had set up all our tents and a large tarp for us to shelter underneath. He had ready a hot fire, and then cooked up barbecued kangaroo for dinner, a meal that had been eaten on these riverbanks for countless generations. Together, around the campfire, we thanked the animal we were to eat.

'May we be worthy of your life.'

THE SIXTH NIGHT

A few years later, I am visiting my friend Savaad, who lives right on the Yarra in Warandyte. His block is thick with tea-tree scrub, low and prone to floods. He takes me down a narrow path to the riverbank, where there is an unusually deep swimming hole. A huge old manna gum leans over the river, with a ladder made of sticks hammered into the trunk. At the top of the ladder perches a rickety wooden platform, and looped onto the platform is a rope tied on a branch far above.

There on the bank Savaad tells me a story.

'I once swung hard off that rope, flying through the air, before letting go, to land like a stone in the river. I went down and down until it was completely dark and unbelievably cold. I turned over and over in the water – I'd no idea which way was up. I panicked, desperate for breath, for a sign of light – I tried to swim but I had no idea which way to the surface. I thought I'd die there.

'After what seemed like forever I realised that only if I stopped struggling would I come out alive. So I calmed myself and stayed as still as I could, and I floated slowly up. I began to see light above me, and I swam for that. I exploded onto the surface.

'I'd made it. I was so glad to be alive.'

In the *Woiwurrung* language, *Warr-an-dyte* means 'the place thrown to'. This name is said to originate from a Dreaming story where *Bunjil*, the Wedge-Tailed Eagle spirit, threw a stone down to the earth, an impact that created the world. A very deep, very dark waterhole was formed, somewhere on the river in Warrandyte.

A beginning place.

It's beginning, right now, as soon as you leap.

WE CAN BOTTLE THINGS

'We are happy when for everything inside us there is a
corresponding something outside us.'
W. B. Yeats

Without quite waking up, or getting out of my sleeping bag, I
dragged my sleeping mat out of my tent. I lay in the morning
sun and pulled my beanie over my eyes for privacy. A rest day
was welcome, a chance to be quiet and alone and cast my
mind back over the six walking days. I did that – the recap –
and my mind drifted back into a morning mist of sleep.

In a waking dream I set out from the rapids at this bend
of the river, in Seacloud, my tiny inflatable boat (I had left it,
I thought, under the stairs at home in Brunswick). Around
the edge of the yellow and blue plastic were my companions
of the air – currawong, magpie, grey fantail, cockatoo, yellow
robin, willie wagtail. And behind me sat an old Wurundjeri
man and an old Wurundjeri woman. Together we floated all
the way down to the sea, passing the places we'd been through
the last six days. Finally we arrived at Williamstown, where
our walk began, and I asked the ancestors – how can I honour

you? The answer was something like – you are doing ok, you are remembering us to many people and you are loving this country as best you can.

Eventually I roused myself. Barefoot, free of daypack and schedule, I explored the bend in the river.

To the northwest of the grandfather's bend it was steep and cliff-like, with hardy bushes and thin trees clinging to the bone-dry stone. To the southeast the slope was gentle, where the path we ascended the evening before led up from the river. With my diary in my hand I took that path down through the red box trees. Dying leaves with the morning sun behind them became small and vivid panes of ruby-stained glass. Mistletoe hung from the eucalypts, the crimson blossom fell in patches on the crackly, bark-covered earth. Descending into the shade of the burgan, dried-up mosses covered the ground beneath the spindly bushes. It felt gentle compared to the parched ridgetops.

At the end of the path by the river a mass of young wattles grew, creating a feathery green room. I found a place to perch that looked over the rapids. The sun hit the churning water. Light broke over everything. A bull ant approached, the same red-brown colour of the wattle seedpods strewn on the forest floor. It looked up at the gigantic mammal that looked down at him. It stopped and cleaned its fangs beside me.

—

In January 1973, the State Government decided that another dam was needed to augment Melbourne's supply. There were drought years in the early 1970s and the accompanying water restrictions were not politically popular. A damming of the Yarra was proposed, to be located just four kilometres above Warrandyte township.

A Bend of Islands man I got to know told me of the extraordinary efforts of a few local people who opposed the flooding of their homes and their beloved stretch of the Yarra. They found a book called *How to Beat the Bureaucracy*. It was written by the English fellow who wrote the television series *Yes Minister*, about the machinations of civil servants, manipulating the government's decisions to make sure that they served them. This book helped the residents launch a spectacularly successful campaign. They somehow convinced the State Government that there was a huge majority of the population ready to vote against them if they dammed the Yarra.

At home after the pilgrimage, I searched for a copy of the 1974 *Yarra Brae – Sugarloaf Environmental Study* by the Melbourne and Metropolitan Board of Works. It is a thick typewritten document with few photos, but one that I found shows the location of a weir. It was to be built right on top of the lovely little peninsula where we camped that rest day. And much of the land we walked through the day before, and the days that came after, would have been inundated.

—

As I sat by the river, Kate came down with a pile of dirty clothes in a clear plastic tub. She took the clothes and put them on a rock beside the river, and then she waded out to half fill her tub with water. Then she came back and squatted in the sun and scrubbed at her clothes in the tub, careful to keep her small cake of biodegradable soap from the river. I watched her, delighted, for a long time. I watched her joy at the life flowing around her, while she worked at her task.

Kate washing clothes was, for me, a symbol. It was a symbol of something I loved. It linked back to behaviours thousands of years old, it indicated, to me, ways that have been lived, sustainably, in place. I had seen women squatting on riverbanks, washing, in India, surrounded by colour, by children playing; there was singing and laughter. It was a celebration.

≈

The Narmada River in India has an ancient pilgrimage route along its length. To walk the river is to take a *parikrama,* a sacred journey on which no food or money can be taken. The pilgrim is required to live in total surrender to *Narmade Mata* (Mother Narmada, the river goddess, daughter of Shiva) to provide whatever is needed. The local people who live alongside the river, their goddess, support the pilgrim's journeys, fulfilling the will of *Narmade Mata*. All along the river, shrines and temples to her grace the riverbanks.

Or rather, they did. For the Narmada is being dammed.

The Narmada dams projects have been at the centre of controversy for decades in India. Activists, mainly villagers who will lose their ancestral homes, fields and the shrines and temples to *Narmade Mata*, have marched and gone on hunger strikes. Some refused to leave when the dammed waters rose, and they drowned in their homes. Others have been resettled in camps in the desert where there is no water – starvation and death by disease are common. Others have no choice but to join the slums attached to the cities, and eke out a life at the very bottom of society's ladder.

Over one million people will be displaced by the thirty big, 135 medium and 3000 small dams planned for the Narmada. If they are all built the river will disappear, to be replaced by a series of silty lakes. Dams throughout India have flooded out around 50 million people, many of them tribal people who live outside the modern economic systems, who make or grow everything they need, or collect it from the forests around their villages, who live lives of independence and self-sufficiency. One man who was relocated, who once collected almost fifty different types of fruits from his now-flooded forests, wonders if his children will ever experience the taste of fruit. Now he needs money – something he never before needed – to buy such things for them.

The reasons for building the dams have been fiercely contested by the anti-dams movement, who cite evidence of corruption and greed.

But one thing that damming the river incontrovertibly does is give a few people a great deal of control of water. Undammed water cannot be sold. If something is free flowing, it cannot be bought.

And selling water is big business, all around the world.

~

Water is on sale now in every Australian milk bar, café and

supermarket. This trend began only a few years ago, but now plastic or glass bottles of water are everywhere. The bottles have to be manufactured, trucked around the country, and then hopefully recycled (but recycling still creates pollution). If you filled each plastic bottle one-quarter with oil, you'd show how much unrenewable fuel was used to create that product. If it were up to me, I'd tie those bottles to black balloons and float them away.

I also discovered that for every single litre of bottled water, up to five litres of fresh (drinking!) water are wasted in the manufacturing process. For some imported waters it's more like seven litres.

It seems if we want water in the future, we've got to stop drinking water™.

Every year, the sales of bottled water skyrocket. Pepsi and Coca Cola are two of the biggest players in the bottled-water market; as soft drink sales level off, more money is spent on promoting and niche marketing different 'waters' – most not much better quality (and some worse) than what comes out of the tap. Melbourne has one of the best quality drinking water supplies in the world. It also has a massive and growing market for bottled water.

Why do we pay for something that comes free? Is it because we want it cold? (Put your own bottle in the freezer, take it out and wrap it in a cloth – it stays icy all day.) Is it because we think it's healthier?

The bottle is a symbol. The bottle is a symptom of a system that sells things with the false promise of experience.

We say, sometimes, when something is especially good,

we'd like to bottle it. Do we mean we want to have easy, immediate access to the rare, the hard won, or the treasured? We can do that now. We can bottle things.

THE SEVENTH NIGHT

Sometimes, the world piles coincidence upon coincidence in a manner that is, frankly, ridiculous.

It is some time after the pilgrimage to the source of the Yarra. I am staying at an exquisite spot in the Bend of Islands for the summer. I walk to the river for an early dip.

Shimmering light streams through the treetops. I am alone in the beautiful river, swimming through smooth water to the rapids. I enter the fast-flowing channel, where I turn onto my back and float downstream. I am carried along until a stone, emerging from the water, stops me with a gentle bump.

I take up the offer; I stand on the dry part of the stone and face the sun, and gaze upriver. I stretch. I am whole and I am illuminated. I extend my naked body, and raise my straight arms out from my sides to meet over my head; they draw a circle around me.

As I stand on the rock, I notice something floating down the river towards me, down the very same fast-flowing channel of water I too had floated on.

It is a piece of rubbish. A bottle.

It too bumps against this stone.

There is a picture on it – of a beautiful river, clean water flowing over stones.

There is a naked woman in the centre of the picture, a circle surrounding her.

There are words on the bottle.

It says 'Organic Springs – Bottled at the Source, the Essence of Pure Creation™'.

The Yarra Valley

Key:

- △ Camp sites
- ∞ ∞ ∞ Roads
- ～ River
- ⌐ Creeks/streams
- ◯ Dam/reservoir

0   7.5 miles

0   7.5 kilometres

Sugarloaf Reservoir

Yarra Glen

Yering Gorge

Stringybark Creek

Olinda Creek

Yarra

Watts River

GREAT DIVIDING RANGE

Healesville

Yarra Grange

Coranderrk

Badger Creek

Blackwood

Mt Toolewong

WARRAMATE HILLS

River

Woori Yallock Creek

Yarra Bridge

IS THIS THE WAY TO WILLIAMSTOWN?

6.00 am: pack up time. It was overcast, and spots of rain drifted down from pink-edged clouds. The birds were just beginning, a rhythm of high pipings. Yet I felt out of rhythm, the rest day having broken the flow upstream. I looked forward to the trance-like march of our feet on the earth, the dreamlike way the hours spread, blown and wide, through each elongated day. As if time, space and the rhythm-loving body were fused; when walking, each heartbeat, each step, each second were like three sides of one thing. Maybe that's why it seemed ridiculous to believe only a week ago we'd begun our Pilgrimage. We all agreed, it truly felt as if we'd been gone for years.

Over breakfast, Don, Cinnamon's stepfather, arrived. Don's passions of bushwalking and skiing and camping and canoeing fostered the young Cinnamon's interest in these pursuits throughout her childhood, so we were pleased to have such a veteran along. Don was to be our support person for the next two days. Jess was going to walk with us for the morning, then walk back, passing his responsibility for the trailer over to Don.

7.00 am: river-crossing time. The rain had settled in. At least when the air temperature is cold the river water can seem warm. Jess chose to come too for the morning, and was first in. But I loitered awhile on the riverbank before sliding down the smooth rock ledge and into the river with Ilan, he and I each holding a side of our fat floating drybag. Squealing with cold and exhilaration, we paddled the steaming river. The river was hissing and bubbling like a cauldron of thrashing snakes – the rain, coming down hard, hitting the Yarra's back.

It wasn't much drier once out of the river. On a slippery rock shelf we pulled on our clothes, raincoats and packs – there was no use in towelling off as the rain kept wetting us. Kate had reasoned that she might as well keep her thermals on through the river; 'I'm not going to be able to keep them dry anyway'.

Don came down to watch us negotiate the first part of the day's challenges, and defying Cinnamon's protestations, and much to her disgust, took photos of us and our ungainly passage. I found out later this stoic fellow was thrilled that his step-daughter would do what he saw as such an intrepid thing, and wanted the photos to remember the occasion.

The first upriver stretch curled right in on itself. On the far side of the big bend was a sizable island crowded with pale towering gums. In front of the island was a long reach of rapids. These rapids were well known, being the most difficult for canoes and kayaks to negotiate, the only grade 2.5 rapid on the Yarra. I had kayaked there as a teenager with a school group – I remember my boat flipping over as I went down and I couldn't right myself. From underwater I twisted my torso and scrabbled violently, ineffectually at the surface. Finally a teacher came and flipped over my boat. The rest of that sunlit trip I was waterlogged, light-headed, exultant in my escaping of death, my wet woollens reeking of mothballs.

We trudged around the fluvial perimeter of Clifford Park Scout Camp. There we saw Don walking towards us, skirting the puddles; he had driven from the Bend of Islands downriver to Warrandyte, crossed the bridge and driven back upstream to find us.

'Is this the way to Williamstown?' he asked cheekily, peering out from under his very effective umbrella. I wished I had one.

The puddles were a pale tan, the same colour as the dirt roads around here, the same colour as the mudstone cliffs we had been clambering along for days. The old fragile stone, made of fine compacted silts, was running out of the earth along the eroded path and heading for the river, which was looking decidedly more turbid as the rain continued.

We passed Don, and continued through the scout camp. When the riverbanks rose up too steeply we backtracked through the forest to find paths that led upstream. It was slow and tiring travelling but we couldn't stop to rest. The cold, kept at bay by our moving, would have caught up with us.

We came eventually to Brushy Creek, where a little wooden bridge made for an easy crossing. The creek looked even more turbid than the river, and with a subtle rainbow of oiliness gained, I suspected, from its journey through the suburbs.

'I had my twenty-first birthday on Brushy Creek, in the hall on Maroondah Highway', Kate reported. 'I grew up just near where this creek rises in Croydon, with Mount Dandenong looking over me.'

We rejoined Warrandyte State Park, the very last section. Our path by the water wound around the base of Mount Lofty, a grandly named hill that not long ago was grazing land. As we walked, Kate noticed me slowing, pale and quiet at the back.

'Come here Mays.' As the rain came steadily down she led me away from the path, out of sight of the others, where she started stripping off her tops.

'What are you doing?' I shivered.

'You aren't warm enough, and we'll never get there if you get hypothermia!' By this time she was just in her bra, and was handing me her innermost thermal layer, heated by her skin.

'No Kate, I'm not ...'

'Just get your gear off quickly and put this on.' I felt humbled that I wasn't better prepared, but never in my life had I walked so long in rain such as this. I knew I couldn't refuse.

I'd been a shy, skinny child, afraid of catching balls, terrified of cold water. Athletics gave me nightmares; shins smashing into hurdles. I played sick on swimming and sports days, I was picked last for teams. It was only when I joined my high school's Outdoors Club, joining in on weekend trips of hiking, caving or horse-riding, that I began to feel at home in my body, and in the world. Maybe I was still trying to prove I was tough enough to keep up with the others. I needed to get over that, and be a bit more responsible.

Sodden, tired and hungry, we came to the end of the bend. There the path turned around and went straight up Mount Lofty – the banks around the other side of the hill were too steep to allow access by the river. As we climbed, the wind picked up, driving the rain towards us. Somehow I found that my hands were in the hands of my friends. There was such comfort in those hands. Linked together the five of us marched up the wide path. I was grateful for the extra energy the group gave me. They helped me reach the top. And I hope I helped them too.

By the time we made the peak of the mountain, an open plateau encircled on three sides by misty Kangaroo Ground Hills, the wind had blown away the rain. We beheld the wide-open floodplains of the Yarra Valley; we saw all the country we would pass through over the following days, until the way vanished into the distant mauve hills.

'Would you look at Mount Dandenong!' Kate exclaimed. 'When I see that mountain I always know where I am.' And who I am, I almost heard her say.

The mountain sat alone and grand in the broad spread of the valley. It was clothed evenly in the blue of eucalypt canopy, and crowned with transmission towers.

'Well, Walkers, this is where I leave you', Jess announced.

'Have you got enough scroggin for your journey?' we girls fussed over him, hugging uncomfortably through raincoats, rain disguising tears. We were losing our special fifth walker. He turned away, and tall, straight and clear, walked back down the flank of Mount Lofty, back the way we had come.

It was not far down to the base of Mount Lofty and the end of Warrandyte State Park. Lower Homestead Road came down to the river from the leafy suburb of Wonga Park, and ended in a car park and picnic area. Many canoeists put in their craft at this place, to paddle downstream to Witton's Reserve or all the way through to Warrandyte town, though no-one was foolish enough to try to paddle through such a rain as was falling that day.

Don surprised us there, driving in with our trailer – which showed great forethought. While I had recovered from my close shave with cold, Cinn was now vulnerable. With the trailer's supplies, we fashioned a shelter between the trees out of a tarp, and lit the camp stove for tea. After lunch we all felt a lot more robust.

Blue sky began elbowing away the clouds as we set off upriver. Soon we came to a gate with a sign detailing the opening and closing hours to the Heritage Golf and Country Club. Beyond the gate a path lay alongside the river, but the gate was closed. I scrambled down the bank to where the fence ended, just beyond the river. I could get through by going under the wire, I figured. I clung to the wire and launched myself clumsily off the bank. Meanwhile Kate walked up to the gate, gave it a push, and my three companions walked straight through, smirking and trying hard not to look in my direction, while I was still hanging by my fingers from the bottom of the fence, dangling over the water.

We walked into the thick stands of fluffy young silver wattles and along the riverbank. Until recently the land was farmed, and it appeared the riverbanks were not long replanted. Soon the golf course ended and we came to a barbed wire fence. It was the start of the Yarra Valley farmlands. We carefully parted the prickly strands and helped each other through.

Along the riverbank, we clambered over or squeezed through fence after fence. We could generally tell when we passed into a new property, because land management practices varied so much. Sometimes the banks were fenced and tall trees grew along the margin, other times there were small plants still swathed in their plastic tree guards. Sometimes there were no fences, and only grass grew, all the way to the water's edge. Never was there anything approaching the ecological diversity we had seen in the steep and rocky gorge country of Warrandyte. And this land would be ineffectual as a wildlife corridor, with ground cover sparse and fragmented, and fences restricting animal movement. And while the water was continuous, the water quality appeared variable. It was obvious the river does not get cleaner and wilder each step away from the city. I'd read that riparian ecosystems can dramatically improve the quality of the river water. Apparently the water flowing through the lower Yarra Valley is less clean than at Warrandyte – for the trees had cleansed it, as it flowed.

We were walking by the edge of a vineyard with a little pump house to take water from the river for the vines, near where a farm road met the water, when we spotted a by now familiar figure approaching.

It was Don, seeking directions to Williamstown.

Despite all the fence negotiation, it was easy walking, and we quickly covered a lot of ground. Up ahead, the landscape was changing, the land steepening on both sides. The secret Yering Gorge. Just in front of the gorge was a trestle bridge high above the water. We clambered up to it; stepping carefully, it rattled beneath our feet. We sat on the bridge and snacked, looking upstream at the gorge and the rapids ahead, the first since Warrandyte Gorge – only that morning, but it felt a world away.

We heard a motor. It was a car, driving up the road towards the bridge. As quickly as we could, we gathered up our things that we'd spread over the bridge, and stood out of the way. A Torana approached – behind the wheel was a woman with a shaved head and a fierce face. She stopped beside us.

'This is a private bridge, which means you're trespassing – what the hell are you lot doing here?'

We explained.

'Really? Fantastic! My house is just up there – come on!'

Eyeing each other with secret smiles, we obediently followed her car to the house. It was an 1857 homestead, and she was the lucky renter. She told us how she watches the eagles from her verandah. We nosed around the old stables for a while, looking at the hand-split timber and the squarish handmade nails. It was fascinating – and so was she – but we had to keep moving. We still had a long way to go and it was starting to get dark.

Back on the rattly old bridge we looked upriver, into the gorge, where the shadowy forest blanketed the hills. We decided that we must cut across the paddocks and miss the gorge today; tomorrow's walk was relatively short, so we figured that we could backtrack and spend a good amount of time exploring then, in proper light. The mystery of the gorge had to wait until another day.

I was torn. So much of me wanted to walk into that darkness. We crossed the bridge and tramped the dirt road, with the enticing dark hills to our left, beyond a row of pines. It was a beautiful evening, washed clean by the day's rain. We jumped the fence to skirt around the base of the hills, and then across wide-open paddocks. A waxing moon was in the eastern sky, and we travelled towards her. As we walked the daylight faded and the moonlight swelled. The vapours began rising from the river; the distant cows were silhouetted against the mist. And so were the occasional old paperbark trees, standing sentinel over muddy holes. What once were billabongs were now simply depressions in the earth, shaped like the resting place of a giant serpent. The story of the rainbow serpent does not come from around here, but I can imagine no other story more fitting.

The Warrandyte park ranger, Glen Jameson, spoke of the wetlands that once covered these floodplains as 'the Kakadu of the Yarra Valley'. It was rich, diverse, a place we would treasure and call world heritage if we discovered it today. I stood with Ilan by a remnant paperbark, imagining this land 200 years ago. We held hands, and transformed our witness into intention – to help renew these ecosystems – and to bring awareness to what has been lost.

It became darker and darker and still we walked through the gentle undulations of the floodplains. We were grateful for the moonlight, glowing through the thickening fog. Eventually we saw what looked like a torch flashing in the distance. We followed it. Was it Don, coming to meet us near the edge of the last paddock?

Someone called to us through the mist: 'Is this the way to Williamstown?'

THE EIGHTH NIGHT

Nightmist and moonlight, and my body walking through it, holding Cinnamon's warm hand. Voice, not much louder than breath, chanting to the beat of our footsteps, a strange little song sung over and over. It hovers close to me in the damp air, it says, 'Birrarung, Birrarung'. The voice, mine, yet unlike me, is it leaving my body or entering it? The mist gathers around us, thickening, rising from the river, a thin floating river. River water, rising to meet us.

So here you are. Walking, walking through this gentlest of waters, where all of our edges are blurred, finally. I can meet you.

SUGAR AND SPACE

Perched on the riverbank, my tent faced directly east. Hot sun streamed in, steaming my belongings still damp from the downpour of the day before. Through the arch doorway, the river appeared as a warped old mirror, doubling and deepening the blue of the sky.

I'd woken up with a sore throat. When I struggled out of my tent, and Cinnamon was there, smiling in the fresh sunshine, I burst into tears in her arms.

'Maybe I can't do this. I don't want to hold you up.'

'Maya, you'll be fine. I've got those Lemsips in my kit – they've got painkillers and vitamin C in them. Just take it a bit easy, hey?'

'Thanks Cinni,' I said, crying a bit more.

'Hey, darling, we won't leave you behind.'

We set out to backtrack to Yering Gorge. It immediately felt strange to go downriver. Tramping through the treeless paddocks, up and down through the dried-up billabongs, two wedge-tailed eagles wheeled above us, circling effortlessly downstream. Bunjil and his mate, inspecting the snake patterns of the billabongs, watching over the world they'd created, as the world went on, creating itself.

There in Yering Gorge creation was unfurling in manifold form. So much diverse life, tightly packed into one place. As we walked around the bends the vegetation told which direction the bank was facing – the northern and western slopes had almost no colour, all was brittle grey, dull brown, bleached and still. The southern and eastern slopes by contrast were lush and green, ferned and feathered. A small path wove between these worlds. Kate and I heard a commotion from a flock of little birds; wrens, thornbills, wagtails. They seemed to be attacking a bush. And then we noticed, silent at the centre, a boobook owl, staring straight at us.

Further on, we came to what our map called the pumping station, squat and ugly as a cane toad, skulking at a bend in the captivating gorge. It took water out of the river and stored it in Sugarloaf Reservoir, to top up Melbourne's drinking water. After the Yarra dam at Warrandyte was defeated, Sugarloaf was built, flooding some of Christmas Hills instead. Yering Gorge was saved.

Just as we passed through the thickest, most secret part of the gorge we heard the splash and patter of waterfalls, somewhere on the steep shadowside of the river, hidden behind a blanket of tree ferns. Ilan moved a little way into the trees and had a pee, quite audibly.

'He's embodying the place,' whispered Kate.

Cinn and I become our own little waterfalls, laughing til we cried.

Heading back, following a slightly different path a little away from the river, we found something we'd never seen the like of.

'Would you look at that tree!'

It seemed as if three great manna gums had started growing in the exact same place, and so all leaned out at an identical angle. In the centre of the three enormous trees was a pile of cast-off bark; long curls like oversized cinnamon quills, and smelling almost as fragrant. I clambered in and nested there among the crunching bark. I lay back with my head against one trunk and my two feet on the other two trunks, and felt very happy with the world. Kate swung on a branch that descended almost to the ground before changing its mind and curving back towards the sky, making the most perfect swing. It was a giving tree, a remembrance of belonging.

'C'mon walkers, there's headwaters somewhere up there, waiting for us!' said Ilan.

Cinn and I were together, ahead of the others. The river was not fenced, so the cattle drank from and shat in the river, just a few hundred metres from the intake pipe for the Sugarloaf dam.

I'd been looking around me as we walked, when I recognised a stretch that I once visited on the opposite bank, on a reconnaissance mission last summer.

'Cinn, remember the wetland I was telling you about, the ones that Glen Jameson reckons are the best example of what this place was once like?'

'Yeah. It's near here, you think?'

'See how just over the river the bush is sparse compared to

the vegetation on either side? I reckon that's where it is.'

We looked back to see if the others were visible. We could see far across the paddocks but the other two were nowhere in sight. So much for Ilan's hurrying us up earlier.

'How about a quick look?' I suggested. It didn't feel quite right without the whole gang, but time was trickling away. So we waded the river. The water didn't rise above the tops of our thighs – much shallower than we'd yet encountered. On the other side, native nettles and swordgrass lined the bank. Gingerly we pushed and hauled each other up.

It was worth it. We'd found the wetland. It was filled with frog song and massive ancient paperbarks. Standing trees shaded a patchwork of grasses, rushes and sedges. Fallen trees formed a criss-cross of bridges; precarious pathways through boggy ground. A flock of wrens passed, like bright pom-poms bouncing from strand to strand along dark-green reeds, sounding their scissory warning calls to each other, their wings purring. Insects buzzed by on pollen business.

We'd found one of the only remnant billabongs on the Yarra – certainly the only one with such an incredible mix of life. The last little bit of Kakadu on the Yarra.

We got back to camp, ate, packed and moved out, finally heading upriver. Through the barbed wire, and into Spadoni's reserve. It was the first piece of Yarra bank accessible to the public since we left Warrandyte State Park at Mount Lofty – many kilometres back. After the often-bare riparian zones of the farmland, it was good to see the riverbanks clothed with vegetation again, although weeds formed much of the groundcover. Spadoni's had been set aside by Parks Victoria as it was the only place on the river where the sweet-smelling Buxton Gums grow; a pretty tree with delicate dust-grey foliage. There was evidence of replanting of the gums, plastic protectors tight around the base of many of the young trees.

Spadoni's reserve was bordered, on the upriver side, by the Olinda Creek, which rose on the flanks of Mount Dandenong. Some of the mountain creeks I had played by as a child flowed into here. To our surprise, it had been turned into a channel, with steepened sides, although not lined with concrete, in the way of channelised city creeks. It was dead straight for as far as we could see. The junction of creek and river was overgrown with vegetation, weeds including hawthorn, ash and various nasty prickly things. As the creek was only shallow, we didn't want to strip and fill the drybags, but when we crossed we found it much harder than it looked. We helped each other across on fallen logs that sank unnervingly when we put weight on them. Clinging to tree branches overhead, we eventually made it. (Later, I discovered that the Lilydale Purification Plant – fancy name for a sewerage farm – discharged its purified sewerage into this creek. And then the pumping station we'd seen earlier took up this water when it pumped from the Yarra. It became part of the drinking water stored at Sugarloaf Reservoir. So Melburnians are drinking treated sewerage, whether they know it or not – even if it is just a miniscule proportion of the supply.)

Drying off and dressing in the paddock on the other side, I was giggling with relief.

'I thought you were supposed to be sick today Maya,' said Cinn, looking weary and drawn herself.

'You made me better.'

We'd hit the four o'clock funnies – when exhaustion starts creeping in as energy drops, and the jokes got worse and we would laugh at anything. This was the time when we often broke open a packet of lollies for a sugar hit. Ilan abstained, warning us it was a short-lived pick-up; we'd slump again soon after. But we wouldn't listen, and after a few snakes Kate and I were chasing each other through the paddocks, drunk on sugar and space.

See those mountains in the distance? The ones mauve and hazy and so very far away? Those ones, there on the edge of the world? Walk there. Just leave the house, and walk, walk through the unfolding days, walk along the oldest path, the first path, walk until you get there.

That was the call I heard, resonating through my tubular bones, echoing low and strong through my body. Finally, finally I had obeyed.

As the day starts to fade, when the evening light washes gently over the valley, that is when the dream of the land is strongest. We are tired, we have been walking all day, we are thin in energy and thick with a rolling joy. The time is endless. So is the land. Neither is true, both are utterly true in the vast spreading moment. Oh my dear companions, this goodness is everything, this freedom is all. I am exactly where I am meant to be. Kate shouted as we ran, 'This is the bold and the beautiful hour'. Full of the magic of the afternoon, I bellow my agreement.

I found out later what she also meant. Four o'clock was the time the American soap *The Bold and The Beautiful* was on the telly.

As we neared Yarra Glen, we came upon a disused railway line running through the paddocks alongside the river. It once ran from Lilydale out to Healesville and then on to Warburton, roughly following the line of the river, passing through Yarra Glen on the way. Then cars made the line uneconomic, and it was shut down. As we needed to get to the other bank, we decided to walk across the old trestle bridge as a welcome alternative to a swim – the afternoon had turned chilly. The bridge was high and narrow, with holes where planks had fallen in. The water below was dark and cold-scented, and shadows lay all around. We walked the railway tracks the rest of the way into town, in the new night.

Right on the river on the edge of Yarra Glen was our destination, River View Cottages, a bed and breakfast kindly donated to us for the night. Coincidently, Kate knew the hosts from her horse-riding days in the Yarra Valley, so straight away there were hugs and stories. After hot showers we had the challenge of finding clean clothes to wear out to dinner. For we had a date with the locals.

Stiff and sore, we approached the Italian restaurant in Yarra Glen. There we met members of the local historical society and the Friends of Yarra Glen Wetlands. We sat around the long table and told stories and listened to those of the remarkable local folk. Many had worked for years revegetating a large area of wetlands by the banks of the river, just over the bridge from town.

The Black Saturday fires of 2009 reduced those wetlands to dried charred depressions, the earth bare and scorched. The silver wattles by the river were stripped skeletal black. You could see where young trees had been planted, for three black sticks that once held the plastic tree guard were still in place – the fire moving so swiftly that the sticks weren't burnt through. While the fires raged all around the Yarra Valley, the Yarra Glen Wetland was one of the only spots where flames reached the river.

The Friends group is back there, replanting again. Seed of natives, seeds of weeds, are blowing in and taking root. Something new is emerging.

THE NINTH NIGHT

Just over the bridge from town, that floodplain with its fertile soil had long been prized. The first graziers came and claimed the best of the valley only two years after the white settlers arrived in Melbourne. In 1837 the Ryrie brothers overlanded and set up Yering Station, and a homestead just near the wetland. Here, across the river from the Town of Yarra Glen, Jaga Jaga, a headman of the Wurundjeri, was tricked and captured, before fifty men of his tribe came to rescue him. It was a rare win for the Wurundjeri, in their struggle to retain their land and their culture, and this incident is now officially recognised.

I am here for the very first commemoration of the Battle of Yering (as the incident became known), 164 years to the day after the event. As part of the ceremony, Sebastian Jorgensen sings the three songs that have been preserved in the Wurundjeri language. The first is the song of Koala man, a powerful lore man, who in this spot sang a song of names, the names of all those who are mountains that ring the valley. This was the knowledge of the clever man, the *Ngurrung Gaeta*, Koala man, who once stood in this very spot, here within the valley of Birrarung. He stood here, in billabong country, where Birrarung twisted like a flashing snake, this is where he called out their names, the names of the mountains. Baw Baw, who stood up, shedding the waters of his flank, so the water runs this way, through the valley, away down to the circle bay.

The songs contain more of the old language of the land I lived on than I have ever heard. The wind is running over us and the sun shines into our eyes. The wind and the sun and the words are heavy; I curl against the earth. I feel my heart shaking me as my blood soughed through, a cross-rhythm to the clapsticks. I close my eyes to the sun.

Am I going to be here, or am I not?

Breathe.

The songs of Koala Man are gifts. What was he giving, singing them, who was listening?

We don't know what he knew. But he knew this world, the mountains standing up when he called their names, standing up for him, standing up, alive, in the mind he had made for them, where he could see them and know them, alive.

The new people come, the ones who listen. They are planting trees. The trees all burn. They will plant more trees. They will foster the seeds that come up of their own accord, after the fire. They will learn from this. They will keep listening.

In this way the stories will grow again. It's not the specific details of the story, it's the fact that the stories grow the people into the land, the land itself claims them, asks them for their songs. That is what we are here for. To give, to give the songs.

What are our songs, our stories? Do they come from science, whose method of driven curiosity has, in the best of minds, borne children of awe and wonder? From evolution, millions of years in the making, making these old worn-away hills, these many many trees, this diversity of plants, insects, birds? Perhaps if it were a science that grows love and listening, humility, and honour. Then maybe our story could grow from a graft onto the older roots; the story of how people, for thousands of years, made rich sweet lives in this place, the longest continuous culture on earth.

PALM SUNDAY

The day began overcast and humid, the low sky heavy with rain. We headed towards the purple mountains, growing in the east.

Birrarung was flowing brown through the farmlands, with a thin string of willows clinging to her banks. Underneath the trees were a few dominant weed species. One paperbark loitered beside a bone-dry billabong – there was no other sign of the original water-loving vegetation. Yet one of our hosts was saying at dinner last night that these billabongs will be resurrected to some sort of life when the autumn rains come – the downpour of two days ago not yet being enough. Around Easter time the rains will come, if it is not a drought year.

A wind sprang up in the middle of the day, buffeting us through the bare treeless paddocks. I liked the wind – it stopped us talking. For a few kilometres we left the river to follow the long-disused railway line to the Abbey – walking fast as we were late for our audience with the Abbot. Ahead of me, Ilan balanced along the thin metal line the whole way. We were strung out along the track, and I walked last, enjoying the solitude and the alternating textures underfoot – smooth sleeper, rough gravel. Blood-red rosehips were splattered through the wild rosebushes that lined the deserted track. And as I walked I picked, then ate the hips for their deliciousness and their vitamin C, delicately nibbling off the tart outer layer so as not to touch the prickly interior. The wind whipped and rustled the reeds below the rickety wooden trestle bridges, bleached from decades of sun. And I watched Ilan balance, even in the wind.

'A story is like the wind – it comes from a far off place, and we feel it.' So say the Kalahari Bushmen, according to Laurens van der Post. What does the wind make me feel? Less present, buffeted, a bit more internal, less in the space around me. I am blown through the paddocks, like washing carelessly pegged. Migraines are the wind caught inside the body, according to traditional Chinese medicine. Perhaps my migraines, which had plagued me for years, will leave me if I tell stories, if I let them out and hang them up to dry on the line, to release the winds now caught in my skull.

On the journey upriver the wind is mostly behind us; mild or warm wind if a nor-westerly, chill if it is from the southwest. These are the prevailing winds of Melbourne. Strong easterlies are rare and the trees are caught unawares, boughs brought down in numbers by a wind that sneaks up from behind.

Melbourne is known for its winds, raging rivers of air, tumbling through the land, flowing over the earth to fill a hollow, to fill a vacuum. Wind carries stories from its past wanderings as scents – the essence of a thing dissolved into the air. Including stories of the sea. Over millions of years persistent southwesterly gales have brought ocean salt in on the winds. The salt is dissolved by the rain, and it percolates slowly down through the soil and strata, becoming part of the geological profile. These winds have been blowing over this valley for an unimaginably long time. This river was old before the Himalayas rose. The Yarra is a Gondwanan river. It existed before India detached itself, floating away to slam into land that would rise from the blow to become the tallest of the world's mountains.

Salinity is not a big issue in the Yarra Valley – as yet. Salinity is caused by the removal of trees; with no deep roots to drink up the groundwater, the water table rises, and brings with it the salts that lie within the soil, salts laid down over millennia by the winds. Advanced salinity is indicated by salt crystals forming on the earth around the water body, and a die off of vegetation. When the soil is too salty to support life.

We followed a driveway lined with sugar gums, their bark the colour of Nice biscuits. Past the immaculate rose gardens, we approached the grand Abbey buildings. We were late, tired, hungry and scruffy – Ilan was wearing what he decided to call his 'the church needs to respond to the needs of youth' clothes; old cut-off pants held up with a fraying tie and a stained T-shirt with strange things sewn on the front. I wondered what sort of reception we would get. We climbed the steps to the entrance, and rang the bell beside the glass doors.

'Could you please tell the Abbot that the Long Yarra Walkers are here?'

We were ushered in to a dark wood panelled hall, and were directed to a simple white room whose windows looked out over the fields towards the river. An elegant, deceptively youthful looking man soon arrived and introduced himself as David Tomlins, the Abbot of Tarrawarra Abbey of the Cistercian order. His ankle-length robes were of heavy cream linen, below a dark brown tunic belted at the waist. He waved us into seats around an oval wooden table covered with a white tablecloth. Kate fingered the delicate embroidery around the edges and gave me a wink. She and the Abbot were the only ones looking relaxed.

David Tomlins offered us tea, which we accepted gratefully; Brother Bernie went to make it. We tentatively explained that, since we were running late, we had not stopped to eat, and would it be all right if we ate our lunch while we talked? 'Of course, of course,' said David. With manners I never knew we had, we unpacked tins of tuna, half-eaten blocks of cheese, Vita Weats and old cucumbers and ratty ends of tomatoes and prepared our lunch on the lids of Tupperware. I tried to listen to the Abbot, while willing the tuna oil not to spill on the tablecloth as Ilan opened the brimming can.

David told us stories. The Cistercians are a contemplative order, who pattern their lives with solitude, prayer and care for the land. The abbey had been on that land for fifty years, and the monks are a strong part of the local farming community. They see themselves in certain ways as being kin to Aboriginal people, as they too are 'people of the place'. Yet they are also part of the international brotherhood of Cistercian monks, part of a worldwide family whose geneaology can be traced back almost a thousand years, and further back than that, too, as part of the Christian tradition.

After lunch we took our dishes down the long passageway

to the kitchen, and tidied up with Brother Bernie. He told us of his work at Tarrawarra, maintaining the pumps that brought water to the abbey. I looked down at my wet hands in the sink. I listened to his voice, a tone almost impossibly gentle. The monks bathe in Yarra water, pumped up from the river.

David then took us on a tour of their chapel and unravelled the symbology of the stained-glass windows. There were stories of fire and water and blood, sacraments of purification and renewal. Within the glass was a character in Hebrew that the Abbot couldn't read. Ilan translated for us. It was *dum*; blood.

In the Old Testament – the Book of Genesis – God created life through parting the waters and raising the firmament – the earth sits poised between waters above and below. The ancient cosmology was that the blue dome of the sky was water, held back by God's will.

Baptism by full immersion is, in part, to signify burial. You are taken down to the river and laid down backwards into the water as in a grave, but held there in the arms of the representative of the Lord. Then raised back out of the water, returned to life, reborn.

Baptism was traditionally performed around Easter time, at dawn, and the first baptisms were done in the River Jordan, in Palestine. The baptised soul would then wade across the river, into the east, into the rising sun. (I have seen pictures of the River Jordan today. It is lined with Australian eucalypts, one of the few plants that thrives in the depleted soils that ring the Mediterranean. Their indigenous trees, the thick oak and cedar forests that grew all through the Middle East, were cut down and any seedlings eaten out by goats a long time ago.) For the ancient Hebrews there was living water – the flowing water of rivers and springs, and dead water, such as the Dead Sea, too salty to support human life. Rain was a blessing from God.

When we left the abbey, David Tomlins saw us off, waving from the wide verandah. As we set off down the slope of the well-kept pasture to the revegetated riverbanks, it started to pour. A short, sharp drenching, then just as suddenly, it stopped.

≈

If a man came to this valley, and lived quietly, mindfully, frugally, and if he watched and waited for the land to show him its ways, and in this way became a farmer and a thinker, who then might he become?

I had been to the Abbey once before, years ago. It was to meet a monk called David Ranson, who had spent eighteen years living and working by the Yarra at Tarrawarra. I wanted to find out more about his work, his exploring of ways that the church could respond to this land, these seasons. He was developing a place-centred liturgy; the celebrations of the year attuned to the cycles of the land. He acknowledged that traditional Christian festivals emerged from northern hemisphere pagan roots; peasants whose lives depended on understanding and respecting nature, people who created rituals for their lives as they are lived in their place. Christmas falls at winter solstice, when much of nature is in hibernation, and people gathered together to support each other, to share food and celebrate the lengthening days after the solstice – the return of the sun and the defeat of winter. Lent, the traditional forty-day fast, was early spring. That was when winter food stocks were exhausted, and little grew. And thus Easter was a celebration of life returning after the hardships and privations of winter and hungry spring; hens laying again, plants growing vigorously after the dramatic spring thaw. Christmas, Lent and Easter fall at opposite times of year in the southern hemisphere, yet to try to change the times of year when we celebrate these festivals, David felt, would be culturally impossible. For the place-responsive aspect of these festivals is only one component of these rituals.

Instead David Ranson began by contemplating what he observed in nature.

The time when our native vegetation bursts with new life is not only spring, but in autumn when the rains bring relief from the withering summer. We have taken on an idea of spring that belongs to another place; spring has come to mean return to life, just as autumn means a type of death, and so we don't tend to notice that Easter falls at exactly the right time in our natural cycle. Similarly, the time when everything dies off and retreats to the roots here is not winter, but over our summer, which happens to coincide with Lent. In summer the heat dries everything out, the ground water table drops and the native trees, especially the eucalypts, push their roots deeper in search of water. The grass dies back; the trees slow their growth and enter into a type of dormancy unless they are artificially watered. The local adaptations are leaves that are leathery to reduce summer evaporation, or in a drought year experience mass leaf drop. Some of the few Australian deciduous trees lose their leaves due to the heat and dry, rather than cold. In Europe, the dangerous time of year is winter, with threats of extreme cold and snow. Whereas here, it is summer that is the risky season, with the constant threat of raging bushfires fanned by extreme heat and northerly drying winds. Christmas bushfires, families together working to save their livelihoods, are not uncommon. At Christmas, water keeps us alive, is our joy and recreation, and hopefully can save us from fire – which is different to the workings of these symbols in traditional Europe. Our autumn rains bring relief, and return life to the land.

≈

Off to Yarra Grange! We were excited about our campsite for that night, because we were staying on the land of Michael Herman, Protector of Sea Eagles. When I rang Michael on the suggestion of a friend, he told me that there had been a breeding pair, Samson and Delilah, on his land for ten years now, and they had raised many eaglets under Michael's proud and watchful eye. Michael thought they were the only sea eagles who nested anywhere on the Yarra. We were sad that Michael was not going to be there that night – and so was he – he was very sorry to miss us, and had complained sweetly about our poor timing to me over the phone (I had dubbed him the Man with the Mellifluous Voice, it was such a rich, low rumble). He wanted to show us the eagle nests; huge messes of branches high up in the very tall manna gums, and the photos that he had taken over the years of these handsome birds. Yet he made sure we would be set up with a good camping spot. He would inform the farm manager of our coming, so as to direct us away from setting up too close to the eagles. Michael was famous in the district for holding magnificent concerts in the grounds of his stately home; he would fly out a famous jazz singer from the other side of the world, and raise money for the Children's Hospital. But now he was sick, with cancer.

Kate thought we must be close when we were greeted by a scarlet robin, little robin red-breast, the first we had seen on the pilgrimage. These tiny blood-bright beings come down from the mountain forests in autumn to spend winter in the valleys, singing along the Songline, wee-cheedalee-dalee. We were crossing paths, travelling in opposite directions. We paid our respects, admired his beautiful breast, and continued along the river.

Over the phone, the farm manager of Yarra Grange had said we'd know when we got to their property because there was a big manna gum down over the river; as we were on the other side he thought we could use it as a bridge. This was a relief, as it was cold and starting to get dark. But somehow the instructions given over the phone that seemed so clear suddenly seemed insufficient. I can get caught out like that – I seem to think the vaguest description will get me to my destination and that I will be fine if I just follow my nose. Sometimes I'm wrong, but faith is such a delicious feeling.

When we finally found a manna draped over the river, the waters were well on the way to submerging the entire tree, so we decided we'd have to swim anyway and leave it not a moment longer, as it was darkening quickly. To help us decide it started to shower, so we scrambled down the bank in the half light and started stripping off our clothes, stuffing them into drybags. We inched into the icy river, the rain wetting us from above. As the water rose around me, so did an unexpected joy, the wild joy of running water. The hard cold rain found my outspread arms and my thrown-back head, the river flowed fast around my body. I sensed that this was what a deeper faith could feel like, and that the world has it, and that I was being given it.

What was it about this river? Was I really going to have an epiphany *every* time I got wet?

THE TENTH NIGHT

As I step out onto the other side, into the shadows at the end of day, I feel clean and fresh and full of beginnings. I can't bear to put clothes on this new person, so I let her walk naked through the open paddocks in the downpour, white skin glowing in the gloom. Then I get cold and put on my coat.

As I walk with my fellow pilgrims to our home for the night, we are guided by a cooee that slips through the raindrops to find our ears. It is my cooee, my call calling me, from the throat of my sister – her voice is just like mine. We are led to a thin bridge of land, the river close on either side. We walk between the gates; shining tall mannas, like sentinels, holding both dark and light. And there beyond the trees is a dear little spit of land, and our friends, and a fire that contains all the colour in the world.

DELICATELY THROUGH THE WILDERNESS

I have a faded sepia photo of my grandmother and her twin – their names were Myrth and Joy – in long white dresses, standing upright among white trees. They were born in the goldmining town of Jericho, on the Jordan River, in the heart of the Victorian mountains not far from the headwaters we were making for. Jericho was named after a Biblical story that tells of the hard road to that place, for this Jericho was very isolated, accessed only by a rough track through mountain forests. When I was young, I heard the stories of dressing up for Sunday walks through the forest where they lived. As I lay in bed on my way to sleep, my grandma told how they searched the trunks of the gums for sweet manna to eat. Manna also means spiritual nourishment, or an unexpected benefit. The family of seven children had a pet lyrebird called Dick who would come for these walks and liked them to pick up logs and stones so he could forage for insects underneath. The family moved into Melbourne when she was six, but all the stories she told me were of the mountains.

When I was little and staying with grandma, I loved to

look at that photo. Then I would go, to loiter, to swing on the wire strands of the old fence that separated grandma's garden from the rest of the world. I was five or six years old, and had already chased through all the shadows of her large and luxuriant backyard, nestled at the base of Mount Dandenong. Beyond the fence was the forest; narrow paths between giant trees. I would drag my little sister to the fence and tell her about all the adventures that lay within the forest, at the ends of the paths, out of reach.

Out of reach, that is, until Trim. Trim was our puppy – in her company our world expanded, as we were allowed to go beyond the fence. Jane, my three-year-old sister, was harder to convince – but each weekend we ventured a few metres further in, before she ran back to the known realm of the house. I wouldn't dream of going on without her. Our bravery grew, as did our puppy, and soon we started to explore the forest paths. Just beyond the fence were the fragrant pine trees, where red and white toadstools nosed through the needles. Then the grove of Blackwood wattles, under which a carpet of rankly sweet purple violets grew. We picked all the violets from a space the shape of our bodies, so as not to crush them when we lay down in the leaves, and looked up at the sun from the violet's world. We rested their delicate flower-faces on our own, drinking in their dark scent. And we waited, quiet as cocoons, looking beneath leaves, seeking fairies.

We galloped along the paths pricked out among the sappy green *tradascantia*, below the ash trees that were colonising the damp silt. We splashed in the tiny creek, clear as bellbirds, tasting of eucalyptus, and shaded by tree ferns like round rooms. The water ran over stones and fine yellow sand and our toes, disappearing downstream into clumps of blackberry, which every year smothered more of the creek. On the other side of the creek was the bush; dry, bright and shining. The paths there seemed without end, yet we were told that they wound all the way to the top of the mountain. Back then, it was the paths that were the thing; the way they wove between light and shade, dipped into gullies or curled around rises. I had a hunger for the feeling of ever onwards, and the elusiveness of destination. Every year we ventured further down those paths. We never made it to the top of the mountain, but no-one ever said we couldn't walk all that way if we wanted to. Years later mum confided that every time we went exploring she waited anxiously for our return, but grandma had insisted we be allowed into the bush by ourselves. Grandma knew, I think, of the comfort and the intimacy to be found among trees.

≈

It rained on through the night. The earth was sodden and the grass a livid green. Clouds hung at treetop level, the air so moist it was almost drinkable. The rain intensified the incense scent of the manna gums, and the carolling of the magpies hung among the water droplets. I wandered off alone before my companions emerged from their bedraggled tents. I walked in the only direction available, back along the narrow land bridge of our peninsula – our almost island. At the narrowest point I looked upriver to where it curved around a bend. The straight gums were white pillars lining the far riverbank. They reflected in the river and lay shimmering there, like a marble aisle of a ghostly cathedral, a cathedral that would vanish if I dared enter.

After brekky we farewelled our support people, including my sister Jane, who had made dinner and cheerful conversation throughout last evening's rain. They were spending the day exploring the area; we were to meet them late that afternoon at Coranderrk Cemetery. As we left we looked out for the sea eagles, Samson and Delilah, and their chicks. We didn't see them, but three brown hawks circled as we left.

Further along the river, still on our host's property, we came to the most intact native grassland I had ever seen, fat clumps of tussock grasses and indigenous herbs. We wondered if the owner of the property knew what treasure was under his custodianship.

We were so sorry to have missed the intriguing Michael Herman on the walk that, a few weeks after we returned to the city, Kate and I arranged to visit him. It was strange to drive from Melbourne and be at his house in a little over an hour, when it had taken ten days to walk there. We drove down the long driveway and shyly approached the grand manor house. Our knocks on the huge white door drew no response, so we walked around the house, calling out tentative hellos. Michael emerged from a little room stuck onto the back of the house, his snug and crowded study. We had tea and talk, and he showed us videos he had made of the sea eagles, and the eagle genealogies he had kept, noting births and deaths, first flights and mishaps. They were his family, it seemed. Then he took us mushrooming. He drove through the paddocks, while Kate and I passed him the field mushrooms we picked through the car windows. Back in his study he wrote in our logbook. We had left a space for him to fill in:

> Congratulations! What a fascinating and educational trip and I want to hear more about it. Today was chat, chat, sea eagles and mushrooms. Come back soon, love and best wishes, Michael Herman.

We didn't see him again. He died a few weeks later.

As we walked the banks of Yarra Grange, we saw a tributary entering the Yarra from the other side – we consulted our maps and found it to be the Watts River. The Watts winds through Healesville – it was dammed to make Maroondah Reservoir in 1927. Healesville shelters right in the shadow of the Yarra Ranges – the mountains pressed up close behind, and so the heavy rains that fell there fed the Watts.

While we were standing beside the river looking at the map it started to spit, so we snuck into a hollow gum standing by the water. It was large enough for us all to shelter inside. When we heard a plop and a splash from the water, we poked our heads out of the tree to see what it was.

'Platypus?' Cinnamon suggested hopefully.

'More likely a carp. Platypus would be a lot more subtle.'

We were keen to see platypus on our journey, but it usually took patient hours of dawn or dusk river-watching. We'd need to be lucky.

When we sat down for lunch I suggested that we work on the logbook together, as we had planned on filling in a page every day of our journey, yet so far we hadn't gotten around to it. I volunteered to be scribe, and scrawled an outline of the river onto the page; an abstraction of the path the watercourse took that day.

'Sorry Maya, I don't want to do it like that,' Ilan said, looking down at the lunch things and slowly making a sandwich.

'Why not?' I asked, lowering my best writing pen.

'You've drawn the river the way that *you* see the river in your head. Now I have to fit in around that.'

'Yes, but it's just a place to start!'

'But you can't presume your picture works for me or the others – it's the way *you* see things.'

There was tension between us when we packed up our lunch things. I walked on, kicking thistles from the earth. I questioned Ilan:

'Isn't my love for you all, my good intentions, enough for you to trust me?'

'Maya, it's not about trust. It's just you don't know my story. It's mine. And it can't necessarily fit into yours. Don't presume that your experience encompasses mine.'

Ilan and I had reached this type of impasse before. Was it true I was trying to smooth over essential differences between us? Maybe my exuberance was overbearing, stopping me seeing into the experiences of others. Maybe, in truth, I didn't want to know the minds of others. Not on the pilgrimage, when so much was rushing in, making itself known to me. Walking along the river was so much closer to the shape of the life I felt I'd been born to live, it was true and precious, spilling me over into fluid contact with all the things of the world. I felt more like I belonged to all things, to my society, my times, these trees, this river, than ever before. Yet the dear person who walked beside me seemed to be saying he was not in my world. It wasn't an easy thing to hear. I wasn't able, as a pilgrim, to believe in separation.

Thoughtfully, I followed the others through tea-tree forest along the riverbank, the ground carpeted with moss. The way proved inaccessible, and we backtracked to a fallen tree, which might serve as a bridge. The tree was high above the water, and very narrow. Assisting each other, and taking it slowly, we made it across with no mishaps, although Cinnamon looked particularly nervous.

Relief at a successful crossing made me careless; I got a huge shock, smack on the bottom, from the high-powered electric fence that was our next obstacle. Stunned and sore I lay on my belly, my face resting in the dirt, hoping the earth would drain away the awful buzz running through my body. The others were not sufficiently sorry for me.

'Da na naaaa.

Da na naaaa.'

'What are you singing Kate?'

She just looked at me sideways, with a smirk, and kept singing.

'It's the theme from *Rocky*,' said Ilan, while Kate sang. 'You know, Sylvester, pounding the streets of the grimy city, training for the fight of his life.'

'Here we are, walking delicately through the wilderness …'

'Over barbed wire fences, through thickets of blackberries, or in the pouring rain, in our heavy duty boots, past the carcasses of sheep, and rubbish upended into the bush...'

'Ok, ok!' I gave up and joined Kate.

'Da na naaaa.

Da na naaaa.

Da na naaaa.

Da na naaaa.

Dunna-naa, na na naa

Da da, da-da, da-da,

Da daaaaa.'

Kate explained, 'I use it with kids on camp, a "let's get into the adventure" sort of thing when they're tired or the going is tough – or to get them out of the whingeing mode.'

'You saying I'm a whinger?'

'Any moment now, you'll be pleading for snakes.'

'Fine idea, let's break out the lollies.'

'Suffer, they're in my pack.' She took off, running across the paddock. I chased her, screeching like a lorikeet.

Ahead of us, across the paddocks, was the drone of the Maroondah Highway. The highway led into Healesville, then continued over the Great Dividing Range, following the path of the Blacks' Spur. The Blacks' Spur, a stunning stretch of road lined with towering Mountain Ash, was so named because it was the route the people of the Kulin Nation took on their return to the Yarra Valley. They had been exiled into the mountains, a place outside the boundaries of their traditional homelands. They returned to claim a small fragment of what was once all their country – a piece of land on the Yarra they called Coranderrk. It became a mission station. The Kulin ran a successful farm there, but were hounded and harassed by the settlers, who thought the land too valuable for blacks.

We came soon to Coranderrk Cemetery; all that is left of the mission. There was a note on the cemetery gate from our friends:

Dear Yarra Walkers, Jane and I have come and gone, giving tribute to all who Rest In Peace after a re-enactment of the Bread and Cheese Club. X Heidi.

'What's this Bread and Cheese Club business?'

The cemetery sat on a rise above the floodplain; the grass was dry and tall and singing in the wind, the eucalypts were waving above. The sun came out and lit the mountains purple and gold. There was one huge white marble headstone, erected, according to the carved inscriptions, by the Bread and Cheese Club. It was Barak's grave.

~

Ian Hunter and I caught up at CERES when I returned from the walk. I filled him in on our journey. In turn, he mentioned that when he needs to make an important decision, he travels east as far as he can go, into headwaters territory, or to Coranderrk to visit the graves of his ancestors. For many years, when his daughters were young, he took them camping up at Reefton, high up in the catchment. He said he liked to be among the mannas and the mountain grey gums.

I listened to his stories, and learned more of his aboriginal heritage. Traditional Language was spoken at home, albeit in a very fragmented and partial way. He expressed that they didn't think of it as Language, it was just how they spoke. They had a large extended family and a supportive network. He said some difficulties within the family came about when money and status became issues, when Aboriginality, and particularly local Aboriginality and therefore custodianship, became recognised, acknowledged and, in some contexts, valued.

According to Ian, all Wurundjeri, indeed all Woiwurrung people alive today, are descended from one Wurundjeri woman, Annie Borate, who was William Barak's sister. Annie, known traditionally as Borat, attended the Merri Creek mission school in the 1840s. She married a white man Adam Clark and had a son, Wandoon, later known as Robert Wandin. Wandoon married a Yorta Yorta woman called Jemima Burns. Wandoon and Jemima are the grandparents of Joy Murphy Wandin and of Ian's mother, Jesse. Jesse spent some of her teenage years living with Jemima in Healesville, close to Coranderrk mission.

As a child, Ian spent time around Healesville and the mission area, and often camped in Coranderrk Bushland, on Badger Creek. By that time the mission land had been sold off. Closed down in 1924, those remaining were shipped off, against their will, to Lake Tyers mission in far away Gippsland (except for a handful of old people, who absolutely refused to leave). Part of Coranderrk returned to Wurundjeri ownership when the Wurundjeri Tribal Council bought the land for a one and a half million dollars. An Act of Parliament eventually returned the cemetery to the traditional owners, in 1991.

In traditional Wurundjeri culture, there were two moieties (kinship groups); wedge-tailed eagle and crow, or Bunjil and Waa in Language. Ian says that this system broke down on the arrival of the Europeans; with the widespread deaths there were few people left to marry, and such loss and sadness that few Wurundjeri wanted to have children anyway.

> … all this mine, all along here Derrimut's once; no matter now, me soon tumble down … Why me have lubra, why me have piccaninny? You have all this place, no good have children, no good have lubra, me tumble down and die very soon now.

This exchange between Derrimut of the Woiwurrung and a Mr Hull on Collins St became part of a report to the 1858 Select Committee on the plight of the Port Phillip Aborigines.

≈

We left Coranderrk by road, to get to the house where we were to stay, a couple of kilometres from the river. We walked for a time on the country highway, overwhelmed at the speed of cars whizzing past us. Then onto a side road, the way to Blackwood, our destination for the night.

When we got to Blackwood we walked through the orchards and vegetable gardens and around the house to the back door. There we found two friends scurrying to and fro on business. They weren't quite ready for us, and made us wait on the dark porch. Finally we were beckoned inside. Their red faces beaming, our friends presented four basins of steaming water, so we could soak our feet. While the four of us sat in a row on chairs against the wall of the kitchen, another two friends cooked dinner on the enormous wood stove. Our friends fussed over us, while the steam of our scented footbaths filled the air. They were all short in stature, and all had short curly hair and broad smiles. Graeme George, our host, tall and lean and sporting a long white beard, stood with his hands in his pockets and admired all the activity transpiring in his kitchen. What a picture it all made; I felt as if we pilgrims had entered a fairytale.

Dinner was a coconut curry, and we ate around a large table in the main room. Shelves in the shadowy corners were filled with books and brown paper bags of saved seeds. Graeme had lived on that patch of land since 1980, and Blackwood has been the setting for countless Permaculture gatherings, meetings and teaching sessions. (Before then he'd been the live-in manager of Healesville Sanctuary, and before that, thirteen years in Papua New Guinea running a wildlife sanctuary.) I had been to Blackwood before, as part of a Permaculture course that Graeme taught.

After dinner, Graeme brought out a stone, and he shared with us a story.

I was cultivating garden beds at the edge of the block, when my digging turned up this stone. It'd obviously been worked – there were marks where flakes had been chipped off. It fitted comfortably in the palm of my hand, as if it were a scraper perhaps. It indicated to me Aboriginal use of this site. I stopped my working and sat down under a tree on a high point overlooking the garden. I held the stone in my hand and meditated on its significance. The word *kaergunyah* came, which meant nothing to me, but I remembered it. Some years later, talking to the Aboriginal man Robert Mate Mate at the museum of Melbourne, a fellow who knew some Language, he thought that word meant 'meeting place'.

THE ELEVENTH NIGHT

It is years before. I am standing under a big old blackwood tree in Graeme's garden, feet sinking into the leaf litter. He has brought us outside to explain photosynthesis, one of the key chemical reactions that underpin life on earth.

'Photosynthesis, powered by sunlight, takes carbon out of the carbon dioxide in the air and turns it into carbohydrates, which is what a tree is made of. And when it is burnt it returns to the air. Ash, left over from a fire, is the stuff that came out of the soil. When we eat food – any food – we are eating what the plants have made out of the air and the sun.'

That air has become us.

Before there were humans there were eons of natural processes, cycles, physical manifestations. And after us, these will continue. And we?

When we are burned, the carbon in our bodies joins with oxygen; we become carbon dioxide and ash. Those few handfuls of ash, the minerals and trace metals that make us, return to the soil. But most of us, most of the stuff of our bodies becomes a gas. Then we return, we return to the air.

HOW MUCH LISTENING
IS NEEDED?

'I didn't know I'd feel this way.'

'But Kate …'

'Yes I know, it's all arranged, I'm only saying that we've been by the river all this time and I don't want to leave her. I'll come, it's just … don't you understand?'

I'd woken early in a room faint with dawn. No sounds of birds or trees or flowing river, no people stirring. The dwelling, solid on the earth, seemed to hover, poised on the slope of the foothills, away from the valley floor, away from the slow fall of river water. I'd felt a gentle tug at my belly, a type of gravity. Yes Kate, I understood. I too felt a pull back to the river.

After breakfast we sat in the big chairs on Graeme's verandah and talked. That day we were walking away from the Yarra up to the top of Mount Toolebewong, where Cinnamon lived in the intentional community of Moora Moora, to have another rest day on top of the mountain.

Then Cinnamon broke the news to us. This might be the last day of her pilgrimage.

'Why Cinn?'

'Look, I don't know, but I'm tired, and the idea of staying at home … I'll have a think, and let you know tomorrow.'

Graeme led us the back way, through paddocks bordered by towering gums, through his neighbour's properties, to the road that wound up the mountain. With us were two of our crew, including my sister. They were to be picked up in their car after a hike with us, after the other crew dropped the trailer at Moora Moora. We hugged Graeme goodbye, and he gave us a bag of fresh herbs and veggies he'd picked from his Permaculture garden that morning. As a living embodiment of his philosophy, he'd given us so much. His philosophy included veggies, so he gave us those too. Yet Permaculture's roots penetrated far deeper than those of lettuces.

〜

Permaculture was initially developed by the Australians Bill Mollison and David Holmgren; the word is a contraction of both 'permanent agriculture' and 'permanent culture'. It's a system of agricultural design principles that replicate the self-sustaining qualities of ecosystems. The idea is that sustainable agriculture will support, enhance and co-create sustainable human communities at all scales – from individual farms up to cities.

Like the Buddha's Buddhism, applied Permaculture is the opposite of belief. It is all about the practice (in Buddhism, the practice is observing the changes in the natural system of the body-mind through meditation). Permaculture requires a practice of consistent, ongoing observation of nature. The watcher aims to understand how their place works, and how they can fit in with the greatest ease, grace and effectiveness. It is a practice with its own charms, one I've never tired of.

I remember beginning as a twenty year old, in my first share house, alternating between my housemate's Permaculture manual and the backyard. I lay for hours in the strategically going-to-seed vegetable garden, face up under the leaves, under the green glow, watching photosynthesis. Then nose in the dirt, smelling, watching the worms, with Bob Marley drifting out of the kitchen.

I have tried to continue my practice. Once, camping by myself for two weeks in Kakadu, I spent my best days lying on the earth, playing with the tail-curling skinks. They were different to Melbourne skinks, which skitter as soon as you look at them. These ones seemed as curious about me as I was with them. I tried to draw them; they kindly came and stood on my paper.

Then they curled their tails.

They curled their tails as if they were in the throwaway habit of describing the spiralling of galaxies. They curled their tails as if they'd taught the Russians ballet. They shook a curl from their hips as if they'd inspired the origins of bellydance. That curl shuddered through their tiny spine in a slow-motion circle, ending, with an impossible elegance, in one tiny flick of the tiniest tip of tail. They shimmied in the sunshine, iridescent.

They stopped their dance, and one looked me in the eye. Its eyeball was smaller that the ball in my ballpoint. Then – and I could hardly believe this – one licked my thumb.

Those skinks were the length of my little finger.

When something that small looks at you so fearlessly and so well, and can dance the pants off the higher mammals … frankly, I think I was the one who felt small.

What has all this got to do with Permaculture? It was, primarily, a humbling introduction to the slow, careful work of attempting to create permanent, sustainable culture in this or indeed any land. It was a chance to ask myself – what is it that I don't know, for lack of looking? How much care, and time, and patience, how much listening is needed, for me to really belong to a world as beautiful as this?

The watching is just the start of something.

—

We walked the steep mountain road lined with tall straight gums. The going was straightforward with no fences, bulls or horses to watch out for. Instead just the occasional car, and unyielding asphalt beneath our feet. And the rain came steadily down. As we climbed the vegetation changed with both altitude and slope – west-facing slopes drier and scraggly.

By the time our two friends were to leave us, my hat was a sodden mess, so my sister gave me hers – a broad-brimmed black felt number that I had long coveted. The rain increased as we gained altitude. A thickening mist drifted through the massive mountain ash, and the cold deepened. My body began to cramp; Kate was wan and pale. She and I were holding on to each other, laughing with an hysterical edge, our spirits high but our bodies protesting. Beside us, Cinnamon was snug and dry in her Oringi's – New Zealand farmer-grade wet-weather gear. Immaculate, organised, always prepared, I wished for the hundredth time that I were a little more like her.

Finally we reached the mountain plateau. As we walked the forest path, Cinn's house in view, a female lyrebird ran across the track in front of us, looking like a mad old tramp with damp coats skew-whiff.

At Cinnamon's cottage one of her neighbours had snuck in and built a roaring fire. We were expected. We shed our masses of sodden clothing, and draped them over Cinnamon's furniture – in moments transforming her spotless little lounge into a washhouse. We fell into the comfy chairs around the fire. It took ages to thaw out.

'How does it feel to be home Cinn?' asked Ilan.

Her smile was broad, warm, exhausted.

The rain finally cleared, revealing a glittering afternoon. Combing my hair, I followed Ilan and Cinnamon to help haul the trailer closer to the house. We came to the lookout. I stopped to admire the dripping and golden view out west. I gazed from the top of Mount Toolebewong back over all the land that we had walked, all the way to the distant sea. The skyscrapers of Melbourne's centre were like a few short blades of grass seen over sand. I found myself speaking aloud to what I saw, addressing all that was spread out below me.

As I spoke, my voice rose and fell like the hills that ringed the valley. My sound trekked down the path we had walked, my words floated down to the sea. I chanted the rhythm of the steps to come, to the land unseen behind me, and I heard my own song come down from the source. The air was thickening. A mystery unravelled in the name of this place, a Wurundjeri word, *Toolebewong*. We Too Belong. We Too Belong.

As I spoke I watched the rain flow off the mountain, gathering into tributaries, I saw all the land as one, all flowing to the river.

And as I spoke I combed my long hair. I untangled knots; I freed the strands until finally my hair was flowing. The movement felt gentle, unhindered. My hair was flowing, pouring down my body. I too was the river.

Turbulent, as if banks had broken and waters were streaming to the sea, I ran back to the house, a flood, precarious, dangerous. But before I had even reached the door, the vision faded. There were my friends, and the trailer. I wasn't needed for that task, after all. So I went to my book, and I wrote down what I remembered of the scene on the mountain, before it flowed completely away.

Cinnamon told us that our dinner that night was to be a community feast at the home of her neighbour, Susannah, who is a chef. I had tasted her delicious cooking before, so I was keen and hungry as we crossed the dark clearing to her house, perched on the edge of the mountaintop, with views down to the valley in the southeast. When we entered her cosy kitchen the room was full of Moora Moora folk. It seems they had been waiting for us, for they gathered in a ring around us.

A tall man with white hair came forward out of the ring; Peter Cock, an eco-psychology academic who was one of the founders of Moora Moora in the 1970s. He had in his hands a bowl of water. He looked into our expectant faces, his laughing eyes played over us. Then one by one he sprinkled us with the water, and welcomed us formally to the mountain.

Afterwards, we moved around the room, meeting

Cinnamon's friendly community, and helping ourselves to dinner. They said we brought the rains; the hard edge of drought, blunted.

I had first come to Moora Moora four years previously for a conference, a gathering called the Sense of Place Colloquium, which was organised by Peter Cock and Monash University. Peter and I had formed a friendship then, and so when I had piled my plate with Susannah's marvellous food, I went and sat on the couch next to him.

'Pete, can I stay in your spare room tonight? Cinn's is very crowded and I wouldn't mind a bit of space.'

'Sure you can.'

Moora Moora is arranged in six clusters with five houses in each, making for a well-designed blend of private spaces and communal contact. Spread over the long ridge of the mountaintop, among the regrowth cool temperate forest, with paddocks set aside for grazing animals, it was an idyllic vision made real. Peter and his wife, Sandra, lived in the house next door to Cinnamon, in Nyora cluster.

'Now,' continued Peter, 'tell me how your pilgrimage is going?'

I was quiet for a moment, trying to collect my thoughts, a bit daunted at having to explain anything to this fiercely intelligent professor.

'Well,' I started, 'it intrigues me that we sometimes say "a journey to the source" to mean something entirely internal – a soul journey, one where we might not leave the house. It's like we've forgotten to do things in the real world. But right now, we are *actually* travelling to an *actual* source, and I feel something coming to life in a different way. It's almost like I am doing this *with* the river, and that somehow it is about both of us. As if when we take the world seriously, the world comes along for the journey too. But its more than that, because of course the river is forever going on its own journey, and we are witness to that, and somehow, just by being there, we get to share in a bit of what the river knows. It sounds a bit batty I know, but …'

'Somatic learning,' he interrupted.

'What?'

'Somatic learning. The body has its own ways of learning, and walking is one of them. The primary thing you are doing every day is walking. Your head isn't going to be able to understand entirely what is happening. In fact, your mind will get in the way of your learning, if you're not careful.'

I paused. Slowly I said, 'I think I know what you mean'.

'Don't think,' he commanded. 'Just feel this experience. Remember that the mind is the secondary source of information – your body is the primary source. So pay attention. We're hooked on the idea of the body as a servant of the mind – just like we think the earth's body is the servant of the human. So when you feel your body's truth, you can feel that yes, the river is there, with you. It cannot not be. Your body is about 70 per cent water, the water you drink is the water of the river.'

What a great way to think about my body. For it was true, I was mostly river. A bit of river with legs, and a flapping tongue, and tricky fingers, and through the pilgrimage I was getting to know my entirely watery self (the Yarra) with the help of all these fancy appendages.

We sat for a while in silence, listening in to other

conversations. Pete tilted towards me, 'You remember Satish Kumar, who gave the introduction to our Sense of Place Colloquium when you first came up here? Remember his story of his peace pilgrimage in the 1960s – from his backwater village in Rajasthan in India all the way to Moscow, Paris, London and Washington – all without money, walking everywhere?'

'Except over the water – yes. Or maybe even there. Amazing man. He was a monk as a teenager?'

'Yes, Jain, very strict. Ran away to join them when he was nine. Not your average kid. Anyway, he's written a book about pilgrimage. I'll lend it to you tonight.'

THE TWELFTH NIGHT

Before sleep, I flip through Kumar's book, *No Destination*. I find this:

> In wandering I felt a sense of union with the whole sky, the infinite earth and sky. I felt myself a part of the cosmic existence. It was as if by walking I was making love to the earth itself. Wandering was my true path, my true self, my true being. It released my soul force, it brought me in relation to everything else. I stood like I stand in front of a mirror. People, nature, everything became like a mirror and I could see myself in them.

Sitting with Peter, talking to him about the words that I found myself speaking while I combed my hair on the mountainside, with a shock I remember.

'Yarra' means both 'flowing' and 'hair' in the Woiwurung language.

A VERY NARROW BRIDGE

We shall not cease in our explorations
And at the end of our exploring
Will be to arrive where we started
And to know the place for the first time

Like a story, like a fiction, I was woken by a voice from the world of dreams. The words of T.S. Eliot resounded through me, like something real.

The weather had closed in around the mountain. The valley vanished, cloud wrapped the forest plateau. I ate breakfast with Peter, and wanted to stay and chat in comfort, to be on the outside of the adventure for a moment, to savour the joy of looking back in. But there was work to do.

Kate and Cinnamon were already bent over the topographical maps when I entered Cinn's lounge. They were checking the route we would take around the water catchment, further upstream. Ilan and I went to sort out food, bringing in all the boxes from the trailer and spreading their contents throughout the kitchen.

There were many decisions to be made as we worked; they came fast and easy, as if there were no choices, just one clear way. Making the commitment to the journey together had meant that the 'group' became more important than the individual, and the journey itself more important again. Being a pilgrim was my identity; it was an archetype fed by a deep well of experience. I was doing something that thousands before me had done, and all of them had known this; that their way was made by the generosity and support of others. I was captivated by my companions, their profound listening and attentiveness to each other and the world. When they spoke, I heard my stories.

Sometimes I wondered if by following the pathway along the river I could open new neural pathways in my brain – pathways laid down by past human experience, but until now untraversed in my own body. The experience of a long walk beside a flowing river, where the tributaries joined and the waters intermingled, was a primary example of submission of the self, a reminder of an old and sacred way.

Yet this was my experience, my way of thinking and feeling. I couldn't presume it was shared.

Cinnamon called us outside, into the sloping paddock in the sun, where a chestnut horse watched us curiously. Cinnamon wanted to tell us her decision.

'I must follow my own stream. I've decided to leave the pilgrimage. I've found the walk far more challenging than I'd expected – both physically and emotionally. I feel not as engaged as the rest of you, and I'm not living from my centre. Instead, coming here, I realise this is where I was always meant to walk to. My little house, this place, they're calling for me to complete my journey here, at Moora Moora. I've walked all the way home – this is where I need to stay.'

We four stood in the grass, in a circle, holding hands. From Cinn's big brown eyes flowed a river of tears. We joined her. The horse came and poked her head into our circle, and tried to lick the salt from our faces.

≈

I first got to know Cinnamon five years previously through some workshops she was running. She had just come back from ten days' training with Joanna Macy, an activist and philosopher of the Deep Ecology movement. Joanna Macy is known throughout the world for her transformative workshops in despair and empowerment. Deep ecology explores the fundamental interconnection between everything. Not as an idea, but literally, observing and attending to the endless cycling of the elements through our bodies; the water that becomes our blood, the earth that is our food, the air that is our breath, and the fiery sun that warms our planet and grows our food. Science teaches that all the stuff of the universe was created at the beginning of time with the big bang, the elements forming in the furnace of stars. Those very same elements cycle endlessly through our bodies now. Physically, we are all as old as the stars.

Deep Ecology puts forward that if we experience our intrinsic connection, we come to know the whole earth as ourselves. We realise that if we damage the earth, we damage ourselves. This knowing, Deep Ecology says, is essential for us to truly feel and understand the environmental crisis and open us up to the depth of our loss – for at our deepest, we cannot forget this interconnection – our bodies cannot hide this truth. When we acknowledge despair and no longer try to hold back our emotions, this release brings with it a renewal of energy and the lifting of the numbing effects of depression. The Deep Ecology group workshops are designed to help us know that most everyone feels as we do, but that it is rare that we have permission to express our true emotions. There is a common fear that the loss and damage of this time is simply too painful, that we will not have the strength to carry on if we allow ourselves to feel all of this. Instead the opposite can happen; the truth sets us free to act with the knowledge that in saving the forest, the ocean, the wild rivers, we save ourselves.

John Seed, the remarkable Deep Ecology teacher who taught workshops at Moora Moora, makes the point that, because the earth is one system, unless you can save the whole thing, you can't save any of the pieces. So any attempt to save a little piece here and a little piece there can only be seen as a kind of a prayer, a prayer for the awakening of people.

In the Deep Ecology workshops, we take the hand of a partner. We are guided to imagine that the hand we hold was once clawed and furred, was once finned; we feel the remarkable evolutionary journey through the body of our partner. For me, there came a shock I'm still recovering from; I knew, without doubt, that the world and everything in it has shaped us to see it. The bird is the part of us that is bird-shaped, the tree is the part of us that is tree-shaped. We have evolved out of this system to be in a body that can say back to the world, 'I see you'.

Cinnamon was inspired by her Deep Ecology training to spread these powerful techniques of healing and action. I benefited from her commitment when I went along to her workshops, and she listened to my sorrow and shared my pain. Together we were made stronger and could continue our work for the earth. But that was years ago, and now Cinnamon was burdened with a complex job, responsible for the environmental education of the thousands of children who visited CERES with their school every year. It was a long time since she had replenished herself, and in her position, she could never escape the brutal seriousness of this time that we live within. Hope can be hard to sustain amidst the erosion of the world we love.

There is a very beautiful song, a Jewish song that I had been singing in Hebrew for years for the comfort of the tune, but with no notion of what the words meant. Ilan translated for me:

The whole world is
A very narrow bridge
But the main thing to recall
Is to have no fear at all

Two days before, as we were leaving Michael Herman's land, we came to a fallen manna gum that made an elegant bridge, narrow and high above the fast cold water. We needed to cross over to the other side of the river. Ilan went first, lightly stepping, graceful and balanced, and was over in moments. Kate and I shimmied across with rather more care. For Cinnamon it represented a major challenge. We supported her as best we could, but I could see she was shaken. She shared later that the difficulty lay for her in fear where before there was none – she had always been physically confident, and couldn't understand the sudden onset of crippling apprehension. She wanted to know – how is it that sometimes we have faith, and at other times it deserts us?

≈

At Moora Moora, there are no dogs or cats allowed. This preserves the domain of the native animals, and the natives learn to work around the humans who share their mountaintop. It is the only place I have ever seen tame lyrebirds. Normally this shy wet-forest bird is threatened by the predations of our pets.

After emptying one too many food boxes, despairing at our over catering, the lack of synergy between the amount we need and the amount we had, my eye was attracted to a movement outside. I watched a lyrebird from the window – I caught her googly eye, and she gave me her glance in return, her skeletal claw hung in the air. After a moment, she went back to her task of digging over Cinnamon's garden beds. Her whole body was engaged in digging, her oversized claws tore through the soil with great energy. All the while her elegant head remained utterly motionless, intent on spotting food. She saw a worm and then pounced – a dart of the head that immediately returned to stillness. I couldn't understand how she could do that – her head was absolutely still while her body, one worm richer, was all activity. How could it be like this?

While I was watching, there was a quick splat of mottled

white behind her; she had deposited a little fertiliser on the garden, in return for eating up its worms. The bird gave her wastes to the soil, the soil made worms; and as I watched, another worm was transformed into bird. Where does Lyrebird begin and end? Her wet black eyes, as dark and deep as soil, motionless as mountains, made of worms.

Her mate has other work as well. Lyrebirds are famous mimics, and they make long compilation songs that include the tunes of all the birds of the forest. If you listen carefully, you can find out who is resident in the forest from listening to one lyrebird, as they voice whipbird, cockatoo, yellow robin, blue wren and so many more. But Lyrebird doesn't discriminate. He bears witness to the whole story. He listens to chainsaws felling the forest, the yowls of feral cats, the aeroplanes on their flight path, and wraps them all in his beautiful voice to create the song of this land. A united flow of music, like a waterfall, carrying all, tumbling through the valley.

Lyrebirds live their lives well in one place, return all to the earth, and tell the whole truthful story in beauty. What a wonderful role model.

In the late afternoon, after we had completed our logistical tasks, Kate suddenly announced that she was setting off, then and there, to walk back down the mountain.

'I need to be back in the valley, close to the river, so I will ring Graeme and see if I can stay at his place tonight,' she explained.

'Well, take care, and we'll meet you tomorrow morning.'

Meanwhile, I was weary of sorting and people, and missed the daily rhythm of walking. I found my beanie and scarf among the explosion of my backpack, and opened the door onto the chilliness outside. I knew where I wanted to go.

I took the way through the forest on the eastern slope. The sun doesn't reach there late in the day, but slants through the topmost branches of the trees. The wattles and blanket-leaf bushes made a tight path, and the soil was spongy below me. I carried my Ganassi with me, a handmade wooden recorder styled on a Venetian instrument of the sixteenth century. About a mile away was the Lodge, the community's common house, the original 1930's residence on the property. There was a room I knew of at the Lodge – a big white dining hall, shiny and resonant, that my Ganassi loved to be played in.

The room faced west, with large windows looking down over the valley, and as I opened the door of the silent space, the setting sun shone onto me. I untied the ribbons that fastened the box of my instrument. I brought it out of its case, and let my fingers flutter over the blonde wood, finding the familiar comfort of the notes. And then I played to the silence until the room was filled with the night.

I walked back along the road in the dark to Cinnamon's house for dinner – Ilan was cooking. It was a special Jewish holy day, Pesach, or Passover, and Ilan had invited us to join in a simple rendering of the traditional celebration. We were honoured to be asked, and Cinn and I gathered around the table in anticipation. Ilan shared the ancient story. Pesach is the day in the Jewish calendar to remember the Exodus of the Israelites from Egypt. It is customary, before the evening meal, to say this: 'In each and every generation we shall remember this day as if it were we who walked out of Egypt'. As if this generation had been born into slavery and then fled to a new land, it calls the devotees to live in gratitude to freedom, and use it well.

For the occasion, Ilan created a new prayer; he asked us 'to remember this day as if it were us dispossessing the tribal Wurundjeri from their homeland'. In doing so, he called upon us to acknowledge this wrong with the conviction of having been a part of it, and work to repair and heal this hurt through our actions. His culture gave him practices that he used to explore justice and the meaning of freedom in this time and place. He had given us a gift, a weighty gift.

THE THIRTEENTH NIGHT

Late, alone, I walk to the edge of the clearing. The moon, one day from full, casts an icy spill over the mountain. From where I stand sheltered by the trees I look down over the Yarra Valley, all the way to Melbourne, and see thousands of lights, each one its own mysterious centre. And I wonder if I can return there with the river's teachings flowing through me.

Above the valley spreads the river of stars, the Milky Way. Some traditional cultures who have known the silence of the pre-industrial world for millennia tell of the songs that the stars sing. That is not something I know. I haven't known a world quiet enough to hear the voices of the stars. Maybe that silence needs to start with me, an inner quiet, a hushed mind. Yet silence within often seems as far away as galaxies.

I have journeyed just over halfway along the path. The source remains a mystery. This mystery is an idea, an aspiration, something to immerse in without holding on, like a river of stars, like a river of water. I can't hold water. But when I let go, I can float.

THE WORKINGS
OF KINDNESS

The almost full moon was setting over the city as Ilan, the lone Long Yarra Walker, set out. So he told me later; I didn't see the moon. I was still in bed.

The night before I'd felt ill and tired, overwhelmed at the thought of the long walk of the next day, and the changes to our little group. Kate had rung, late in the night, explaining how on her journey down the mountain alone she had sprained her ankle, and had walked on her injured foot the rest of the way to Graeme's house. She was doing ok, she said, but thought she should not walk the next day, to give her ankle a chance to heal.

'She can't recover from a sprained ankle in a day,' I said, when Cinnamon got off the phone to her.

'She reckons she can, she thinks it's not a bad one,' Cinn replied.

'She's too tough, that one!' I exclaimed, thinking of her limping kilometres to Graeme's. In her place I would have flagged down the first car and pleaded for a lift to the nearest doctor.

I hope she's right that it's not a bad sprain, I thought. We were going to be without Cinnamon for most of the rest of the journey – to lose Kate as well seemed too cruel. Perhaps I should be a little more careful. I wasn't too healthy myself, and the journey of the fourteenth day was far longer than usual; first down the mountain to Coranderrk Bushland, then along Brushy Creek to where it joined the Yarra, then a full day's walk to Woori Yallock – over 30 kilometres. I decided to drive with Cinnamon to the base of the mountain, where we would meet Ilan and Kate. I didn't like the thought of getting into a car, but I felt that I owed it to the pilgrimage to take care of myself, in order that I reach the end. Pilgrims, dropping like flies.

We met at 8.00 am that morning at Coranderrk Bushland Reserve at the invitation of Graeme. The bushland was officially part of Healesville Sanctuary but it was off-limits to the general public. Graeme, however, having once managed the sanctuary, gained permission for us to accompany him.

Previously, the bushland had been part of the original Coranderrk mission – their hunting territory, which extended up to what is now Graeme's place and beyond. It had never been cleared, and was one of the few large remnants of dry sclerophyl forest in the Yarra Valley. Almost all of that type of bush had been cleared for agriculture, as it grew on the fertile alluvial plains of the valley. We'd have encountered this forest type through much of the Yarra Valley if we'd walked 200 years earlier. Coranderrk Bushland was our first experience of it. As Graeme unlocked the gates I considered the strange reversal of these times – the natural environment, which had been here for hundreds of thousands of years, was now a fenced fragment, which only a few privileged souls could see.

And it was a privilege – it was beautiful. In the early morning light the sun streamed through the mix of eucalypts to the forest floor dense with tussocky plants; lomandras, gahnias and grasses tall and dark and feathery. The fragment was large enough to feel expansive – we could see long distances through the naturally open bushland. We ambled along; Kate had joined us to see this special place, and her heavily bandaged foot meant a gentle meander through to the other side, where Graeme opened another set of gates for us. He had brought us through to Barak Lane, the entry to Coranderrk, and the road we four had walked up a few days before. This time only two of us would be continuing on.

There was silliness and sweetness between us as we said our goodbyes. We knew we would be seeing them again – Cinn had decided to do some day walks with us, and be an extra support crew member – but it wasn't going to be the same. We asked Graeme to take photos of the four of us – or five of us, as we posed with Kate's ankle a feature in each shot – the latest character in our drama. Kate was feeling very sad to be missing part of the journey along the river; it was ironic, as she was the one who was so keen to get back to our water pathway. She made us promise that we would tell her all about it when we next saw her. We had made arrangements for her to get a lift with the trailer down to Woori Yallock, and meet us that night at our host's place, Yarra Bridge.

Ilan and I headed west down Barak Lane, back towards the cemetery, holding hands companionably. The sun was at our back; our long shadows lay before us. Walking with our cheerful shadows, Ilan's wearing a feather in his hat, mine with shadow-lengthened plaits, it seemed like there were still four of us, after all.

We lingered at the cemetery. We stood again by Barak's grave and the plaques of commemoration. It was only two days since last we were there, but it seemed much longer, and we had more stories and sense of this country. My understanding of what had been lost, but what is still, mysteriously, being given, had grown in that short time.

Eventually Ilan and I crossed the fence into the paddocks and sauntered down to Badger Creek. It was a dear little waterway, with many fallen manna gums making a weave of tree bridges. We crossed them back and forth all the way down to the Yarra. We felt like kids out on an adventure – playing all the way. The wattle-coloured weather continued as we turned south along the river and walked the open grazing country. Mount Toolebewong followed us on our left as we walked; indeed, its long north–south ridge defined the course of the river. And coming up in front of us to our right was the other definer, the Warramate Hills. The Yarra lay between them.

I had watched the Warramate Hills over the days we had wound through the Yarra Valley. Beside the much larger Mount Dandenong, they were the only forested peaks within the bowl of mountains that contained the valley, and I'd wondered where the Yarra lay in relation to them. Of course, our maps could have told me, but they were a poor type of knowing compared to feeling the land roll out beneath my feet.

We were sitting on the riverbank watching the brown Yarra

and eating our lunch, when we heard the sound of a tractor approaching. Ilan jumped up;

'Old fellow, driving this way.'

'I hope he got our permission letter!' I scrabbled around, collecting up our things. It was warm, so shirts, shoes and socks were spread out over his riverbank. We stood together and waved at the machine approaching. The man climbed down from the seat and limped over to us. Ilan reached out a hand.

'Hello, we're the Long Yarra Walkers.'

'Weren't there supposed to be four of you?' He took off his hat and scratched at his thin white hair. Our two short shadows lay underneath us, silent watchers.

'Yes, that's right,' said Ilan. 'There's a bit of a story there – injuries and the like. We were wondering how would you feel about telling us a bit about what it's like living and working here? You've been here a while?'

'Sure have, round about thirty years now …'

Ilan took out his little recording device and collected the farmer's stories, as he had done at a few places on the journey. I stood back and watched them, the old man and the young one, both all in blue, standing by the river in the sun. Ilan the dancer, the mover, was (quite unconsciously I think) mimicking the stance of the farmer – bent and intent. Then I saw my friend too grow old, somewhere by this river, and I hoped that one day, a young man would come and listen so attentively to him. He would have a good story to pass down.

Further along, a woman spotted us from her house on a rise, and came down to accost the trespassers. We explained; she remembered the letter and was suddenly the gracious host. She walked with us to the pipeline bridge, a secret bridge over her property, the place where the water from Maroondah Reservoir was piped in to Melbourne. She used to walk this bridge to get to school in Woori Yallock. She told us that a soldier was stationed there for the whole of the First World War, to safeguard Melbourne's water supply. There was a tiny little hut built for him by the water, and he lived there, alone, for four years. The only activity he saw was the seasonal flow of the river, then undammed; a spring flooding, a summer trickling river.

Ten or so kilometres further on we stopped on the riverbank, and looked into the water with a delight long awaited.

'The bottom! We can see the bottom.'

The turbidity had settled, and for the first time on our journey, we could see all the way through the river. In the clarity of the water, we could see the river pebbles, smooth, old, precious things, rattled around to roundness.

Behind us the lowering sun over the fields, in front of us the clear water and the far bank, thickly wooded, sunset-glowing manna gums leaning out from the green. We sat and rested there. I lay curled around Ilan – he rested his arm gently on me.

'Ilan, I'm a bit scared. I feel a migraine coming and my medication is in the other pack.' Which was ironic – I'd only left mine behind because I was carrying Kate's pack with the first aid kit – which had nothing I could use to stave off my symptoms. The migraine had started to churn my belly and scramble my brain – my muscles were gradually tightening, drawing sharp lines into my neck and jaw. Beyond my own discomfort, sometimes my strong reactions to the symptoms were difficult and uncomfortable for others and I hated the guilt this brought.

'Maya, you don't need to worry. I know you when you've got a migraine and I'm not afraid of it. It's ok for you to just "be" with it. I'm here if you need me.'

It was such a gift he gave me with those words. I let what he said sink in, and felt a clear release into pure, unburdened pain.

'Ilan.'

'Yes?'

'I don't think I've ever felt so safe.' Held in the arms of two beautiful friends, this man and this valley. Walking into the oncoming evening, the spread land soft and gold and welcoming, I felt a fierce freedom in my chest, as my heart expanded to hold new happiness.

—

It was just a year before the pilgrimage when Ilan and I first met. At that very first meeting we began planning all sorts of creative projects. He rang me up the next day. He sounded confused.

'I don't even know you, why are we going to do all these things together?'

'Because we want to!' I replied. 'We're into the same things – we want to make things happen. Don't we?'

'Yes, I suppose. I mean, yes! But let's spend some time getting to know each other first.'

That certainly happened – I needed a housemate, he

needed a house, so he moved in to Brunswick. I was excited to have my new friend close by, to share the many things we both loved – plants and maps and cities and dance and music and performance and growing food and how all these things could come together to shape a culture of belonging. I presented him with armloads of my books to read; he asked me endless questions. We went down to Merri Creek together, and he showed me ways of moving, ever more subtly, through the land, following instincts I never thought to notice. And he showed me ways of being, for he brought presence and integrity to his listening, his speaking, and his actions (except, that is, to the housework!).

But the next day he'd be on guard. Shutters rolled down over his large blue eyes. On a good day, I asked him about it.

'You're only bothered by it because you know how open I can be. You're used to the intimacy, but I can't be like that all the time. Sometimes I need to take my own space.'

I was to learn about that. At home, about a month after the pilgrimage, he told me he was moving out. I was devastated. He explained why he couldn't live with me:

'I'm an Aquarian – a water bearer. In my home environment I need to be able to rest and have my pots open and dry. You are flowing like water, and I feel that you want to fill my pots all the time, so I need to pull the covers over my pots to keep them dry. Which is tiring for me. It's not the space for rest I want in my home environment.'

It took a couple of years, but we sorted it. We've both softened, and I've quietened, partly due to the long introverted journey of writing this book, of deepening into my own questions, fears and fascinations instead of firing off ideas and opinions to anyone who, like Ilan, was kind enough to listen. We're closer friends now, maybe because I've emptied myself enough to be able to better hear others. I've learned something of how to meet Ilan's authenticity, to rise to the ambitions he has for friendship. And I know something, now, of the importance of space.

Up the drive to Yarra Bridge the moon was behind us. Ahead stretched our companions; our long moon shadows. Still we were four. Beyond our shadows we could see a figure coming towards us. It was Kate, just then scouting for us.

She led us to a clearing on the rise – by moonlight we could see the river lay both to the east and to the west, the old house located perfectly to appreciate both views. Kate had set up our tents in the clearing near the back door. When we told her off she blustered, 'Well, what was I going to do all day?'

(In fact, she had been quite busy – we later found out that she had hobbled around the township of Woori Yallock just over the other side of the river, passing by the office of the local radio station on the main street. She entered, introducing herself as one of the Long Yarra Walkers, and they sat her down and interviewed her then and there, live to air.)

'Come meet Sarah and Andy, they're fantastic,' she said proprietorially.

When we entered the house we were, for a moment, overwhelmed with the light and colour and people after our time in the moonlight. Sarah and Andy, a few years older than us, had kind and open faces, and immediately felt like friends.

On the table in the old kitchen were set pots of curry and rice, and we slipped into our seats. I felt a little overcome by the kindness of these strangers – while realising that the workings of kindness means there are no strangers.

THE FOURTEENTH NIGHT

I take my migraine drugs; I return to the world. We talk with our hosts late into the night around the lamp in the lounge. They share a story of some friends, an elderly couple, who also called themselves pilgrims. The couple lived with faith as their guide, without money, yet giving generously of themselves. Sarah and Andy were struck by their clarity and calm, and are fascinated by what it means to cleave to a pilgrim path.

So am I.

Later, at home, I hear the story of a woman in the United States who, in the 1950s, set off to walk across the country for peace, with only the clothes she stood up in, a fold-up toothbrush and a comb. She changed her name to Peace Pilgrim. She took no money, and never asked for food or shelter – only accepting these if they were offered. She kept walking. She walked for 28 years and covered around 40,000 kilometres. She said she never suffered from hunger or heat or cold; her faith meant she did not suffer. Countless times she was arrested for vagrancy, the crime of having no home in which to live. Always, not knowing what to do with this smiling silver-haired woman, they let her go. And everywhere she went, she spread her message of peace.

The idea of her shakes me, a blaze in the mind. Shall I leave my home and walk for all my days, over the land, into the land, into the greatest of possibilities? Into endlessness and transformation, living change, and being peace.

And if courage fails me, how do I live in my one small house, with this challenge flung out, ringing the air, pealing truth?

The Upper Yarra

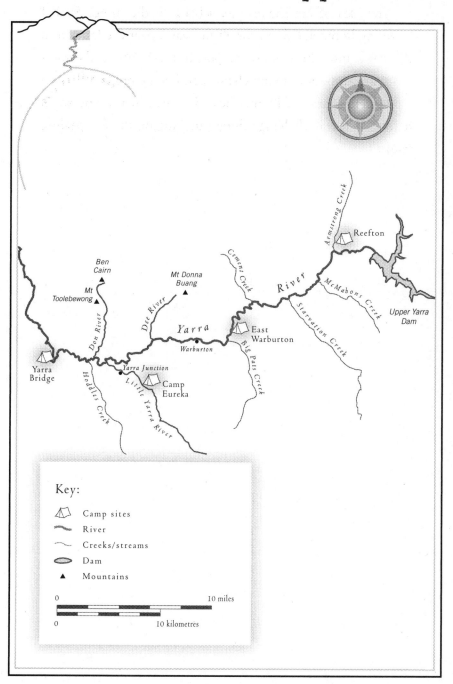

Key:

- 🏕 Camp sites
- 〰 River
- ⋯ Creeks/streams
- ⬭ Dam
- ▲ Mountains

0 ——————————————— 10 miles

0 ——————————————— 10 kilometres

GOOD FRIDAY

I was hibernating in my feather cocoon when the beeping began. It was my alarm, set early, so I could join Ilan in his Bodyweather dance practice.

He appeared at my tent door. 'You coming?' As we walked through mist away from the clearing and into the bush, he gave me instructions for the practice. First we do a warm-up, from head to toe, and then we stand quiet for ten minutes, to feel into the atmosphere of the place. Then, for another ten, we will dance whatever comes to us from the place. And that's it.

We came to a suitable spot on a wide path among the burgan. That tea-tree species grows thin, peeling and spindly, branching out into a small-leafed canopy above. The trees held the air, and the mossy path muffled our feet. Following Ilan's example, I sprang into a vigorous full-body jiggle. After waking each muscle in turn, we came to a halt, panting slightly. I closed my eyes. There was a faint smell of the tea-tree, a stronger smell of moisture and mist. I felt the earth under my feet and the slope of the land as it bent down to the river far below, and the sound rising up from the water where it flowed over stones. The moss beneath me was holding moisture, and holding seeds.

As I held still, I sensed in the burgan scrub a waiting – a stillness before the riot of a richer ecology. That quiet place would be changed when the eucalypts and other species now nursed in the moss came to prominence, and the burgan faded away, long bones sinking into the soil, the soil that they had made from their own bodies. And so I danced this, the stillness of the trees, the seeding and the sprouting, the arching out over the river below to cleanse and cool the nourishing waters, and then, at the end, the returning to the soil. As our time ended, I lay my body out on the moss. The moss bed was softer and sweeter than my sleeping mat. And damper.

Ilan and I walked back up to the house. The mist was clearing – blue was visible beyond the thin layer of low cloud, and it was going to be another lovely day. When we returned for breakfast, the sunshine was pouring in through the open door to the farmhouse kitchen, and a black cat, green eyes narrowed to vertical slits by sunlight, basked on the threshold. (Last night Andy and Sarah told us the story of that cat: 'she vanished one day and the children were distraught. After she'd been gone a few weeks the kids said, "we're going to find the cat". And they found a black cat in the bush and brought her home. She wasn't the cat we'd lost. But the children were happy, not minding that she wasn't the same'.)

The smell of hot cross buns reached out through the doorway – it was Good Friday, a holiday for our hosts. Their four children were away with friends, and Sarah and Andy were using this time to start packing up their house. They were leaving in a week. After renting for ten years, their lease was finally up.

'Hey Maya,' said Andy, 'I've got a song I'd like to play you'. 'Sure,' I said, curious. I followed him into the lounge room, where he crouched over the stereo.

> When I die, put me in a barrow
> Take me down to the banks of the Yarra
> Dig a hole both deep and narrow
> Bury me by my brown Yarra

'Do you know it?' he asked me.

It was my special song, written by Melbourne band the Whirling Furphies, which I sung, alone, to the river.

I ran out of their kitchen. I ran out into the sun, and stood by our trailer, and cried an unfamiliar gratitude, alone. Not alone, magpie sat above me in the tree, singing too.

After Easter buns, after photos, Andy and Sarah walked with us to the edge of their block. Down the slope to the river under the shade of the burgan, they pointed out the terrain they had freed from the weed *tradascantia*, and its creeping return where they had stopped their labours. Andy knew this work well; as a landscape architect, he was implementing a re-creation of the riparian vegetation on the former bank of the Yarra where it ran through the Royal Melbourne Botanic Gardens. That bend cut off from the Yarra is now a billabong. When the replanting is established, that billabong will be in better ecological condition than many of the wetlands and riverbanks we'd seen on our journey. He and Sarah had cherished their custodian duties to their upstream bit of river too, and were brimming with emotion at the thought of leaving. We stood with them by the clear Yarra, tea-tinted with tannins, a bright rippled mirror. After telling a tale or two, Sarah and Andy fell silent, and together we listened to the gentle chuckle of the river. They turned and held each other, but looked at us, their faces wide open. Maybe they were so happy to have us with them because they could speak of their attachment to their spot on the river with three pilgrims who so understood river love. We were like a parting gift to them, arriving in the last week of their ten-year sojourn, washed up from the river. They, in their empathy and understanding, were certainly a gift to us.

We loitered together by their boundary fence. We found an elegant grass-green bug on the worn wood fencepost and we watched it intently, too shy to look at each bright other, for all our eyes were shining with water.

With Kate back, it was three pilgrims who set out into the beautiful morning. The farms upstream from Woori Yallock looked healthy, there was recent revegetation and the river was fenced from stock. In the paddocks were treats – big field mushrooms. We collected them, rubbing their stems to ensure they didn't take on a yellow tinge – a sure sign of poison. I placed the delicate mushrooms in the top of my pack; I hoped they would last the day, so we could eat them for dinner.

We came to a dead tree, fallen into the river, but balanced like a seesaw on another downed tree. We took turns sitting in the leafless crown while a companion swung us close to the water. We sang as we played:

As I went down to the river to pray
Studying about that good old way
… Oh sisters let's go down
Down to the river to pray …

We paddled in the rapids. I sat on the sun-warmed stones and watched Ilan dance in the shallow river, the water white with scattered sunlight.

I thought of that gospel song I love, simply because it mentions a river. I don't know much about praying, although I know how good it feels to bring my hands together and let my body be filled by the idea of kindness, or humility. It is a Christian song; I don't know much of Christianity at all, but it shapes my life anyway. Good Friday is sacred to me in a very particular way. It is because there are no cars. It's a public holiday, so people are not rushing about, and you can walk on that land reserved for cars, you can walk down the very centre of your street. And the silence spreads over the land.

Christmas, too, has that same sacred silence for the first few hours of the day.

One year, early in the morning, I rode my bike through the blissfully empty streets to Yarra Bend Park. The red gums were flowering, they smelled like buttery toffee. Down by the river was a dead silver wattle. All of the sap had slowly leaked out of the tree. All along the undersides of the branches, globules of honeygold, red and amber sap had congealed into hard transparent spheres. The dawn sun, streaming low, lit the black skeletal branches decked out with their sappy orbs. The sun hit the balls of sap; the sun shone out from the centre of the crystal-like globes, and gave me my own private Christmas tree.

We walked across the river flats, across paddocks, as vegetation along the river was too thick to allow us to walk beside the water. We passed between manna gums older than European presence in this land. Giant limbs lay fallen across the paddock. We found a door in a hollow tree. Of course we had to peek inside; it was a pit toilet, installed many years ago, by the tumbledown look of it.

We stopped to have lunch under one of the generous trees. Kate took the opportunity to take off her shoes and unbandage her ankle, letting it breathe awhile.

'How's it feeling?' Ilan asked.

'Not bad, not bad,' she said, in her 'I'm not going to take myself too seriously' voice.

On we went. Ahead we could see a creek coming down to join the Yarra. I looked at the map – it was Hoddle's Creek. Would he have named it after himself, on his river journey, all the way to the source, in 1845?

We were wondering where and how to cross the creek, when a herd of feisty black cows with sharp horns spotted us and came running. We didn't stop to negotiate – we took off up the paddock, and, chucking our packs hastily over, dived through a wire fence. Panting, and bold now that we were safe, we looked back at the beasts, who were working against their momentum to avoid crashing into the fence. They snorted and huffed at us, as we waved goodbye.

By jumping the fence, we had found the Warburton Rail Trail. It was part of the disused rail line that we had criss-crossed through the Yarra Valley, but in that stretch it had been adapted for the use of pedestrians and bicycles. It was heading in the right direction, and there was a bridge crossing

Hoddle's Creek just ahead, so we decided to follow it for a time. The minor risk of being bowled over by a cyclist seemed trivial compared to being speared by stampeding cattle.

Ahead, the Yarra swung alongside the rail trail, just as we arrived at the Warburton Highway. On the other side of the road was a building familiar to me – the Launching Place Hotel. I knew it from my childhood, as this highway was the route we took to get to my family's holiday destination – Camp Eureka (where we were to stay the coming night). I remember asking mum what Launching Place meant – she said it was the place where the timber cut from the tall forests was launched into the river, to float to the sawmills downstream.

The rail trail crossed over the Warburton Highway, but we didn't, we stayed with the river. Just ahead of us was Don Road, the end of the road up to Mount We Too Belong. We'd come a long way alongside that mountain, and finally we were leaving it. Its distinctive shape had been a marker on our many days through the valley, but the south face of the mountain was unfamiliar to us.

As we walked the mountains crept in tighter around us, enclosing us to the north and the south, and the river ran in the cleft she had made for herself, coming towards us from the east.

We passed through a paddock where some horses were watching a man and a young boy fishing, and we soon came to the junction of the Yarra and the Little Yarra. We scrambled down to the edge of the water, and I scooped up a handful of the coarse quartz sand that lined Little Yarra's bed. The water ran clear, fast and cold; it was the river of my childhood. Our destination lay that way, but we decided to walk between the two waterways for as long as we could, to stay within sight of our larger Yarra. We continued across the paddocks and came to a road that ran between the rivers, through the lush green riverflat. We straggled across the width of it. A small white car drove up behind us, beeping its horn. It stopped beside us and a woman, in her sixties perhaps, wound down the window and asked:

'Are you the Long Yarra Walkers?'

We confirmed that we were, then an imperious voice in the passenger seat called out,

'We've been calling you on your telephone all day – why haven't you answered?' We had put a mobile number on the letter we had sent out to all the landowners whose properties we might be crossing – so we assumed that these women must live around here and were trying to head us off from crossing their land (we usually turned the phone on at the end of each day – if we remembered!). But this was not the case at all.

'We've been driving around looking for you lot – we've got some stories for you!' came the voice again. We bent down to see its owner; there was a white-haired woman in her nineties. She had insisted her daughter drive out to look for us, because she wanted to tell us about the country. She was the daughter of one of the original squatters in this area, who had taken up land between the little and big Yarra Rivers in 1890.

From the car seat she launched immediately into storytelling, while we peered in through the car windows. She gestured to the lush green landscape around, 'All of this land here was useless, covered in trees, so he ringbarked the lot of them first'. She told us a little of farming life in the early days, of how she loved her work, tending the cows, the chickens and the pigs. We asked about native animals, and the bush around; she talked more about her chickens. We couldn't draw her further on the subjects we were keen to hear about; of the changing landscape and the growing dominance of European farming and tree getting. And we would never know of the life of an early settler, and the difficult carving out of a known method of survival, right over the top of unrecognised Wurundjeri pathways. She came to tell us stories, but it was where words failed that I think I learned the most.

She wrote in our logbook:

At that time the Victorian Government allocated 20 acres to each applicant. Some managed – others faltered. Although I have been away from this lovely farm for 45 years my heart is still very much here between these two lovely rivers, the big Yarra and the Little Yarra. I'm fascinated about the source and origin of these two rivers.

We thanked and farewelled our visitors in their little white car. On ahead, the rail trail met up with our road. We consulted our map again; this was where to turn off, to leave the Yarra and instead follow the Little Yarra. We waved goodbye to the mother river, bending away from us across the paddocks. We took the rail trail and headed south.

Very soon, the shady path came to an old trestle bridge, where the old rail line had straddled the Little Yarra. That was where we must follow our tributary. We jumped down the steep embankment, squeezed through a grove of close-growing young elms and over a barbed wire fence. After some muddy ditch leaping, a few fence skirmishes and some quick-smart cow-avoiding tactics, we were looking rather bedraggled. There was not a word of complaint from Kate about her ankle, but I could see the day was starting to take its toll on her indomitable cheerfulness. And then she remembered.

'Oh gawd. We didn't ask for permission to walk here.'

She was right. We hadn't.

'Well, we don't have too far to go now, and the light's fading. If we don't look at them, maybe they won't see us.'

'Can I check the map, see how far we've got?' asked Ilan, as he leaned against the padlocked gate, there in the fence we were about to cross.

The map wasn't there. It had been kept, throughout our adventure, in a clear plastic holder attached to the top of Kate's pack. It must have been torn off somewhere in the last mile of scrambling.

'Wonder where it's got to? Untidy to lose it, but no big deal really – we just follow the creek – and you know where we're going tonight, don't you?'

'Yeah I do. It just feels funny; no permission, no map. None of the legitimacy we've been parading around with us.'

≈

No land is innately fenced. It didn't happen all at once, but in England, over 800 years or so, the land was shut up into parcels. Enclosure, as the practice was called, divided land with fences, ditches or hedges. As the industrial revolution powered up in the late 1700s, this slicing was vigorously encouraged and legalised by the governments of the time. Lords and landowners were quick to take economic advantage.

There was more money to be made in fattening sheep for wool than the traditional use of peasants growing subsistence crops.

Those who resisted the forced enclosure of the land their family had lived upon for generations were branded criminals. Some were sent to Australia as convicts. With no land on which to grow their food, many thousands of farmers faced the stark choice of either starvation in the country or gruelling work in the mines, or in the mills or factories of the industrial towns.

In Scotland, the dispossession of people from land was even more dramatic. They were called the clearances – the forced removal, sometimes by the army, of thousands of furious Scots, in order to set up vast sheep runs. To this day, half of Scotland is owned by 0.01% of the population. And many of the newly landless Scots boarded the ships for Australia, including some of my ancestors.

The farmers, predominately illiterate in written matters, were probably highly literate in their understanding and connection to the land. Leaving the land, what of their culture was irrevocably lost? Perhaps this culture was in part supplanted by a culture of class anger. Marx, working on *The Communist Manifesto* in London in the 1850s, drew on the history of the enclosures of the commons to demonstrate the development of capitalism, and its effects on the powerless. Yet he addressed the new working class of the industrial age, not the peasants and their land-based traditions and culture. The energising comradeship of communism with its timely call for justice and equality offered an alternative to urban Christianity, and quickly gathered adherents all over the industrialised world. It believed, heroically perhaps, in the workers, and ideals. But did Marxism believe in a wider net that held the people? Did he believe in the great holding given us by the arms of the world?

Some of the sources I scoured suggested that enclosure marked a revolutionary change in how the world was previously viewed; that prior to enclosure, the peasant farmers had no concept of land ownership. The ruling class most certainly did – they promoted the notion that the traditional peasant ways of life were primitive and the people lazy, irresponsible and unproductive. The landlords justified the clearances as a necessary evil to civilise and improve their estates – and the peasants.

Back to Yarra River country, where squatters, including ex-convicts and landless Scottish and English migrants, came in with their hard-won knowledge of land ownership. They claimed this land. Their sheep wandered over the unfenced land, and ate out the Wurundjeri staple food crop, the murniong daisy tubers. The records suggest that most settlers considered the traditional Aboriginal ways of life as primitive and the tribal people as lazy, with no notion of responsibility and unable to produce anything of value. Those pronouncements disguise, fairly obviously, a forgetting. This forgetting was necessary if they were to take over the land of others.

I wonder, now, what else was forgotten?

I remember listening to the voice on tape of an Irish storyteller and historian talking about the Celts. He spoke about the Celtic knowledge of eternal time, a magical world alongside this one, a realm where time moved differently, a place of indescribable beauty.

I wondered whether the realm he described came out of the experience of living deeply connected to land. Was this realm referring to a flowing sense of being part of all life? Was this knowledge (foundational, I imagine, to a land-based culture) lost during industrialisation, when the emphasis shifted to the machine?

Maps as we know them came to prominence when landowners sought to monitor and patrol their parcel of earth. The maps we used on most of our walk, the Melways ones that I am so fond of, are mostly areas of white. That is private land. There is a thin amount of green, indicating places of public access.

On every map there is a key, also called the legend. The key is the explanation of symbols, a thin blue line for a river, hatched blue blobs for billabongs. We looked for it – our map had gone.

Within fate is the invitation. I opened it. This is what it said:

Lose the map. Throw away the key. Walk the land, and know those marks as real things, a lived life. Give your body a chance to remember and doors shut tight inside will open wide, as wide as the green land and the blue of the sky.

Before and after this moment in time, there is the land, land with no locks. No keys no fences no gates no reinforced barbed wire six feet high. There is just the land stretching all the way to the mountains, and behind, all the way to the sea.

Unlock the world.

Be the key. Be the legend.

We walked on, and, as it happens on a pilgrimage, we came to a water lily garden, lotuses in full flower everywhere. A peaceful man sat among them; he'd planted them, it was his garden, open for visitors. He was happy to let three pilgrims cross from island to island via his little wooden bridges, but it seemed his true attention did not stray from the flowers. They lay over the surface of the water. The Buddhists, whose culture thrived in India before the Mongols and then the British invaded, revered the lotus. They observed the lotus, and the lotus told them its story, a timeless lesson, learned from a clear-seeing contact with the real world:

The lotus has its roots in the mud,
Grows up through the deep water,
and rises to the surface.
It blooms into perfect purity and beauty in the sunlight.
It is like the mind unfolding to perfect joy and wisdom.

We walked further into the valley, dusk light saturating the scene, sweetening colour. We stopped, as if to meet the silence. We stood in an ungrazed paddock and gazed at the dark line of trees ahead. Nothing moved. Old blue mountains had lain down on either side of us long ago, gently cupping the valley. They watched. Kate turned and turned, drinking in the valley. She told us how she once lived on the other side of the creek, at a residential school camp, with her puppy Theo, and how they would walk out at this time of the evening. I too knew this stretch well; we were about to enter Camp Eureka.

As we walked along the creek into the Camp, I drifted into a memory of sitting by the water with my mum while she told me this story.

'This creek is called the Little Yarra, and if you follow it down it joins the big Yarra, which flows all the way into the city and then out to the sea.'

I can see her pointing to the bank on the other side of the creek.

'See how the sides of the creek are falling away? That's because there are no trees to hold them in place. When I was little, the creek was narrower. One day, maybe that whole paddock will wash away.'

I remembered imaging that; the land scoured by water, and the creek growing wider and wider.

My grandparents had taken my mother and her siblings to the Camp when they were children. Once the base of the Eureka Communist League, the Camp was set up to provide cheap holidays for the working class back in the 1940s. It was intended to be an experience of communalism; built collectively out of rough-hewn bush timbers, cut on-site by the holidaymakers. Twice a year for many years we would come to Camp in the car, first with mum, then, when anxiety and depression constricted her movements, our cousins.

My grandparents were drawn to communism after experiencing the poverty and inequity of the Great Depression. My grandfather became a prominent union leader, and at that time, in the 1950s, the American suppression of communism under McCarthy spread to Australia. Police raided my mother's house a number of times when she was young; a terrifying experience for her, the youngest of the family. Her father, a man driven to fight for the workers, died of a heart attack when she was twelve. He was giving a speech at a union gathering; Bob Hawke tried to resuscitate him.

My mood as we entered Camp had some of my childhood excitement about it; I was so keen to share it with my friends. We walked past the high-roofed, open-sided mess hut, built in the time when up to a thousand people would come, back in the 1950s. We walked through the dining hall and into the big kitchen. Among the Camp folk were sitting our support crew, including Jessie, Ilan's girlfriend. We said hello to our mates, Ilan threw his arms around Jessie, and I went and met the Camp regulars.

'Hello, we've walked from Melbourne!'

The woman standing there at the bench, a woman I had known all my life, looked at me coolly, and said 'Oh you did not!' and turned away.

I stood, staring, frozen. Dark and heavy ice lodged in the pit of my belly. My brain was strangely blank; for long moments I could not bring the bits of my brain together to comprehend what it was that she said. Did she not believe in the pilgrimage? How, after negotiating my pilgrim self through the city and suburbs and farmlands, and everywhere finding succour, could there be dismissal, right at the centre of my world?

My eyes are swimming with water. I am a child, denied. I am my mother, confined by her agoraphobia, the fear of leaving home. I am my grandmother, hiding in shyness. I am all of us at once. I am broken. I am drowning in my own dark river of memory. I am flung into the flow, I cannot escape it.

Breathe.

I cannot swim against this dark water, deep and swirling with dangerous coldness, but I must do something.

And then it comes. Of course; I was taught this skill as a child, here in the Little Yarra, learning how to be safe in the water. Of course.

I can float.

All of the past is coming towards me, a flood of consequence. As the pilgrim had seen, the sheltering trees planted alongside the river can change the quality of the water, can cleanse and purify the flow. What is done now will change the future, will heal the past. Thank you my river for this, for in my attentiveness to you I have learned what is needed. Thank you little river. I can hold you, even though you are water.

This is where the heart rises. This is where the heart rises with the flow of the water, where there is a way, where there is a washing away, a washing away, bless the sweet water.

What happened to make me fall apart?

Why did my pilgrim world break into pieces with those few abrupt words? It felt as if she denied the existence of the pilgrimage, yet I didn't stop to ask, to find out what she meant, for I had already fallen into an abyss. That this happened at a place resonant in family memory was, I knew, no coincidence. Being in pilgrim mode, open and receptive to each moment, perhaps had certain dangers. The pilgrimage, an interweaving of the personal and the political, the inner and the outer landscapes, was more than just a search for meaning. It was also a quest for healing. The breakdown at Camp Eureka was my chance for breakthrough.

I remember as a child asking my grandmother what our

religion was. She replied, 'helping other people'. I liked the sound of that, but as I grew, and as I watched my mum's lonely struggle for mental health, I started to see gaps in the concept. The fight for justice and transformation seemed to be all 'out there'. The personal seemed non-existent, and care and attention to each person and their unfathomable depths almost iconoclastic.

In contrast, there is the society that I live within, the society that had made the fences, and they had said yes, you can walk the river, you can cross this land, and pass through the fences. I come from a family and subculture striving for social and environmental change, a subculture that sees itself as opposed to the ways of the mainstream. It was profound for me to 'get permission', it opened in me a new sense that society could change, understand and accept its past, and grow towards wholeness. People all along the river supported our adventure. This was reconciliation; I was no longer part of an angry opposition, continuously fighting for justice. I had journeyed instead towards complexity, subtlety, acceptance and peace.

Until that moment in the kitchen. For with those few careless words, the child self, the hopeful self, was broken.

THE FIFTEENTH NIGHT

What if I take my broken self to the river tonight, if I walk back down the narrow path, the waning moon lighting my way, between the shadows? Between the shadows cast by tall white trees, I take my little self to the Little Yarra, and with me are my mother and my grandmother. I walk between them. I take both their hands, and we walk together, until I am grown. We sit on the tiny beach of river sand, and mum tells me the story once again; of the riverbanks that wash away because there are no trees to hold the Little Yarra together.

I wade alone into the cold river. I take my fear and place it there in the moonlit water, and the fear washes away, all the way down to the sea. The fences fall; they ravel themselves away as if they were never there.

I cross the river, and I plant trees on the other side.

BIRRARUNG, RIVER OF MISTS

Next morning, Karina, my friend who campaigns on forest protection for The Wilderness Society, gave me a shell. She wanted me to take it to the source for her; she had collected it at our launch by the bay. I was happy to. I put it in my pocket, beside my limpet shell.

Cinnamon arrived to walk with us for the day. In the mess hut kitchen we had a large happy breakfast with our big gang of friends. The field mushrooms we'd collected the day before went deliciously with our eggs. With so many goodbyes, it took a while to leave. Then everyone decided to walk to the Little Yarra with us anyway. We tramped to the creek where we said our final farewells.

Downstream we went, drifting in the sunshine, following the meanders towards the confluence. Two black horses kissed beside a tiny island. Full-hearted joy bloomed from beauty; I felt whole once again.

Back at the rail trail, we turned upriver, searching for a good place to cut across the paddocks to the river. We took advantage of the smooth straight track for a while, and I guided

Ilan, who wanted to try walking with his eyes closed. Because he couldn't see, I watched spider webs for him; strands loose and shimmering through the air, carried along in the same direction as us by the delicate westerly breeze coming up the valley. Then it was my turn to be guided blind. Birds sang as I crunched along the grit path, sun-warmed though a scented world.

'I didn't get much sleep last night!'

'We know, we heard!' I smirk below my blindfold.

'Louis is coming tonight', he countered.

'That's quite enough Ilan.' Louis was my on-again, off-again lover – we were staying at his uncle's house that night, in East Warburton.

Back with Birrarung. Shafts of sunlight stabbed through the thick eucalypt canopy, to land on rapids and turn the river to light. Kate and I leapt off a slate outcrop covered with strappy lomandra tussocks, into the clean tannin-dark water. The pain of cold was intense, I shrieked with something approaching panic and flailed for the edge. The river's sides were sheer stone. I swam fast upstream until I found an accessible bank.

Giddy and tingling, reborn, I followed after the others. We found small paths hugging the river alongside the south bank. Some pieces of bush were lovingly cared for, others were weedscapes, all were speckled in sparkling early winter light, held together under the darkness of the overshadowing eucalypts and rainforest understorey. The water was now shadow-blackened, then reflecting the forest to itself, dazzling where it shot the sun up into our eyes. Blue hills wedged tight around us. Like walking through a vivid dream, the path went on and on. I hoped it would never end.

Up ahead we saw three men at a wood splitting machine. The biggest bloke was pushing through the logs with his beer gut, in one hand a tinnie, in the other a sausage. We bunched up together on the path, a little shy of approaching. Kate took the initiative, she marched in and presented us and our mission. The big bloke introduced himself as David Finch, and he and his two mates were using a hydraulic splitter.

'Turn that machine off!' bellowed David to his friends. 'These people are making me sweat just to listen to them.' He turned back to us with a grin, wanting more details of our expedition. He told us that he used to work at the Upper Yarra Dam, and had secret maps to show us – secret ways to find the source.

'Go in gate 20, road 12, but as soon as you hear a car – you'll hear them coming – off into the bush with ya ... don't leave anything behind, they'll never know you were there.' A conspiracy to get us in to the closed catchment! Regardless of his encouragement, we knew we wouldn't break trust with Melbourne Water.

He offered us sausages from the barbeque by the splitter, and obviously had many more stories to tell. But we needed to keep walking – we'd only walked half of the way to our next campsite – it was nearly 5pm and dinner would soon be waiting, somewhere far ahead.

Ilan tempted us on by promising to buy us snot-blocks from the bakery.

'I don't want one if you're going to call them that.' But we arrived in Warburton too late for custard slices – the bakery had long closed.

Through the town, European trees glowed in the glory of autumn colours, and grand and shabby Victorian buildings were set against a backdrop of blue mountains that stepped steeply up to the north and the south. I thought I knew this place but I was not prepared for so picturesque a scene.

Past the shops, on the far side of Warburton, David drove up with his young nephew in a ute, with split wood in the back. He shouted out of the window at us,

'Finally found you! I want you to see the high water flood marks up by the oval.'

Nephew Nathan was turfed out and Kate jumped in so she could show us when we got there. As she sat in the passenger seat she turned and gave us one of her winks, and I could see how she was bringing her cheeky pilgrim self to this encounter. For Kate it was more about saying yes to what was being offered, rather than insisting on getting to the headwaters entirely on foot.

I introduced myself, Cinnamon and Ilan to our new eleven-year-old walker.

'Funny names?' I offered.

'It's all good,' he replied with a worldly expression.

While Kate was in the car she discovered David knew her grandfather Dick Dalton – he was the principal of Warburton high school when David attended. He also remembered her mother. When we met up with them at the oval, David wasn't going anywhere – Kate had become something of a long lost daughter.

At the oval he introduced us to Ted Chisholm, an 84 year old from the Warburton Progress Association. With deceptively youthful olive skin, dark eyes and neat hair, it was his back that gave his age away – it was so bent he could barely look up to the many trees he had planted. His face was directed to the ground, and perhaps his vision sprang from this stance. He had put all of his money into beautifying a stretch of the river, and was beloved by the town for it. This task sustained him after his wife and both of his sons died. He was so proud of his awards and the letter from the Prime Minister, which had arrived just two days before. As we walked with him through the twilight along the waterway park he had made with his community, many people enjoying *passegiata* greeted him by name.

We passed under an avenue of thirteen massive redwood trees planted in the 1920s. It was almost dark and there was still a long way to go. We left these custodians, David stalwart beside his friend; his next mission to make sure Ted got home safely.

When Melbourne people think of the Yarra, many have an image of her as far up as Warburton, but for most that is where their cognitive map ends. Warburton shelters in the crook of the valley, nestling low where the water flows. The mountains stand up all around, silent elders. None of us really knew the Yarra beyond that point. By starlight for the last few kilometres, we strode along the centenary trail, by the water, the valley enclosing us. I felt safe and held in a darkness infused with the scent and sound of river, stars glinting faintly below. They'd fallen in the river.

Walking in moonless tall forest darkness, yet stepping out boldly, I felt attuned to the environment; I believed my senses, not dulled by torchlight, would warn me of any danger. But there was something beyond that. Being a pilgrim was a liberation, an extended experiment in trust; whatever unfolded was meant to be. For as the day before had taught me, even the traumatic had its place, its way of guiding. I let go of concern for myself and held faith with my body in space. Walking entwined enhanced this; my arms encircled Ilan. In this experience I felt myself expand to encompass my friend beside me, my friends behind me, the path ahead of me, the forest and the river beside me, the black sky and the stars above me. I found myself chanting little songs about Birrarung, the river of mists, to the rhythm of our footfall, four feet falling together, over and over again. This was the happiest time, the dearest time, on our way to whatever home awaited, on our endless journey to the source.

≈

A few years after the Walk, I travelled down to the Otway Ranges for a course called Nature Philosophy. It taught the skills of survival; shelter building, tracking, plant lore, fire making and water sourcing. Three Australians taught the course; they'd learned their skills in the forests of North America. Their teachers had learned from Native North Americans. Our teachers told us how they regularly went out into the bush for days at a time with nothing other than the clothes they were wearing and their knives. By the end of the course, I could believe it. They made us do things I'd thought impossible – including walking near naked, blindfolded, through the forest for hours on a freezing night. We made fire (yes, literally rubbing two sticks together), we splattered each other with mud to blend in to the bush, and then practised slipping unnoticed past our companions. Then our teachers explained that all of this was detail. They said that there were just two things we really needed to know. How to use our eyes, and how to use our feet. If we could perfect those skills, everything else would fall into place.

First, fox walking. Stand barefoot and look ahead, extend one foot forward and place the outer edge of your foot slowly onto the earth. Then roll the flat of your foot down, sensing the surface, checking that it's safe, without putting weight on your foot. Then, when you know it's ok, move your weight forward. Then do the same with the next foot and so on. Your torso mustn't bounce up and down. Make sure to place your feet on either side of a line imagined on the earth. Minimal disruption movement. Practise all the time, until you can run like a fox.

Second, wide-angle vision. Hold your two hands in front of your face, soften your gaze and extend your hands slowly till they are outstretched, or until your eyes can only just see your fingers. Then bring your hands back to your face, and take one up, one down, again, until you can barely see them. That is your wide-angle vision. Now hold that gaze. Move, fox walking, with that gaze, without shrinking your sight back to a focussed point. Keep it as wide as you can. They said if you try hard enough to look behind you, you will find, eventually, that you almost can.

Now this is where it gets interesting. Gently, observe the sensations in your brain. If you are holding wide-angle vision, you'll find that somehow it feels a bit smoother, more tranquil, in the space inside your skull. That is because wide-angle vision automatically alters your brainwaves to alpha frequency.

It's an innate capacity of the body; it's a skill that many people use to enable different qualities to come to the fore. The course emphasised that aligning the brain to alpha frequency was a survival tactic of indigenous people all around the world, of those dependant on their hunting and gathering skills to find food to survive. Alpha, they suggested, enhances attunement to the land; it fosters close listening. It slows down the frequency emitted by the mind, allowing for greater permeability and interpenetration with the surroundings. It is closer to the brainwaves of animals, so when we are in alpha they cannot 'hear' us as easily; long ago hunters found it's therefore easier to approach them, asking for their life with grace and gratitude, the human gifts.

Alpha brainwaves are common to children under the age of five years, artists at work, scientists making cognitive leaps, readers utterly captivated by the perfect poem, listeners to a flawless sonata. Alpha is the frequency of the meditator, the lover, and those drawn into trance by dance or drumbeat. Or those entranced by the rhythm of footfall, over and over, for hours, days, weeks.

≈

Finally, after about two hours of trekking in darkness, we arrived at the cluster of houses known as East Warburton. We were staying at Tom and Tanya's home, a wooden cottage within the tall forest. Their two small children had long gone to bed, excited, as the Easter bunny was to visit the next morning. Tom's nephew Louis was busy at the stove cooking up kangaroo in chili and coriander. I hadn't seen Louis during the entire journey, so I dragged him to the couch and poured into his long brown arms, and rested there awhile. I wanted him to ask me questions, but he held me silently.

'Don't you want to know what it's been like, you rat?'

'Yes I do, but I want to know through experience. Can I walk with you tomorrow?'

'Of course you can. Yes please!'

THE SIXTEENTH NIGHT

I am exploring the open wooded hills near the headwaters of Diamond Creek. It is the large property of Louis' family, and we are climbing the dry ridge at dusk on the way back to the house. I turn around to see the view as we emerge from the darkening valley, and over on the side of the next hill, quite some way away, a few people gather around a fire, on the adjacent property, under the stringybark trees. I burst into tears, and run to Louis, and try to explain.

'I can't go there! I want to be able to walk there, to just walk and walk through the land and be allowed to, to be able to walk for days, and to visit all the campfires!' Somehow he knows exactly what I mean, and can comfort this surprising pain, this unexpected outpouring. How many of us feel the desire to belong to country, to the whole terrain, in a way that even ownership of a large tract of land cannot satisfy?

I see now that the pilgrimage was an attempt to make this real. In part, it succeeded. And now I sense, far deeper, how much we are missing.

FIRST SIP

Louis and I woke early – magpies were warbling on the verandah. The interior of the little wooden house glowed pre-dawn grey all the way to the high-pitched ceiling, the bell-like pealing of the magpies faded to silence. The house, a tiny mountain, a chapel, a world, and we safe inside.

We crept out and watched a thin mist rise from the river. The soil on the banks was rich, dark with water from the rains. This was the gift of the autumn break – a resurrection of fertility, a gift of water. Easter Sunday.

When we returned, the children were bouncing through the garden hunting for chocolate eggs, with small baskets to collect their harvest. Inside, the house was busy with packing. It seemed to take ages that day; or perhaps I was simply more aware of the process, as the night before Kate had confessed to me of the difficulty of traipsing late into the night, with her ankle only partly healed. I was keen to respond to her request for us to leave early, so I was trying for maximum efficiency. Louis' gesture of serenading us on his viola as we packed did little for my sense of purpose – instead I got narky with him.

While we were eating breakfast, Ilka arrived. She was our

housemate from Brunswick, and had come straight from an Easter dawn service on the Yarra in Kew, where they ate fresh loaves and cooked fishes in memory of past miracles. There in Melbourne at 7.00 am the fog was heavy, but as she drove up the valley to meet us her car climbed above the mist and into the sunlight.

Five of us set out – Cinn had returned home the night before, but we had Louis and Ilka instead. We crossed the road to the river; the undergrowth grew thick, but there curled a small track. It was too dense and winding to see far ahead, so we were surprised by a rattly old trestle bridge appearing after a few bends. Perfect for Poohsticks, the stick-racing game Winnie the Pooh and Piglet played in their Hundred Acre Wood. We held a terribly thrilling game – I dropped my lens cap into the river in the excitement. Kate scrambled down the bank, took off her pants and waded in to search for it. It had gone. Another piece of plastic on its way to the sea.

Just beyond the bridge the path became messy. The beautiful rainforest had been illegally bulldozed for a trail bike track, gouging at the soil. And beyond that, the way was overgrown by blackberries. We retreated to the road.

The valley closed in; the contour lines drawing together as we climbed. There were few houses. We saw no people. Where were the custodians? Where were the people to clear the blackberries and tell stories, to make a little footpad path to follow, all the way to the headwaters?

We ate lunch back by the river at the Cement Creek Road Bridge. We ate all our Easter eggs. That time I agreed with Ilan about sugar – too much chocolate was bad for pilgrims. With sore tummies we headed back to the main road after lunch, as the forest, even without blackberries, grew impossibly thick for the pace we must maintain. The road had little traffic, and led through high meadows. Soon the paddocks and clearings ceased. All around the tall forest grew and the road stayed close to the Yarra. The river's sides were the only relatively flat land; the hills pressed in steeply.

Soon we came to a road from the north that bridged the Yarra. The bridge was barred to traffic, for it was the entrance to the O'Shannassy Reservoir. As we approached a man was locking the gate.

'The Yarra Walkers I presume.' He ambled over and leaned on the bonnet of his ute.

'Which one of you is the granddaughter of Dick Dalton?'

'How did you know?'

'I'm a mate of Dave Finch.' Our wood-splitting friend of yesterday. We should've guessed.

We lingered for a time while he told us a bit about the O'Shannassey dam. It was constructed in 1928 on the O'Shannassy River, which ran into the Yarra just by the bridge. It held a significant amount of water back from the Yarra. Now it is one of the series of dams that supplies Melbourne with water.

Saying goodbye, we continued and came to Little Peninsula tunnel and, soon after, Big Peninsula tunnel. Like Pound Bend in Warrandyte, two tight bends bypassed by dynamiting rough tunnels. Gold seekers changed the course of the river three times in the search for gold.

—

My great-grandfather Jack Goode was a worker in the gold mines in the mountains just beyond the Yarra's headwaters. Not long after my grandmother was born in Jericho, the family relocated to a ridge of the Great Divide, in the Thompson catchment. They lived in the highest town in Victoria, Aberfeldy, where the mountains undulate away in all directions. My grandma remembered her mother hooting to the owls down the valley; they would come at her calls.

A few years before the walk, Greg, my sister Jane and I took grandma on a road trip, to visit the place where she was born. When the gold ran out, Jericho was abandoned, and swallowed up by the forest. Aberfeldy still exists in name, although it's almost a ghost town. Once thousands of people lived where now just a handful of houses sprawl among paddocks. We found enough clues to lead back to where grandma had lived. The flagstone and a rosebush were all that was left of the house. Trees gathered around, where not long ago they had all been cleared; fuel for the furnaces that powered the gold-extracting machines.

We stayed that night at the Woods Point pub, an old wooden building attached to the side of a steep valley. Grandma and I went up to the bar to buy drinks. There by the bar on the wall above her head hung an antique photo of a small group of miners, posing stiffly before the entrance to an underground shaft. Grandma pointed out one of the men. My great-grandfather.

〜

Further again. The Yarra had contracted to a narrow stream of water. She ran between trees, clean and clear over the rocks, thrumming and thwacking like a talking drum. I drank my first sip of river water. It tasted, wonderfully, of nothing much at all.

Late that afternoon we revived ourselves with takeaway beer and chips from the Reefton pub. The smoky wooden room was jammed with older men bearing very large beards, some in that blurred state of drinking.

The pub was moved from Reefton when the gold was all mined out – the pub followed the miners down the hill. It is still called the Reefton pub, though it is not very close to Reefton. Unfortunately for our road-sore feet. Sharing one stubby, we walked on to Reefton through the dusk.

The last hours passed below a narrow river of stars; its dark banks were the forest's canopy above the road we travelled upon. As we strode steadily uphill, Ilan asked me what I had been thinking. He does that sometimes, and I am always grateful; often I don't know what I am thinking until he asks, and his sensitive listening brings ideas to life. So we talked of how, much to my surprise, the long day felt a little lonely with less human habitation. I thought I always preferred wilderness.

Later, back in town, I rang Myf, a linguist friend who was writing a dictionary of the Kaytetye language spoken north of Alice Springs. I ask her about the word wilderness. She said in Kaytetye there is a word *akngenpe,* which is a place where people haven't been to for a time, and as a consequence it is lush with plants and animals, and there is plenty of food to eat. Myf asked Alison, a Kaytetye woman, if wilderness would be a good translation for the word; Alison said no, because wilderness means a place always without people, which cannot be a good place, for then who would look after Country? Country, in this sense, is a word from Aboriginal English, and it refers to a sense of land perhaps not often experienced outside Aboriginal cultures. It refers to much more than landscape; it is the people and how they live there, the spirits that reside there, the stories that belong there. It is a word that feels up to the job of the complexity and humility required to properly belong. It is a word we would do well to borrow.

After trudging for what seemed like forever we reached the bridge that crossed the river to meet the road that led into Reefton. We searched our packs for a torch, to read the signs and find which dirt road led to Wendy's house. Reefton contained just a few residential streets, wedged among ash forest on the ridge between the Yarra and Armstrong Creek. We easily found her street, but it wound on and on, and still we climbed. Very tired by then, we began to lose our rhythm; we held each other's hands to help keep pace. I asked Ilka why she had chosen such a hard day of walking to come and join us on. She primly reminded me that the first draft of our timetable, the one still stuck on our fridge at home, had slated that day as one of the shortest of walks, and so she had chosen it accordingly.

'Oh sorry Ilks!'

'It's ok, but I haven't had the warm up like you lot.'

Eventually we saw a dancing light coming towards us – a torch swung in a hand. A voice called out, 'Are you the Long

Yarra Walkers?' It was Ruth, Wendy's neighbour.

'Wendy sent me out to look for you, she was wondering where you'd got to.' We reassured her we were all ok.

'Oh that's a relief! You're nearly there – it's just half a k further up the hill.'

When we finally arrived Wendy's little cottage was steamy and full of delicious smells – our dinner she'd kept hot. She was a friend of both Cinnamon and myself – we were to stay two nights. The next day we'd prepare for our full-pack journey around the edge of the catchment and visit the Upper Yarra Dam. We would then return to her cottage for another night before setting out on the mountain paths.

I had first met Wendy at the Sense of Place Colloquium at Moora Moora four years prior, and we'd stayed in touch. Recently she'd moved from inner Melbourne; she had a strong desire to be in the mountain forest, near the river. Wendy grieved for the damages wrought on the world's ecologies, but had been given hope by the writings of eco-theologian and philosopher Thomas Berry. Berry's life work has been the promotion of the universe creation story – the version given to us by science, a version he says is at least as miraculous, as astonishing, as any pre-scientific religious story. It is so beautiful, he declared, that anyone who really knows it would work to preserve the richness of life on earth. She had travelled to the United States to meet him, and was promoting his work and his inspiring story in Australia. Wendy was thrilled to have us staying at her house, and we, in turn, were energised by a host so attuned to our quest.

'Oh, what a wonderful journey – you must tell me

everything!'

In the light of the kitchen we got to meet Ruth-the-neighbour properly, as she was joining us for dinner. A short woman with a mop of white hair, she had recently retired from her work as an Anglican minister. She worshipped now with a local group in Warburton, and that morning had driven down the mountain for the Easter dawn service. She said she had told her spiritual community about our pilgrimage.

'Such a journey is in the true spirit of Easter!' they responded. Apparently they prayed for us.

Feeling a little overwhelmed by all the attention, I swerved my questioning onto Ruth – could she tell us more about her church's Easter rituals? In her low and musical voice, Ruth described the Easter Sunday dawn service.

First they kindle a fire outside, and then light a special candle from its flame. They carry that candle into the church, where tapers are lit. By the light of these they read aloud the first chapter of the bible; Genesis, the creation story – the making of the ordered world out of chaos. After it is told, the sun rises through the church door, which faces east in order to catch the sun the equinoctal sun, the Easter sun. The world has been remade. In the new springtime (well, late summer/early winter down this part of the planet), they turn on the lights in the church and ring the bells, filling their temple with life.

Ruth then shared that she had recently left her position in the church, partly because she felt there was a disconnection to the land, to the world we live within. Now she lives in the forest, learning to listen, learning to become a custodian.

THE SEVENTEENTH NIGHT

It is sometime after the pilgrimage. I am by the water's edge. The sun is setting at the end of the river's bend. A brief sun shower bursts, and as each drop meets the river the impact is a spark of gold. Water, catching the sun. It looked like thousands of specks of gold had suddenly fallen into the water. Prospectors dredged, dammed and mined the Yarra for such treasure, and thought it spent. But it seems gold has a way of returning.

I am watching without ceasing when the water is broken from below, and golden rings spill out around a small dark shape. Something takes a breath. Then it arches its tiny back and sinks. It returns to the task at hand, feeling along the riverbed for nourishment, feeding on what lives or falls in the water's depths. It is a platypus, the first, the only platypus I have ever seen in the Yarra.

MY BODY, MOSTLY WATER

When I awoke each breath rattled through ragged lungs. The minor cold I had carried for days had intensified and settled in my chest. I vowed to ignore it.

Outside my window Wendy had lit a fire in a circle among the trees and the mist. She was feeding the flames. Kate was sitting on a stump, cradling a mug and enjoying the fire. I joined them. While we sat, the mist thinned, and sun peeked between the eucalypts.

Kate was sharing with Wendy our visit to Coranderrk Cemetery, and the thoughts inspired there. She felt that it was helping her to understand that reconciliation was something to live, it was the actions that she took, and her positive approach to the idea. Wendy responded, saying that the river and land are the only things big, wild and old enough to help us through to reconciliation. For her, reconciliation meant we have to listen to the land, as well as to people.

After farewelling Ilka and Louis we spent the morning organising our things for the last leg of the journey, the hardest part, carrying all our gear up through the mountains. Our packs were bulging – I manoeuvred the heavy load onto my back in stages, testing its weight. We were to be travelling for only four days through the mountains, but the weather could be severe at any time of year, so we'd packed plenty of warm things. On a reconnaissance trip Jess and I had made about six weeks earlier, at the end of summer, it had snowed!

Cinnamon arrived as we finished. She was going to come with us on our afternoon excursion to the Upper Yarra Dam. It was only a few kilometres upstream. Cinnamon, Wendy and Ruth were going to drive there while we walked the last little reach of the river before the dam. Just as Ilan, Kate and I were about to set off, I made a decision.

'Cinn, can I come with you? I just don't have the strength to walk today. I'm too congested. And with the pack walking coming up tomorrow, I reckon I need a bit of a rest today.'

It was hard to admit, but I reasoned I had already got in a car once on the journey, and it was only a tiny bit of Yarra that I would be missing. I knew I was being sensible, and for all our sakes it was important to be healthy, especially once we were out in the mountains. Even so, I felt cold and lonely when Kate and Ilan set off without me.

Wendy, Ruth and I squashed into Cinnamon's little car. Driving would give us extra time, so Wendy was going to take us to her favourite spot on the river, a short way upstream. She brought along a string bag filled with garbage bags.

'What are they for?' I asked.

'You'll see when we get there.'

We drove down Wendy's dirt track and back to the Woods Point Road, which we had walked in the dark the night before. We crossed over the Yarra and turned upstream towards the dam. Not far along the road, Wendy directed Cinn to pull over, to a track heading downhill.

'Out we get.' Wendy led the way through a lush forest with a ferny, mossy understorey. The midday sun barely penetrated the rainforest canopy; all was a dimly glowing green. The track widened as we approached the river, where we found an unofficial camping spot. There, just by the edge of the clear splashing rapids, was a mound of beer cans and soiled disposable nappies.

'Why people would come to such a beautiful spot only to trash it I simply cannot understand!' sighed Wendy, who got to work filling her garbage bags with the refuse.

'Did you know this rubbish would be here?' I asked, as I picked up a bag to fill with cans and other recyclables.

'There usually is! I mean, it's obvious people like coming here, so what is going on in what passes for their heads? If the rain had got here before us, all these shitty nappies would have floated off down river.' She stomped off down the bank, weary and furious.

And yesterday I'd been drinking river water, thinking it pure, just downstream from Nappydump Bend.

We spread out and gingerly picked up all the rubbish we could find. It was strewn up and down the mossy banks, between slick river stones and knobbly tree roots. When we were done, we sat by the riffles, smelling the scented earth. I'd have happily stayed there forever. I'd be perfectly situated to abuse the next beery baby party that showed up.

Once we were back in the car, it took just minutes to reach the gates of the Upper Yarra Reservoir. The forest had been cleared, there was lawn and European trees. They were planted in parklike order, and at the end of their autumnal display. We spied Kate and Ilan ahead of us on the grass, and we parked. Then the six of us set off down the lawn to the thin strip of rainforest retained alongside the river.

There was a path by the water, the Yarra just a stream. After only a few minutes of walking I started feeling very weak, as if I couldn't pull enough oxygen into my lungs. Cinn asked me how I was feeling – she reached out for my hand. Kate came and held my other, and Ilan hers. The four of us pilgrims walked on. Wendy and Ruth were some way behind us.

We rounded the curve of the path by the tiny Yarra. And there in front of us was a concrete wall, a mass of grey extending up and up, dwarfing the forest, looming over the valley. We stopped, holding on to each other tightly, as the wall towered over us. I found I was crying. So were the others.

They were such simple tears. They kept on coming, a bursting. I found, once again, that I could breathe.

We retreated. We turned back and walked away from the wall, back down to where the tiny river runs through the trees. The four of us sat like injured children along a log across the dammed Yarra, and we looked into each other's tear-stained faces. We said nothing of what we saw. Instead, we thanked each other; we acknowledged how far we had come on this journey together. We took off our shoes and paddled in our river, and laughed at each other's antics, and then were quiet.

When we were feeling better, we put our shoes back on and turned back to the task. We walked back up to the wall – Wendy said later that we looked like hobbits approaching

Mordor. We shouted with the bravado on the far side of tears, we shouted at the tall echoing wall, 'Let us in, Frank Lawless!' Mr Lawless was the manager we had been speaking to at Melbourne Water. It had been his duty to say no to our request to enter the closed catchment.

We climbed around to the top of the wall, past the Stalinist-style architecture of the dam, the 1940's engineered concrete. And there, ringed by mountains, suspended within the mountain, was a vast lake, so big the ends vanished around the flanks of the hills. Raven's cries echoed over the open water. Ilan thought he heard a rumble beneath the lake. All I perceived was the rough buffeting of the cold breeze lifting off the water. A tiny blue wren, cuteness with a perky tail, perched in the chain fence, bobbing between the links. I smiled despite myself.

The fence separated me from a Yarra I didn't know. I looked upriver, uplake, upvalley – to the mountain's ridge we were heading for the next day. It would be a whole new phase of the journey.

THE EIGHTEENTH NIGHT

I have hardly begun to fathom the work of telling the truth, because the well of truth descends deeper every night. To get to the bottom of the well I dive into the water, where I will trust I can hold my breath and last longer than the night before.

Some nights I can breathe underwater.

Submerged, I ask,
    'How old are you?'
    Water, all water, is formed when stars, coming to the end of their life, explode. In the unimaginable heat and the immense pressure all the heavy elements come into being. When stars go supernova, stardust plumes over the universe, elements spread wide, and water molecules dance through the vacuum.
    Here in this corner of the galaxy, around this sun, stardust and gravity joined to make a planet. In among that stardust was water. More water has come here over billions of years by way of meteors, ice-encrusted comets. But that's it.
    Water is not made on this planet. It is cleansed and purified

by the cycles of earth, by the way temperature changes it from ice to liquid to gas, but it's the same water, going round and round and round.

Most of me is water. Most of me is a substance cycled through all living things yet unchanged for billions of years. I am, it appears, very, very old.

The mind bows to the body. Together, they rise.

The night mind has caught the tail of mystery, and now must hang on for the ride.

On my journey to the source, I ask to learn from the river. At the dam wall I see the pent-up river, the halt of free flow. I see my body, mostly water, reflecting the Yarra. My request to be a student of the river is granted.

Yet what is the nature of this river? It is a dammed river, a river tamed, made purposefully small and manageable. That dam, that water supply made my city, and my city existence, possible. Yet it is squeezing and constricting the wild of my country.

When we were at the dam, Cinnamon had showed me a photo of how the Yarra used to look like from that spot. She had photographed an old photo in the Parks' office just below. It was sepia, yet finely focussed; it showed the river running through a tight valley, massive trees cloaking the mountains steep around. Two images, and time. All things change.

One day the dam will no longer be here. The river, so old, knows other ways. My waterbody, as old as stars, knows that too.

THE PATH INSIDE

We danced around the fire in Wendy's bush clearing. Breezes too delicate for us to feel were shifting the smoke, so each of us in turn picked ourselves up and placed ourselves out of the drifts. Constant realigning, as we swung and changed and tried to come to a decision about where to go – how to overcome the obstacle of prohibited access. We had just discovered that the route we thought we could take – Boundary Road, around the edge of the closed catchment, was actually within the restricted access zone.

'How did that happen? How come we've just discovered that now?' asked Ilan, his voice tense.

'When we looked on the maps at Moora Moora we didn't pick that up from the topographicals. It's written on there, but in such tiny writing,' explained Kate.

'And, you know, I think we were all still hoping that somehow we'd be able to walk through the catchment,' added Cinn. 'That's made it hard for us to really nut through the possibilities.'

'We stuffed up didn't we Cinn, in not thinking this through properly.'

'We just wanted to believe Melbourne Water would understand.'

Kate rang David Finch for advice. He then rang around the Melbourne Water workers he knew on the ground. Apparently they had been warned to look out for us, to prosecute us if they found us trespassing.

'Persecute us' came the slip on Kate's tongue.

It seemed we had two options.

We could drive straight to Baw Baw, and then walk down the mountain until we approached the edge of the catchment, near where the longest tributaries run, to get as close as we could to the source. Or we could walk from Reefton down to the Alpine Walking Track near Warburton, and then head up towards the source. That track links up to Baw Baw, and so we would eventually get to our endpoint on the mountain. But that way would add an extra five or more days to our trip, and we were not prepared.

'And remember, Kelly's Lodge on Baw Baw is putting us and our friends up on the Friday and Saturday nights. We can't ask them to change that generous offer, and I don't feel right to not show up, after they've booked us in. Not that I feel right about driving either.'

'I'm afraid that I've got a wedding to go to on the Saturday, the day we planned to leave Baw Baw. I can't not go. I can't take any extra time,' said Kate.

'There is no way we can walk it then, is there?' Ilan almost shouts in frustration. 'I'm going off for a while, I need to think about what I want to do.'

I wanted Ilan to stay, for us all to think through the

situation together, but I knew better than to argue with him. I put out my hand to him as he walked away – he pushed past me, his eyes veiled, as impenetrable as blackberries.

I trudged off by myself too. I headed towards Armstrong Creek, which ran along the other side of Wendy's road, to find a place to sit and think. I thought about sources.

We had been walking for weeks through land rippled and crumpled, layered and smoothed, worked by wind and water. From all of that country water had flowed, drops to runnels to streams to tributaries. The land upriver of us was just the same, and would branch out over and over again, ever more intricately creased. All those carved ways would carry water, and at the end of each of them, a source. Thousands and thousands of sources. The longest ones all ended in the closed catchment, out of reach to us, but we could walk around the edge, and peer down into the forest. It was all we could do.

Then I remembered another source. It was one we'd initially identified as the longest tributary. Later, looking closer, we'd realised that particular tributary, one that rises on the flank of Baw Baw, was originally part of the Thompson, but had been rerouted with a short aqueduct, in order to direct more water into the Yarra. Yet it lay outside the closed catchment. Maybe that was where we could end our quest.

Eventually we all returned to Wendy's house to face up to the inevitable drive. Kate and I would go with Cinnamon – she'd deliver us up there, and stay the night. Ilan would make his own way (Ilka had driven his car up from Brunswick and left it there for our return journey). He'd meet us on the mountain the next morning – he felt he needed some time alone. I sympathised with him – while walking the whole way was an idea important to us all, due to my sickness and Kate's injury, he was the only one who so far had managed it. He had not gotten in a car for nearly three weeks – each step so far on the journey was his own.

We got in Cinnamon's car and drove around the valley, to access the headwaters from the other side, by going from the top down. I thought of the ancestors, left behind as we sped off in the car. I felt I had betrayed them – that they were the silent, unspoken victims of Melbourne Water's prohibition. I was devastated as I sat in the back seat of Cinnamon's car, thinking that I had betrayed the spirit of the journey. I promised myself that when I got to the source I would call out to the ancestors, I would look down over the valley and the dam and ask for them to join us there. This was a break that I wanted to mend.

⁓

Cars, by their nature, their speed and momentum, are innately dangerous to softer, slower life. It is estimated that globally at least 1.2 million people every year die in car accidents, (one-third of the population of Melbourne) and something like 50 million are injured. We cannot know exact numbers, but hundreds of millions of animals are killed every year as well. My instinct to mourn for the wasted lives of the animals rotting beside the road feels socially silenced. Visiting Tasmania, I was astounded at the number of squashed and bloody corpses littering the road, and the seeming invisibility (or is that inevitability) of this to those sitting in the bus around me.

Does it have to be like this? Travelling by car, do I take on the nature of the car? The values that society now promotes – personal mobility, individuality, personal wealth via economic growth – might these be linked to the needs of the manufacturers of machines?

It is estimated that more people have died in car accidents than in all the wars of the twentieth century combined. It is difficult to relate to the sheer number of deaths by car because we are all so utterly implicated – we all use them in some way. But that is different from choosing them. We cannot just wish them away, for the world has been reshaped to accommodate them. Up to 70 per cent of all land in some suburbs is devoted to cars. About the same as the percentage of water in our body. We call the principal road networks the arteries of a city.

I've never learned to drive. I couldn't bring myself to do it. It seems to go against so much of what I've truly wanted from life. Partly my decision was about the role of cars in heating up the earth, eating up the air. (The fact that we were pilgrims at the time of Australia's invasion of Iraq – a country that happened to be rich in the substance needed to drive all those cars around – was a nasty irony. Our country's attack on Iraq was – just quietly – one of the reasons why we were not permitted to enter the closed catchment. A dam is a site of national security, something terrorists might bomb or poison.)

At the heart of it my choice is not so abstract. For me, not driving wasn't about restricting my movement. It was about preserving the beauty of places in their intricacy, the gentle subtlety of foot upon the earth. Thus I became an urban designer, promoting car-free cities. I can be a difficult employee, when frustration with the way things are rises up to drown my hopes for what we could be.

I remember sadness first rising as a child, being in a car and watching an old, old woman, bent and slow, pulling her shopping trolley behind her as she walked on the footpath beside the six-lane highway. I knew, then, that my loyalty was with her, and I would not drive. I would not pass her by.

On bad nights, I plan the bombing of freeway bridges. I'm wearing a slinky black outfit, no-one gets hurt, the rubble falls neatly into the forgiving river. Everyone is overcome by the beauty of the new silence, and Melbourne decides to leave it that way.

Without the 'convenience' of being able to jump in a car to get around this huge and sprawling city, I've learned other ways. The combination of bicycle and train is pretty efficient. And then there's hitchhiking, a way that requires a certain wakefulness and trust, curiosity and gratitude. When I lived in the country for four years without a car, a place too remote and hilly for my bicycle, I came to love how hitchhiking asked me to remember these precious ways.

But I don't much like being in cars. The smell, the speed, the sense of being away from the ground, cut off from interaction. There is something about them that doesn't seem real enough. I've always wanted something more true, more beautiful, than cars could offer me. I went to Nepal, and walked for a week through mountain villages, and I was in ecstasy. There in the mountains there was no us and them, no hurtling separation, there were no cars.

One long hot day, wanting to remember such times, I

trekked alone over the mountains of the Mount Warning caldera in Northern New South Wales, to get to the town on the other side. It was a fifty-kilometre journey by road; I didn't feel like hitching on such a hot day, and it was less than twenty kilometres through the forest. So I set off, uphill, heading north, through the rainforest. I got lost on the mountain paths, and covered in ticks. Leeches clung to my forehead; when I brushed them off the blood ran down my face. Eventually I found my way back to the path, and made it to the ridgetop for sunset. Long-strided, exultant, down the other side, through the gums, along the track to my home for the night; I got there, myself, the way humans have always done. It was not everyone's idea of a good time, but it was as real as I hoped I could be.

To listen to the birds, to be in my body the way they are in their bodies, and enjoy doing what I do alongside all the other creatures, the trees being trees, the hills being hills. To walk permeating and permeable, open, thin at the edges. To fall forward, letting my foot catch my fall, again and again, a slow fall always saved by the momentum of body rhythm. Falling, into the open arms of the world.

Keep going until you get there. Just keep going. Walk all the way to the breathing land. The world was quiet for a very long time. Our busy brains gather and stack the past and the future into a thick foaming chatter. Yet silence lies close. The quiet links back to the ageless, the innate belonging over aeons, back to our evolution out of all time.

There is so much more time when you walk. It is counter to external appearances, but inner experience has its own truth. We do less, but we *are* more.

It is difficult to remember this in the world thus shaped; our society seems not to value this path of belonging. Cars are just one of our tools that take us away from deep time. Walking was the only way, for so very long. This was who we were for thousands of generations, and if we forget this, I fear that we may forget our depths, the way they arc back in time, and the way we may yet dream into a whole future.

~

We stepped out of the car after our long drive into darkness and icy wind. We stood there beside the car for some moments. I shivered, and felt confused, displaced.

'Where are we going to camp?' I murmured, half to myself.

Just then, a man came around the side of a wooden building, and strode up the slope towards us.

'What are you lot up to?' he asked, surprised to see three women arrive on the mountain at night, in the off-season. We sketched our story, and the disconcerting turn of events.

'Well, we've got a place you can stay if that'd help at all, it's pretty comfy – one of the lodges where they put us, the summer crews. But first come and have some beers with us; we've got a fire going down the back here.'

With those words I felt my body relax into the peace that was my more usual experience on our journey. In his generosity, he was recognising us as pilgrims, and demonstrating yet again the spirit of kindness and welcome that we encountered everywhere.

The three of us followed him back down the path and,

rounding the corner, came upon a crew of workmen sprawled on seats around a big campfire. There were beers handed to us before introductions. They were the regular summer work crew, who lived there between snow seasons to repair the ski runs, maintain lifts and get everything ready for winter. Some of them had been coming up for many years to live summer on the mountain. We exchanged stories.

'So the Yarra comes out this way? Who would have thought!'

They wrote in our logbook.

'Well done for walking so far in the wind and in the rain. Thank God we didn't have to come looking for you. All the best from the Baw Baw crew.'

After one drink we bowed out, keen to eat and get a good sleep. We were shown our spacious accommodation. Dinner was simple; we reconstituted one of the dehydrated meals that Ilan and I had prepared before we left Brunswick. Kate and I then collapsed in the couches in the living room, while Cinnamon went to get a book. She brought out her copy of *Always Coming Home* and presented it to me – she knew I loved it.

That book by Ursula Le Guin is about a 'reinhabitory' society set in the future; people who become indigenous to their place, yet who remember through their myths terrible times of environmental destruction and despoliation. It depicts a people who know their valley intimately, and who travel ritual journeys along their river to the sea and to the headwaters. These people come to understand themselves through their interactions with their place and its inhabitants; the birds, animals, trees, stones, mountains, even the weather is a character. It is my very favourite book; in the last decade I had read it continuously and voraciously. I was keen to share with my companions some of the special excerpts that meant so much to me, stories that contained much of the inspiration for the journey we were on. And so I opened it up, from the back for some reason. There I found a poem, at the end, like a last thought. It was called *Stammersong*.

> I have a different way, I have a different will,
> I have a different word to say.
> I am coming back by the road around the side,
> By the outside way, from the other direction.
>
> There is a valley, there are no hills around it.
> There is a river, it has no banks.
> There are people, they have no bodies,
> Dancing by the river in the valley.
>
> I have drunk the water of that river.
> I am drunk my life long, my tongue is thick,
> And when I dance I stumble and fall over.
> When I die I will come back by the outside road
> And drink the water of this river, and be sober.
>
> There is a valley, high hills around it.
> There is a river, willows on its shores.
> There are people, their feet are beautiful,
> Dancing by the river in the valley.

There was a whirling in my mind, as I felt the boundaries

between experience and fiction melt away. 'I am coming back by the outside way, from the other direction.' There we were on top of Baw Baw, we came by the outside way, from the other direction – out of the catchment then back in.

I read it aloud to my companions. We looked at the book in wonder.

'How weird. I've never seen that poem before,' I said. 'It's like it has only just been written, written exactly for us to read, right now. It's been waiting for us.'

Le Guin calls *Always Coming Home* her most hopeful book. Her voice is shining and bitter throughout. And she ended it with that poem.

THE NINETEENTH NIGHT

What I see in *Stammersong* shines, dappled but strong, on the very path I tread. In a broken time, in a time broken by fences and roads, my path – of course – is the 'outside road'. I did not come into a culture that knows the world as whole. The 'inside road' belongs to the time before the sort of separation we have with the real world.

We must come from the outside back into the wholeness of the world. There is no inside road anymore. The inside road is drowned. There once was a track all the way up the Yarra Valley – the Wurundjeri probably walked that way for thousands of years. Even my great-grandfather may have travelled to Jericho on that track.

The inside road no longer exists. It is under the dam. The old way is covered with water.

Oftentimes I longed to be in the place Ursula Le Guin had created out of nothing but words, a place where people lived strong and whole and vivid lives. I wanted to know what it meant to fit into the world, where I would know only to take that which can by the grace of life be replenished. I would always come from the outside road, but I was determined to glimpse the valley.

Then I had a chance to start my education in earnest. I went to live on the river at Collingwood Children's Farm.

Over the hot evening I am watering the garden from rainwater we've collected off the roof in buckets. Inside the buckets there is much squirming; the bent-double acrobatics of mosquito larvae. I pour the water and the wrigglers onto the tomato plants, and I can almost see the fruit swell with this food and drink.

I sit down in the garden bed, picking cherry tomatoes and popping them straight into my mouth, sweet tangy explosions. Before long mosquitoes find me. I watch one dig her proboscis into the skin on the back of my hand and suck out my blood. I don't disturb her eating of me; she gets rounder and redder, as if she were growing a tiny tomato at her centre. Now she has the nourishment she needs to lay her eggs in the water buckets. I will empty them, again, onto the tomatoes, which I will eat, while her daughters (the ones who got out of the bucket in time) eat me.

To be eaten and to eat, to go round and round in this place, shows me a solidity, shares with me a fluidity that I have long craved. So simple, so neat, so accountable, I am soothed by my belonging and giving to this place.

There are places on my skin where small itches make themselves known. The itch of my skin is the price of the fit. To be aware of the itch is a reminder, a nudge backwards to the huge internal itch that drove me to come live at the farm, and devote myself to the garden. The itch was the irritant that drove change, an inner jangling that made me search for where and how I could belong. The itch is a knowing that must be followed. The itch reshaped me. It made room inside me, a space where change can happen.

The itch tells me there is something to respond to. But often it feels as if there is nothing I can do. There is a lesson here. There is a paradox.

The paradox works something like this. I must be utterly accepting of now, being kind with what is. I must also respond to the itch, I must act. I must remember I am beyond time, knowing nothing, simply being. But I can only do that within time, knowing something, and full to the bursting with red round sweet desire.

Mountain Yarra

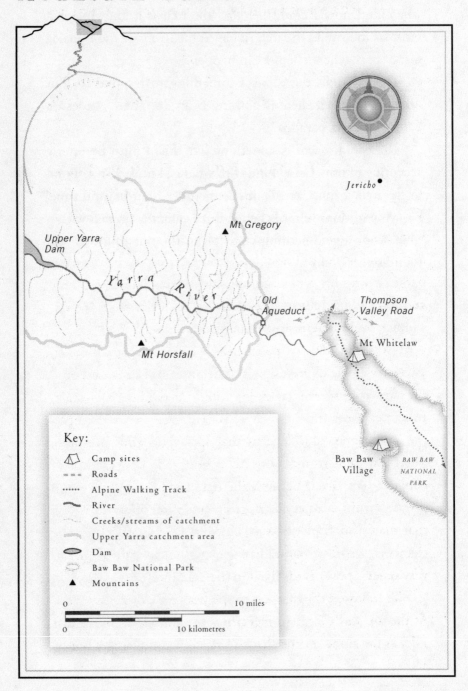

Jericho

Mt Gregory

Upper Yarra
Dam

Yarra River

Old
Aqueduct

Thompson
Valley Road

Mt Whitelaw

Mt Horsfall

Baw Baw
Village

BAW BAW
NATIONAL
PARK

Key:

- Camp sites
- Roads
- Alpine Walking Track
- River
- Creeks/streams of catchment
- Upper Yarra catchment area
- Dam
- Baw Baw National Park
- Mountains

0   10 miles

0   10 kilometres

TINY RIVER RISING

When we left our lodgings early the next morning, we wondered about Ilan – did he get up to the mountain last night, and where did he stay? We found him in the main car park, putting his tent back into his car. He had arrived late and pitched his tent on the grassy verge of the road. He was smiling, looking refreshed from his time alone.

It was a fine day, crisp and clear. We marched out of the ski village, over the cleared slopes of the downhill runs, and onto the cross-country ski tracks that wound around the mountain. In winter those trails lay snow covered, but we walked upon the alpine grasses and herbs that spring up after the thaw. The snow gum trunks were richly adorned – the colours of copper, gold, silver. Beneath the trees lay a thick covering of diverse shrubs, leathery, dark green and often prickly. I sensed that many small plants were old, but kept in check by the elements, a sort of naturally occurring bonsai garden. It was very quiet – fewer birds lived in the cold forest.

We followed the markers to the peak of Mount Baw Baw. At the top was a large stone cairn – we climbed it on the east side, as the stone on the shaded side chilled our finger bones.

We perched at the top of the cairn like four crows and admired the view. Baw Baw is not a high enough peak to be above the tree line, but the cairn raised us just above the crowns of the snow gums. We could see the undulating blanket of the gums, and the eroded, age-blunted blue peaks of the Great Dividing Range endlessly unfolding to the east and north. We spread out our topographicals and mapped our route through the hills laid out around us. We were to cross over the Baw Baw Plateau to where it joined up with the Alpine Walking Track. We planned to follow that track until darkness fell and we could hike no further.

The sun warmed our backs as we sat there companionably, high on the cairn. We could've watched the view for hours, but it was time to say a final goodbye to Cinnamon and get on our way. Even though she had ostensibly left the pilgrimage many days ago she had returned at crucial points to support the journey. We clambered down the cairn and each gave Cinnamon a goodbye hug, her huge eyes upwelling.

The three of us turned down the path on the north flank of Baw Baw. We descended into a broad clearing; a frost hollow. In the hollows the trees hold back, they ring the gentle earth amphitheatres like an audience about to be ushered in for theatre in the round. The play today and every day was the story of the birthing river. For this was where the rivers rose – all along the Great Divide the rivers emerge from these hollows in the high earth. Trees cannot grow in the hollows, for there the frost settles, and the frost will bite any gum seedlings that dare sprout.

We had been walking along the path for an hour when our track ended at the Alpine Walking Track. Our destination was to the west, but just to the east we spied a clearing. It was a mountain saddle; a low point on a ridge that became a funnel for winds over the mountains. The wind had shaped the trees to a low height, and so there were great views back to Mount Baw Baw. One tree stood out above the wind-clipped bushes – a bold tree, a strong tree. The intensity of its colours were greater than all those around – the bark was vivid pink, burnt orange, ochre. We were drawn to the extraordinary gum, and clambered within its branches and each found a perch.

Ilan was sniffing. 'Can you smell smoke?'

I inhaled and found that I could detect a faint fiery whiff.

'I was thinking that the air wasn't quite as clear as it should be. Definitely there's smoke about,' added Kate.

Unused to full-pack carrying, I was exhausted by mid-afternoon. When we came to a grassy clearing with an old stone fireplace, and Ilan suggested we camp there, I enthusiastically agreed.

'It's not as far along as we had hoped to get to today, but it's such a great spot, I'm tempted,' said Kate. It really was lovely – by the fireplace we glimpsed down into a frost hollow, and very faintly we could hear the sound of tiny creeks, rising and trickling among the mosses. 'But it means we'll have a very long walk tomorrow – we need to get all the way to the source and then back here before dark, remember.'

'We won't have our packs though, so it'll be easier than today.'

'Still, we'll have to leave very early in the morning.'

On our map we identified that we were at Mount Whitelaw.

'What a name!' sighed Ilan, his pack dropping from him

with a thud.

The headwaters of the Thompson River murmured beside the boulder on which I sat. The tinkles of the stream only made more striking the quality of the air; the air, suffused with quiet. A gentle, alive quiet, like feathers.

I could see Ilan in the distance, curled up in the last evening sunshine, on a granite boulder on the other side of the meadow.

Sunset. Pink replaced gold. Blue gave over to grey. Heat bled fast away.

I loved being there, but I was a little out of sorts. The discontinuity of the car trip, I thought. When we got to our river's headwaters I would visualise the whole Yarra journey. In my heart I would carry the elders through. I would mend this break.

The temperature continued to plummet.

What could I learn from the tiny river rising beside me, to help soothe me?

Flowing. Ever new. Each moment alive. Gently, persuasively, moving around obstacles. Precious lessons. I stood up, shivering, on my boulder, pressed together my hands and bowed to the stream.

After dinner, we sat in a row in front of the fireplace – the chimney a remnant of a high country hut. We took it in turns to sit in the middle, wedged snugly between companions. We talked about returning to our houses, and how we could keep something of the magic of the pilgrimage alive in us. Kate spoke of her idea for a quilt project. She would ask people all along the river to create an image that expressed their connection to the Yarra, and then she would stitch them all together. She thought she would send out A4 size pieces of cloth for people to make their art on – to the schools and groups we had met on our way up the river.

I thought then of the possum-skin cloaks that the Wurundjeri wore, how dozens of skins (roughly A4 in size, but don't insult a possum with that crude summation) were sewn together with kangaroo sinew. Patterns, patterns that told stories, were then inscribed onto the skin sides of the cloaks. That got me thinking of what a friend told me about Celtic initiations; of how each person would be required to make a cloak for themselves from feathers they collected upon the paths they walked.

I decided I would collect feathers for Kate's quilt, to sew, in patterns, upon the A4 pieces of cloth. Everywhere I go, I will pick up feathers.

THE TWENTIETH NIGHT

I am standing on the boulder within the meadows of Mount Whitelaw. I watch the last gold light spilling through the silhouetted trees on the ridgeline, and like it always does, this sight pulls at me, an inexplicable yearning. As a teenager, I followed this sun, into the water, into the bay, always reaching for something.

Back then, I'd follow whatever I could find of the wild, and the ways it had of slinking through the city. At the back of the old streets that ringed the bay were laneways, long and straight, cobbled with bluestone. At certain times of year, the setting sun aligned with the lane, vanishing at the very end, and the laneway blazed, revealing a beckoning path.

But it is the sunset glow through trees on a ridge that over and again catches at me. Often it's when I'm in a friend's car, being driven through the country somewhere, that I'll see the sun vanishing behind a string of hills. And in that moment, all of me is longing to burst from the car, to follow the light before it leaves the world. I'll lean my face against the window and wonder at the beginnings of tears in my eyes and the ache in my heart.

Then this pilgrimage, the way along the river. The ache intensifies.

TWO SHELLS

I woke in the darkness before dawn, within the silence of the mountain. I cradled some precious minutes of my own, talking to my journal about the big day ahead:

Today we journey to the source. We walk to the boundary of the bioregion, the far reaches of the catchment. But coming in from the outside road, from the other direction. We cannot pass through the water catchment. This land is cut off from people – so the essence of wildness – clear, pure, fresh – can be given to us. Hold these thoughts in mind today Maya – of the great good in locking away the water catchment, and the complicated way we relate to ourselves as a creative/destructive species.

Ready first, I asked the others if I could begin by strolling slowly along the misty path. The gums were patterned a dreamy grey. I trod into the quiet weight of the fog, my footfalls like heartbeats below. All around was the work of the mist; the delicate decoration of the spider's webs.

Each strand in every tiny web was strung with water droplets. Every drop reflected all the others. The mist had shown the extent of the spider webs, of how they were everywhere, linking everything. I saw how they held the world together.

Cobwebs laced between the snow-toughened stems of the bushes. Slow grown, cold-nipped, the twigs had been shaped into wiry calligraphy. In contrast, the new leaves of the snowgums were neon signs in hot pink and acid yellow, magnified by water droplets collecting in the curve of the leaves.

For a moment, I thought I could read what the signs were saying.

I was getting lost in the wonder around. At every tree or stone or web I wanted to linger. We had so far to go, I could not do this; I was holding everyone up.

Ilan and Kate walked past, ahead of me, down into the tall forest. The trees were vast and old, the forest spacious, leaving room for a thriving layer of tree ferns, wattles, myrtle beech, hazel pomaderris. Like spotlights in a gallery, sunlight shafted through gaps in the canopy, lighting up a branch, a gathering of ferns, a gnarled trunk.

High above, the mountain gums were waving in the wind. And since on that day I saw them, I saw they were waving at me.

The path led towards a tunnel of young silver wattles, their feather-like leaves catching the water, gracefully bowing under the weight of thousands of raindrops. Just as Kate and Ilan entered this bower the sun burst through, turning each drop of water white-gold, bringing the bower ablaze. I gazed in astonishment as my companions vanished into the glittering tunnel.

There is a song from Native North Americans I'd learned:

I walk with beauty above me
I walk with beauty below me
I walk with beauty before me
I walk with beauty behind me
I walk with beauty all around me
As I walk the beauty way.

The silence deepened and roared. I followed my companions along the beautiful way, and through the glittering tunnel, and I too vanished.

Yet the way goes on, and we walked there too. Eventually we reached the Thomson Valley Road, a wide carving through the forest. This we had to follow to find our source. It was taking us longer than expected and we were behind time. The night before, when we discussed arrangements for the day, we decided we'd need to be back at camp before nightfall. The paths are not well marked and the weather is treacherous, so we daren't risk walking at night. Kate had set the time we must turn back in order to make camp in daylight, and she was firm about this. So we had a swig of water and a hurried mouthful of scroggin, and continued. Ilan set a fast pace, Kate held his hand and she held mine, almost dragging me along. We strode that way along the forest road for many kilometres. And time marched as we did. Eventually, each one of us realised we would not get to the source we were aiming for. But we all said nothing, and just kept walking until the last possible moment. At 12.15 pm, our turn-back time, we stopped dead in the middle of the road.

How do I tell you what happened next? How can I break it to you, after travelling all this way together?

'No! We've got to go on! This is not the place!' I shout to the others, and pull on Kate's arm, looking fiercely ahead.

Ilan broke first. I turned and saw his face darken, and then crumple. And then he wept.

We were standing at the edge of a clearcut, a massive logging coupe. The ancient forest around us was gone. The forest had only just been destroyed; it was still smoking from the burn-off they do when they finish their cut. There were piles of ashes, red embers beside the road. There were the bases of once great trees, now blackened stumps. There were trees cut down and not used, just burnt and left there. Senseless, stupid, heartbreaking destruction. This is what happens in our water catchments.

Until Ilan cried, I had pretended not to see. I dared not see, it would destroy all that we had done, turning the pilgrimage to ashes. Somehow, something had gone very wrong. But then, when Ilan cried, I knew I could not avoid this. I saw it.

And as I saw, something changed. Deep inside me, I felt a space enlarge, open up, unfold, reach out. Something beautiful and strange was growing inside. *What is this? How can I feel this now? What am I feeling? How dare there be anything but pain?*

And then I knew what it was. Truth. This was what truth felt like. In this pain I had found a part of myself I had long refused. *This is what I am, this is what we are, this is what we do. This is the source, the true source, as much as anything. It must be so, or else we are outside the world. Pretending the world is a sweet little path by a river is not truth. Not mine, not truly, no matter how badly I want to live inside that fairytale.*

The journey had been a path of healing, of living in beauty, an enchantment that could make me strong enough to bear this. That path was the means of bringing me there, on the twenty-first day of our pilgrimage, to the twenty-first century where I live. The journey was saying what needed to be said, over and over again.

Kate said, 'We've got to look at this. This is reconciliation'.

She was right. There is no other way.

So we walked into the coupe. We walked through the ashes, over the smouldering coals. As I walked I tried to understand, I strove to truly see, but my eyes were blurred with tears.

I remembered the shell that Karina, the Wilderness Society campaigner who worked to try and stop logging in our water catchments, had given me on Easter Saturday, back at Camp Eureka. She had asked me to take it to the source for her. This is where we had come in our allotted hour.

I placed the white shell on a blackened stump, on the burnt body of a forest giant. I saw then it was a broken shell, curved, thinned by time and the waves. A bone-like shell.

I bent down to the scorched earth and took some warm charcoal into my hands. I brought the ash to my face, and smeared it over each cheek. We walked slowly to the highest point, and looked west, down over the very top of the Yarra Valley. Like a gong struck, I rang with meaning. This is the story and we have been given it. This, now, is the story of our sacred journey.

~

This is not, however, the whole story. For the way goes on, and we went there too. Our journey didn't end at the logging coupe.

On the edge of the destruction, back towards the way we'd come, we glimpsed a tiny creek still whole, and we made for that. I followed my companions off the logging road and down into the gully, shaded by myrtle beech. I remember how they walked, my companions, gently back into the forest, quietly over the trees felled by the construction of the logging road. Into the forest carpeted with moss and ferns, they carefully picked their way. I watched them walk lovingly, placing their feet with care, as they had done throughout the journey, as they continued to do, over all this country, all the long days beside me. They are my teachers, and I love them.

We sat on a nest of fallen bark, the song of the creek beside us. The faces of my friends were smeared with charcoal, streaked by tears. We talked sparingly. We picked at some food.

Slowly, we came to a decision. We would search for the aqueduct tributary on the slopes of Baw Baw, the source beyond the source, belonging somewhere between the Yarra and the Thomson catchments. It was on our way back, it was there by the path, and so, coming to it, at the end of our journey, it would be a true source. Just like the logging coupe.

We set off. I was struck by a renewed wave of sadness as we walked. I felt injured inside; bruised and winded, and so very tired; I slowed and finally stopped. Like a child I stood in the middle of the road, crying, head bowed. Ilan looked back and saw me. He came back; he stood in front of me, his head bowed too.

'I'm sorry we left you behind,' he said gently. He took my hand and we walked on up the road.

We reached Kate and she took my other hand, and together we kept going. Through the healing of their hands I found strength returning. We walked fast, back along the road and then to the path through the forest. Back through the bower, its glory veiled, as was the sun, hidden behind clouds. Higher we climbed, out of the tall forest and back to the snowline. Through the pure stands of snowgums, calm and quiet. The forest, in its harmony, seemed more like one vast tree than a multitude. One being living in a world of wind and sun, rain and snow. These trees are my teachers, and I love them.

We walked the narrow track, past granite boulders big as houses, through the alpine meadows, the frost-catching hollows. We walked on up the mountain.

We got to the place on the path where we needed to turn off, to find the source. Ilan said that he didn't want to go down there. He was ice, cutting with his grief, the grief that he'd carried silently from the coupe. Fear hit me hard in the belly, fear that we may not be together, that after all this way he would leave the pilgrimage, right at the end. I wanted to scream at him. Instead I turned blindly off the path, straight into the trees, sinking into thick moss, heavy as stone. Kate followed. And then he came.

We walked across earth that had felt few human feet, earth so delicate that our boots tore at the moss. I needed to put my sadness and confusion to the side and tend to the task. I must walk respectfully. The land showed me how to be.

We walked tenderly through the dark cover of the myrtle beech, and came down to the clearing, the frost hollow. On three sides the trees watched. The basin spilled gently down towards the west, open to the lowering sun.

It was hard to stand, so it was the most natural thing to do; we lay on our backs in the sphagnum moss. Like a living blanket, moss covered the cradle of the birthing river.

A river was being born below me. Water falling into the forest, into the moss, percolating slowly through the layers. Sphagnum moss lives for thousands of years; this the water runs through.

After a time of lying alone, simply breathing, we reached out and curled into the arms of each other. We forgave one another, we forgave the world, everything and all. I was sitting facing west, holding them, when the setting sun shot free from the clouds, through the trees.

A shaft of light entered my eyes, and the distance between me and the sun was nothing. The time between the beginning and the end was nothing. The distance between me and the ancestors vanished – they were there, beside us, within us, they had always been there.

A flock of currawongs carolled in the distance, and their warbling veered and played around the ridges before it fell, like gold, into us. They sang on, and on, and on.

We eventually unclasped each other, and I took from my pocket the limpet shell I had plucked from the waves at the bay. I placed it in a small clear pool of welling water, seeping from the moss. Tiny spats of rain fell from clouds racing from the west. Brought by the wind from the way we had walked.

Perhaps that very rain was picked up over the bay, the bay I swam in as a girl. I felt the cycle, the end of the river returning to the source, falling softly, so lightly, upon my face. And suddenly, out of the very blue, I saw the source in the sky above me, in the everchanging clouds. Embedded in this cycle, I return. My thoughts fall into the ancient moss, to lie there for as long as the world turns. Nothing is lost. Everything changes. I am safe in my whirling home, my turning world. Salt rain falls from my eyes and rolls into the moss, to join the tiny river.

I have walked all the way home.

And there is no roof over the sky.

THE TWENTY-FIRST NIGHT

We return to camp, and while Kate and Ilan kindle a fire I go to fetch water. I turn away from the new flames and walk the jubilant darkness. Out from the shelter of the snowgums and into the wind that howls through the hollow, tearing at the trees. These winds feel dangerous, as if, were I to open my mouth too wide, they would enter and fill me, a throng of dark and strong and limber demons, and they would hurl me over the mountains. I stand, mouth open, heart beating, hoping.

I crouch at the stream to fill our bottles, the water cold and sharp. I drink great gulps from the iced-metal rim of my bottle, and I shriek as the cold hits my brain. I shriek again for the pleasure of it, for the way my sound joins the wind's roar, to blend with the tempest.

Returning, I squeeze through the wind-pruned shrubs, sharp with thorns that pierce my clothes and find my flesh.

They don't hurt me. They cannot. I am too much of them. I am not other, and there is nothing, nothing in me to defend.

ABOVE THE ROLLING MOUNTAINS

The next morning at our camp on Mount Whitelaw I made tea and breakfast for my companions. Then I wandered. I sat alone on the cold earth in the sun and listened to the mountain. The wind of the night dissipated; the shedding skins of the snow gums clacked gently against their trunks. And then stopped. Mountain light scissored through the trees; all were striped brilliant and black with sun and shadow.

I moved through the alpine meadow, among the tiny streams, the pure cold water. I drank. It would become red blood for awhile, inside me. Tiny green crickets leapt at my footsteps. Through the mosses I wished myself light, for the earth gave underfoot. I could not stop long without making an impression.

I found a granite stone to perch on. I looked into pools of water collected in the moss. There I saw myself reflected. After days of not seeing me, there I was. I was a little sad to see her. I did not want that body to be the sum of me. I wondered if I could hold on to the soft, spreading sense of knowing who I was. I feared I would forget.

My reflected face lay there in the pool of water, yet that water, even as I watched, seeped away, into the runnels where white stones lay, and slipped away into the young rivers. Dammed maybe for a while, but never for long. Maybe this, maybe this, I could remember.

We packed up quietly. A boobook owl watched us as we hoisted our packs and left the campsite. Currawong came and chased the owl away.

My backpack that last day felt twice as heavy, even though we had eaten all the food. My steps were clumsy and heavy on the path, yet I strode wide, determined not to lag behind. I walked closer to my companions than sense would allow; I tripped and landed heavily, and burst into tears. They helped me up and walked on in front of me. I had to let them go.

We came into Baw Baw Village, the sun setting directly in front of us. We walked towards the sun, down the grassy slope, blue clouds, gold clouds, above the rolling mountains. We walked separately, each making our own way back into the rest of our lives, through dark shadows thrown by trees.

THE RETURN

The fourth of April, 2004. Back at the Timeball Tower on the first anniversary of the Walk. There was a new Parks Victoria sign, naming the place the Point Gellibrand Coastal Heritage Park.

'You are standing at the most important site in the history of Victoria,' the sign tells me. 'Here at Point Gellibrand, Victoria's first permanent settlement and seaport were established in 1835.' Another creation story, it seems.

I sat on the beach once again, and scanned the sand for a limpet shell. I wanted to renew my vow, to find what I'd once given to the source. But I couldn't find one. That has already been done. Instead, a heron stalked the shallows, and scattered pieces of mother-of-pearl shone and sparkled in the sunlight. Once again, just like the year before, the wind raced over the water. Rivers of air rushed through. Far across the bay, sunlight glinted on red cliffs. Just for a moment, then the world changed, just like it always does.

The high dry grass that Ilan and I walked through is gone. Now there is a fence closing off all the land between the station and Timeball Tower – the raw earth is scraped of every bit of vegetation, and the land is studded with survey pegs, ready for something new.

Allstate Temporary Fencing says the sign.

I read it again.

Temporary Fencing. All states. Temporary.

≈

The shape of the land I live in; the circle bay, the snaking river, the mountains, is memorialised in a traditional creation story of the Yarra. That story preserves the memory of the rising of the oceans and the drowning of the great plain that is now Port Phillip Bay, but once was Neerim. Perhaps I will live to see another rising of the oceans, here in my home. What is the story we may tell of this happening, ten thousand years from now?

≈

There is more than one traditional story that tells of the creation of the Yarra.

Melbourne Water finally said yes, we'll let you in to see the river in the closed catchment. In a four-wheel drive, a thoughtful man took us around the Upper Yarra Dam to where the flowing mountain Yarra runs into the vast silence of the dammed river.

We walked the floodplain, where the clean water rushes over riverstones. And at the place of meeting, where the river joins the dam, there on the moist earth and in the water lay many feathers.

By the confluence, nestled in the grass, was a small white egg. Hatched neatly at the top, it brimmed with rainwater. It brought to mind the other Dreaming story I'd heard regarding the origin of the Yarra – of the magic water pot the children tipped over which became the river. The hatched egg in front of me; I saw it, a tiny water pot.

I cannot know what that story once meant – its layers of meaning are gone with the detailed Dreamings, the networks of stories that held the people and land together into a sacred pattern.

I met up with Joy Murphy Wandin by the river at Federation Square. I told her something of the pilgrimage. There by Birrarung, I saw that the once-clear estuary was there in her eyes, alive, living, flowing. She gave me something to mind, while I am here.

I found my little water pot, delicately balanced, there in the mountains. A water pot, not spilt, no river made from this. Into this little pot I will cry, all the tears not shed, all the sadness of what we've done to our world. Maybe one day it will tip, and the waters will flow, and the dams will no longer be there to hold it back.

There are many stories, stories great and wild, given to us by the oldest of things. The river, the sun, the turning world, tell them every day. This world has given them to us to mind while we are here. This is the unfathomable generosity of all things. They are of the deepest, truest comfort there is.

Will we, I wonder, have the courage to choose the story of life?

≈

One day, I took the book *People of the Merri Merri* off my shelf, a book about the people and the language of the Wurundjeri-Woiwurrung people. The sun poured in through the skylight and fell on to my hands holding open the pages. I found the following:

> Tharangalk-bek means 'wooded country in the sky'. When a person died their spirit wandered over their country for a while before passing into the Tharangalk-bek. The spirits entered Tharangalk-bek via the Karalk, the pathway of light that shone from the sun's rays at sunset.

I see that stories belong to this world, and we stumble through them, we live them, unknowing. Then one day, we may find that we belong, after all.

And so then we flow. We flow all the way to the sea.

EPILOGUE

There in source country, we found a landscape that looked and felt like a war zone. There is a systematic and violent invasion of the forests, by governments, by logging companies, by a system that keeps us in 'comfort'.

Trees draw carbon out of the air and build their beautiful bodies over hundreds of years. From tiny breathing seedlings grow towering forests, made almost entirely from carbon dioxide, the gas that, when airborne at too high a concentration, will kill us.

It takes approximately 400 years for a Mountain Ash forest to recapture all the carbon lost after logging. Most of each tree ends up as woodchips, to become paper, which, being 'disposable', is destined to rot or burn, and that carbon enters the air. About 20 per cent of global greenhouse pollution is caused by logging and tree clearing, even greater than the emissions of the global transport sector.

Some of the most carbon dense forests in the world are the ash forests of Melbourne's water catchments. Every year an area of this forest equivalent to 150 Melbourne Botanic

Gardens is logged and carted away; the remainder is sprayed with a combustion agent and burned. The logging industry claims that logging is good for climate change because young regrowth forests suck up more carbon than old growth forests. What they fail to mention is the massive carbon loss that occurs when the original forest is logged. In Victoria they are still logging trees over 500 years old. Deforestation in water catchments is also drying up our water supply. As a result of the logging of five of Melbourne's water catchments, we are losing 1000 litres of drinking water every second, because young regrowth forests drink water that would otherwise flow into rivers and dams. Every year, logging in water catchments means we lose as much water as 350,000 Melburnians use annually.

⁓

When I first heard of climate change I was in the back of Dad's Kombi; we were crossing Queens Bridge over the Yarra on the way through the city. He drew a picture in my mind; of all around us, flooded. I was about seven years old at the time – Dad's scientific and political interest meant that he was aware of the threat of climate change decades before it was commonly acknowledged. He said that we could stop it happening, but that everyone would have to change the way they did things.

It's a strange thing. I've been waiting for people to understand the threat of climate change and to come together to act in the service of life for as long as I can remember. Yet even now that it is common knowledge, action is still deferred.

Capitalist economics is the story that implements the destruction of the forests. A system of thought developed when the world seemed infinitely large, the assumptions at the heart of it led Grimes up the river, and made a new type of world on top of this old, ongoing one. There in the forests we saw the workings of the system; the natural world going in one end and products coming out the other, or, in the dark, accurate words of one commentator; capitalism – the conversion of the living into the dead. But growth economics is a story that is hitting the wall of its absurd premises, and there is about it a manic clutching to something that more and more people cannot believe in.

The word economics comes from the Greek *oikonomikos*, the management of the household; a vital task. *Oikos* means house. The sister-word, ecology, means the study of the house.

How can we truly study our home if we haven't yet decided that this is, in fact, home? And how can we manage our home if we don't understand its limits, if we don't bother to balance the budget?

Sometimes my grief is like self-throttling, my hands at my throat, at the dismembering that is our world's fate, as cars and houses and televisions get bigger while the natural world shrinks. The places to go for contact, for pure unmediated being with the wind and the clean water and the tall trees harbouring intricate layers of life, these places are disappearing all over the planet. As the world becomes more difficult to live in will we all be harder pressed? As the ecologies simplify, so too this mind? The heart's depths, clogged with cloying silt, the run-off from denuded land?

These are my fears.

There has already been so much forgetting, and the asphalt continues to pour, and the ways are made smooth, and fast, and forgetful. The colonial ideas Grimes rowed up the river with are even now being laid out over this damaged, yet still dreaming, earth.

We have been made by our history; enclosures, colonisation, the scientific revolution. In the process of gathering up land, cultures, knowledge, much has been forgotten. There are mysteries locked within us, they have been there all our lives, deep, deep inside. What can we hope for? What can we imagine?

As I walked along the river, I discovered many people practising how to come home in this land. People of wise restraint and love of beauty are combining new ideas with old ways, learning to thrive in the valley of Birrarung. And beyond the valley, throughout the world, cosmology and physics are sharing new stories we could embrace; the dramatic tale of the birth of the universe – this manifold experiment with form. The outrageous mystery of how we evolved from stars, that what we are made of is – literally – stardust – is a tale of such magnificence that we ought never recover from the wonder of it. Add to this the strange and precious happening that I am here and you are here and then one day we're not – I feel this tale is too serious and too lovely to be anything less than the ground of each and every story.

The animal instincts of hunger and security can be moderated when we look to other things in the world to support us. We need true stories to build true culture. We need a lean ethos, not for abstinence's sake, but for a clear-eyed understanding of how the natural world works. And for this understanding to flourish we need encounter, we need experience of the ends of ourselves.

Spiritual traditions the world over emphasise the importance of *having* less, in order to *be* more. Pilgrimage is a time-tested experience of this. It is a cultural form preserved from the wisdom of hunter-gatherers, from people for whom the entire terrain was home. It is an initiation framework that, innate to the form of a long slow trek, requires acceptance, awareness, connection and humility. I was not particularly endowed with these qualities before I set out, but the river gifted me with a first sense of them.

There is something, alive in the world. Sometimes I name it truth, sometimes love, or peace, and I know it by the feeling within my body. There is an internal enlargement, a new spaciousness in the fibre of my being, a timelessness that spreads wide. This flows out of an encounter with mystery, with beauty, when truth, truth far deeper than any human notion, floods through me. I think it could be called the sacred.

Being a pilgrim gave me first an opportunity, then, gradually, an obligation, to be attentive to the sacred. As pilgrims, we were participating in ways of being that the river had taught since the beginning. Aboriginal people have lived their daily lives in something akin to pilgrimage; tracking Country, singing the Songlines of Birrarung. When I walked in the shadow of their ways I felt a gratitude greater than any I'd known.

Indigenous wisdom developed over thousands of years of

trial and error. What would it take to initiate the culture so recently arrived into this land, into awareness of cycles, living in balance and attaining sufficiency without excess?

I read the stories that indigenous people the world over have tried to share with the colonising cultures. When I walked the river these were the stories that made most sense. Now, these are the stories that best explain what I felt. For indigenous people know, I think, that the real world is not a metaphor.

Barwool gave instructions to each person to make the river by walking it; to discover, upon completion of their quest, that their whole self has been sung into the path since the very beginning. Barwool made the path for others to follow, but this making is a strange and dangerous business. If you think you can make the whole world, separating yourself from the ground of being, you will unmake everything, as Grimes and his story have shown. You have already made the world. You just didn't know it. Walk the river, walk the path, and you will see what you once did, you will make the river, in the only time there is, which is right now.

There are memories older than the seas rising ten thousand years ago. There are memories that stretch back to the very beginning. We use our bodies and this land to remember. We use what and where we are; we use what is to hand.

All through the mountain forest are nests, where unhatched eggs wait under feathery bellies. There is an image that haunts me, and unlike everything else in this book this image is not something I've experienced. I must imagine. This is important – we humans can do this – we can and must imagine:

I follow the evening chimes of the currawong, I find her nest, I borrow her baby, unborn.

I hold the warm, speckled-pink egg of the currawong. I roll it gently between my two cupped hands. What am I looking for? I cannot start at the beginning, I cannot get to the end of this egg. Always it curves away from my knowing. And in holding the egg with such care I am the one who cracks. I am broken so small that I can see inside the egg. I see the path has come from forever, and goes on forever. I become so soft and careful that I know I will not fall. This journey follows the subtle curl of the way that is forever unfurling. The way is shining.

The egg, the path, the river, the sun. All wild things are ways in; they are metaphors for mystery. But we are here only because they are not metaphors. The real things made our bodies; our minds, our hearts. We can think, we can feel. We can remember.

Memory lives in the wild speaking world, it is there in the water, it is percolating, still, through the mosses, and emerging, clear of voice, at the source.

There are things I know in my bones, but have been unable to voice, for the words fall straight through the gaps in my thinking. And that is as it should be; we are more than our minds. Those things I know are held in my body; I must listen to the heart-songs, soughing through flesh, sounding my bones.

There is the chance of returning. The Walk felt like that, it felt like home. The Walk was a way of being that went on and on, rich and welcoming, like the path to the sun.

So follow the path. Journey to the source. For these are not just metaphors; they are instructions.

ACKNOWLEDGEMENTS

At the end of the twenty-first day, after we'd reached the sources of the Yarra River, of Birrarung, we returned to our camp in the growing darkness, elated, unburdened. And as we walked we called out the names of the many who helped us reach our destination. Some people we called out their name many times over, such was the debt and the gratitude. These are those names.

Firstly, to Joy Murphy Wandin and Ian Hunter, Wurundjeri elders. In the fire of their passion to spread knowledge, compassion and understanding they are like Mountain Ash aflame, each spreading many thousands of fertile seeds. They are the soul below this city.

Thanks to Parks Victoria, for their vision, their care for the places we love all along the rivers, and their support of our project; in particular Kate Glenie, Alex Holt, Glen Jameson, Chris Hardman, James Vincent, Ric Young and Joanne Nelson. Thanks to the custodianship of Melbourne Water, who, in the end, let us in, and to Neville Rattray for showing us the treasure he guards so well.

Thanks to the local councils along the way, especially the cities of Hobson's Bay, Yarra and Manningham, and the Shire of Yarra Ranges, in particular Rob Dabal for smoothing our pathway through private lands. To the government authorities who are sustaining the vision of a walking track along the entire length of the Yarra – may it come to fruition!

Thanks to Pankaj Srivastava, Sudha Srivastava and Pandu Hegde in India for information about the Narmada dams and river pilgrimage, to Luke Chamberlain of the Wilderness Society, Amelia Young of Environment Victoria, Ian Penrose of the Yarra Riverkeepers, and Anne Boyd of Earthsong journal.

Thank you to our support people and guest walkers: Alison and Les Wardell, Greg Milne, Noel Blencowe, David Naylor, Nancy Sposato, Amanda Flemming, Anthony Morrey, Nic Morrey, Polly Christie, Carolyn Shurey, Bronwen Wilson, Victoria Marcelis, Annette Herschtal, Jane Ward, Mal Marcus, Heidi Sanghvi, Jess Huon, Mara Ripani, Jeremy Shub, Mal Eden, Louis Eliot, Ruth Harrison and the late Don Hutton. And extra special thanks to Jess Abrahams, our fifth walker.

A huge thank you to all of our generous hosts: Collingwood Children's Farm, Havenho, Graham Cock of Yering, Norm Cronin of River View Cottages in Yarra Glen, the late Michael Herman of Yarra Grange, Graeme George of Blackwood, Moora Moora, Sussanah Luebbers, Peter and Sandra Cock, Sarah and Andy Laidlaw, Camp Eureka, Tom and Tania Neil, Wendy Garrett, the Baw Baw summer crew, and Tony Fisher of Kelly's Lodge on Baw Baw summit.

To others we met on the way, whose work for and love of the river we found so inspiring, thank you for allowing me to share something of your stories: Malcolm and Jane Calder, Viewbank and Ivanhoe Primary Schools, Tarrawarra Abbey, Friends of Yarra Flats and the Yarra Valley Tree Group, Cam Beardsell and Mick Woiwod. And to those whose stories interwove with the pilgrimage, I wish to express my gratitude and love, especially to my sister Jane, my parents, Yvonne and Eric Ward, and my deeply missed grandmother, Myrth Yarker.

Thank you to Bagryana Popov and *Tales from the Hidden City* for sparking the first flints of inspiration to walk the Yarra. Great gratitude to the supportive and inspirational circles of Finder's Lodge, Uni Girls, Sangha, the Social Ecology Masters Program at the University of Western Sydney and the Sense of Place Colloquia.

To those who gave me personal permission to quote their material, trusting without seeing my use of their fine work – special thanks to Michael Leunig, Satish Kumar, and Frank Jones for his song *My Brown Yarra*.

I'm very grateful to the warm and wise readings of various stages of this book by Aliey Ball, Martin Rush, Kari, Jesse Dunbar, Lisa Jobson, Fran Woodruff, Vyv Rodnight, Kynan Sutherland, Andrew Walker-Morison, Peter Cock, Peter Shepherd, John Cameron, Michelle Croker, Stefano Fioretti, Isabel Ellender, Peta Christiansen, Myf Turpin, Cam Walker and Henrik Hass. Thanks also to the elders who have given encouragement and shone light onto the winding path: David Abram, Deborah Bird Rose, Satish Kumar, John Cameron, Carol Perry, David Tacey, Pete Hay, Carol Birrell, Mark Tredinnick, John Seed, Nicolas Rothwell and my treasured fellow walker Freya Mathews. Especial thanks to Susan Murphy's great holding, and to Meredith Elton, Wendy

Garrett, Jan Morgan, Annette Herschtal, and the extraordinary Harry Williamson for sustained support and guidance.

Over the time of writing this I've lived within the most magnificent of communities – right at home. At Villapola and the River House I have been enriched and supported by the company of Ilka, Ilan, Tim, Holly, Gerard, Rach, Tamar, Belle, Beck, Tess, Fiona, Daniel, Pippin, Meredith, Simon, Sage, Karina, David, April and Caro Stefano.

Thank you to Rain, for the way you walked our river, in grace, alone and quiet. The secret soul of the river needs champions such as you.

To my dear fellow pilgrims, Ilan, Kate and Cinnamon, without whom there would have been no journey; two hands, together, in front of my heart.

And lastly, my gratitude to the Yarra herself, to Birrarung, River of Mists, who calls us back to the everflowing ground of being, who reveals, endlessly, the pattern we live within.

REFERENCES AND RESOURCES

Some of these books informed me of outer landscapes, some helped me map my inner lands. All of them I commend to you. For any further information or resources please visit www.mayaward.com.au

Alexander, Christopher, *The Timeless Way of Building*, Oxford University Press, 1979.

Beardsell, David and Cam, *The Yarra River: A Natural Treasure*, Royal Society of Victoria, 1999.

Berry, Thomas, *The Great Work*, Harmony, 2000.

Eidelson, Meyer, The *Melbourne Dreaming: a Guide to the Aboriginal Places of Melbourne*, Aboriginal Studies Press, 1997.

Eliot, TS, *Four Quartets*, Faber and Faber, 1942.

Ellender, Isabel, Christiansen, Peter and Faithfull, Tony (eds), *People of the Merri Merri: The Wurundjeri in Colonial Days*, Merri Creek Management Committee, 2001.

Fukuoka, Masanobu, *The One Straw Revolution*, Rodale Press, 1978.

Grahame, Kenneth, *The Wind in the Willows*, Methuen, 1908.

Hanley, Clifford, *The History of Scotland*, Hamlyn 1986

Harvey, Graham, *The Forgiveness of Nature: The Story of Grass,* Vintage, 2002.

Holmgren, David, *Permaculture: Principles and Pathways Beyond Sustainability,* Holmgren Design Services, 2002.

Jay, Antony, *The Householder's Guide to Community Defence against Bureaucratic Aggression,* Random House, 1972.

Jensen, Derrick, *Endgame: The Problem of Civilisation,* Seven Stories Press, 2006.

Keith, K, Mackey, B. and Lindenmayer D, *Re-evaluation of forest biomass carbon stocks and lessons from the world's most carbon-dense forests. PNAS* 106, 11635-11640, 2009.

Kumar, Satish, *No Destination: An Autobiography,* Green Books, 1992.

Le Guin, Ursula, *Always Coming Home,* Harper and Row, 1985.

Leunig, Michael, *Introspective,* The Text Publishing Company, 1991.

Macy, Joanna, *Coming Back to Life: Practices to Reconnect our Lives, Our Work,* New Society Publishers, 1998.

Macy, Joanna and Seed, John, *Thinking Like a Mountain: Towards A Council of All Beings,* New Catalyst Books, 2007.

Massola, Aldo, *Bunjil's Cave: Myths, Legends and Superstitions of the Aborigines of South-East Australia,* Lansdowne Press, 1968.

Mathews, Freya, *Journey to the Source of the Merri,* Ginninderra Press, 2003.

Reinhabiting Reality: Towards a Recovery of Culture, SUNY Press, 2005.

O'Donohue, Anam Cara *Wisdom from the Celtic World,* Sounds True Audio, 1996.

Otto, Kristin, *Yarra: A Diverting History*, Text Publishing, 2009.

Prechtel, Martin, *Long Life, Honey in the Heart*, HarperCollins, 2002.

Pilgrim, Peace, *Peace Pilgrim: Her Life and Work in her own Words*, Ocean Tree Books. 1982.

Presland, Gary, *The Land of the Kulin: Discovering the Lost Landscape and the First People of Port Phillip*, McPhee Gribble/Penguin, 1985.

Rose, Deborah Bird, *Nourishing Terrains: Australian Aboriginal Views of Landscape and Wilderness*, Australian Heritage Commission, 1996.

Roy, Arundhati, *The Cost of Living*, Flamingo, 1999.

Swimme, Brian and Berry, Thomas, *The Universe Story*, Harper San Francisco, 1994.

Snyder, Gary, *A Place in Space: Ethics, Aesthetics, Watersheds*, Counterpoint Press, 1995.

Van der Post, Laurens, *A Story like the Wind*, Penguin, 1972.

Woiwod, Mick, *The Last Cry*, Tarcoola Press, 1997.

The pattern, the pattern has been given in its entirety.

The water flows all the way to the sea;
it is lifted up and blown back to the source,
purified by the sun, sweet again.

The pattern here is locked into the land by gradient,
etched in, fetched home by wind.
At the end of the day the sun in the west,
the pattern of fire and water, wind and stone thereunder.

The sloping bones of the earth comforts the water that falls gently
to the bay,
and holds my body here below;
motionless and moving,
flying with winds, flowing with water,
transfixed,
transfigured.

Maya Ward was born in and has lived most of her life in Yarra River country. She has worked as an urban designer, permaculture teacher and environmental educator, public art designer, musician, performer, festival director, poet and writer. She now divides her time between inner-city Brunswick and planting trees on her block by the Yarra in Warburton.